The Preacher as Liturgical Artist

Metaphor, Identity, and the
Vicarious Humanity of Christ

Trygve David Johnson

CASCADE *Books* · Eugene, Oregon

THE PREACHER AS LITURGICAL ARTIST
Metaphor, Identity, and the Vicarious Humanity of Christ

Lloyd John Ogilvie Institute of Preaching Series 2

Cascade Books
An Imprint of Wipf and Stock Publishers
199 W. 8th Ave., Suite 3
Eugene, OR 97401

www.wipfandstock.com

ISBN 13: 978-1-62564-017-8

Cataloging-in-Publication data:

Johnson, Trygve David

    The preacher as liturgical artist : metaphor, identity, and the vicarious humanity of Christ / Trygve David Johnson.

    xviii + 202 p. ; 23 cm. — Includes bibliographical references and indexes.

    Lloyd John Ogilvie Institute of Preaching Series 2

    ISBN 13: 978-1-62564-017-8

1. Preaching. 2. Liturgics. I. Title. II. Series.

BV4211.2 J59 2014

Manufactured in the U.S.A.

Table of Contents

Foreword

In this third millenium of the Christian era men and women called and ordained to preach the gospel of Jesus Christ in His church face formidable challenges, arguably more numerous and complex than in any previous generation. You would think that it would be easier as the wisdom and example of skilled and devout preachers for 2000 years now have accumulated into traditions that preserve the good seed for Kingdom harvest while threshing out the chaff of silliness that commonly clogs up so much religious/spiritual language. But it doesn't work that way. Perpetual vigilance is required.

Dr. Trygve Johnson, Dean of the Chapel at Hope College (Michigan), is nothing if not vigilant. And articulate. He uses words accurately, reverently, and imaginatively—the adverbs that characterize the best sermons when preached. His basic concern is to introduce a new identifying metaphor for the preacher—Preacher as Liturgical Artist.

The usual identifying terms for the preacher for most of our history are the Preacher as Teacher and the Preacher is Herald. These have served us well. Augustine is put forward as the classic example of the preacher as teacher and Karl Barth as the modern master of the preacher as herald. Both identities are rooted in the Scriptures that teach the truth of God taught by Jesus and prophetically proclaim the revelation of God in Jesus.

The introduction of the metaphor of, Preacher as Liturgical Artist, shifts our attention from what a preacher does and says to who he or she is. Augustine and Barth, with their numerous progeny will continue to be faithful and trustworthy companions to the preacher. But given our century's rapid shift in expectations, cultural adaptations, and technological developments, Dr. Johnson assembles images and metaphors that show the way for preachers to cultivate a homiletic identity as a "skilled artisan who absorbs a tradition and whose skills are grounded in a larger framework of participation in God›s ongoing work of creation . . . [and] takes human imagination and creativity seriously, but not as rivals to God."

Two items anchor the metaphor of Preacher as Liturgical Artist: Jesus and Trinity.

Jesus became flesh and lived among us. He lives among us still. Nothing in this message we preach can be abstract, a disembodied proposition. The preacher as artist gives witness that everything in this Gospel is livable, the way Jesus lives it, the way we live it. Nothing in our preaching can be dissected and then as bare bones of truth reassembled in a church museum with the bones identified with labels. The preacher as liturgical artist brings truth and goodness and salvation in metaphors and gestures and stories that the Word not only became flesh but becomes flesh. For, as the poet Christian Wiman reminds us, "Christ speaks in stories as a way of preparing his followers to stake their lives on a story, because existence is not a puzzle to be solved, but a narrative to be inherited and undergone and transformed person by person."[1]

And Trinity. Trinity is the most comprehensive and integrative framework that we have for understanding and participating in the Christian life. Early in our history our preachers and teachers formulated the Trinity to express what is distinctive in the revelation of God in Christ through the Spirit. Trinity is a theological formulation that provides an immense horizon against which we can understand and practice the Christian life largely, personally, and relationally. Without an adequately imagined theology it gets reduced to the cramped world reported by journalists or the flat world studied by scientists. Trinity opens us up to an immense world, seen and unseen, of God creating, saving, and blessing in the name of Father, Son, and Holy Spirit with immediate and lived implications for the way we live. Trinity is the church's imagination at work to take in the Kingdom of God in all its arts and relationships. At a most practical level it provides ways of understanding and responding to the God who enters into all the day-to-day issues we face as persons and churches and communities from the time we get out of bed in the morning until we fall asleep at night, and pulls us into participation on God's terms, that is, on Trinitarian terms. It prevents us from getting involved in highly religious but soul-destroying ways of going about living the Christian life.

Trinity articulates the conviction that the God we worship and proclaim is personal and relational, each "person" in active communion with the others. Father, Son, and Holy Spirit are not abstract truths but personal

---

1. "Hive of Nerves," *The American Scholar* (Summer 2010) http://theamerican scholar.org/hive-of-nerves/.

metaphors. There is nothing about God that is impersonal or non-relational. If God is revealed as personal, God can only be known in personal response. We need to know this. It is the easiest thing in the world to use words as abstract truths or principles, to deal with the Gospel as information. Trinity prevents us from doing this. We can never get away with depersonalizing the Gospel so as to make the truth easier, simpler, or more convenient. As our imaginations become accustomed to the Trinitarian dynamic, the metaphor of preacher as liturgical artist provides us with a perspective of self-understanding better able to cope with the relentless depersonalizing, "thingifying," and functionalizing that have come to characterize not only our American but our ecclesial culture.

"Trinity" has suffered the indignity among many of our friends as being treated as a desiccated verbal artifact poked and probed by arthritic octogenarians of the sort skewered by Robert Browning as "dead from the waist down." In reality it is our most exuberant intellectual venture in thinking about God. Trinity is a metaphor that provides coherence to God as God is revealed variously as Father, Son, and Holy Spirit: God is emphatically personal; God is exclusively known in relationship. Under the image of Trinity we discover that we do not know God by defining him but by being loved by him and loving in return. The consequences of this are personally revelatory: another does not know me, nor do I know another by defining or explaining, by categorizing or psychologizing, but only relationally, by accepting and loving, by giving and receiving. The personal and interpersonal provide the primary images (Father, Son, Holy Spirit) for both knowing God and being known by him. This is living, not thinking about living.

Trygve Johnson himself is an incredibly inventive preacher, theologically astute and biblically comprehensive. He has mined the books and vocabularies of the best artists, poets, theologians, and pastors who are our contemporaries in Kingdom work. He has assembled the dynamics of their imaginations in ways that invite us to become participants in this artist colony of preachers with a fresh focus on Jesus and Trinity. Think of this book as a companion equipping us with the best our generation is thinking and praying under a freshly minted identity—Preacher as Liturgical Artist.

Eugene H. Peterson
Professor Emeritus of Spiritual Theology
Regent College
Vancouver, BC

Preface

"What Is the Matter with Preaching?" This was the title of a *Harper's Magazine* article written in 1928 by Harry Emerson Fosdick, the celebrated preacher from New York City's Riverside Church.[1] More than three-quarters of a century later, Fosdick's words still hang as a significant question over the modern pulpit. Indeed, it is hard to find a homiletics book of any sort that does not begin with either a jeremiad or apology on the state of preaching. Something is wrong. But what is it?

This book will attempt to engage this question. Fosdick's own answer was that preaching suffers because sermons do not address the big questions on people's minds. In other words, preaching fails to engage the culture people are living in because preachers are too preoccupied with talking about "what happened to the Jebusites."[2] Others will tell us that preaching suffers because of a loss of rhetorical skill, homiletic technique, personal charisma, or even biblical knowledge. Some may argue that the problem with preaching is theological, that we have lost confidence in the God of revelation and, as a consequence, the kergymatic witness of Christian proclamation; others may view the problem as being so focused on the kergyma that we have lost any sense of concrete human experience.

"What is the matter with preaching?" Much is at stake in this question. How it is answered reflects not only assumptions about the vocation of preaching but also the place of preaching in the event of God's self-revelation in Jesus Christ. What if the problem with preaching is a consequence of not *how* or *what*, but rather *who* is preaching? In other words, what if the answer to the question begins not with technique, or even the message itself, but with the fundamental identity of the preacher?

1. See Fosdick, "What Is the Matter with Preaching?"
2. Ibid., 10.

This book suggests that one answer to the question of what is wrong with preaching is that preachers are working with inadequate metaphors of identity, what we will call "homiletic identities," that fail to encourage a more faithful preaching in the image and practice of Christ. Identity shapes practice; if you know who you are, you know what to do. If you do not know who you are as a preacher, then your preaching suffers.

This book asks not what is the right technique to master, but rather what is the right homiletic identity to be mastered by. The task before us is to consider the significance of metaphor and identity in homiletic practice. Preachers need an identity that fosters the creative and aesthetic dexterity to speak into a malleable and ever-changing cultural context. This book will explore possible identities for those charged with the vocation of preaching by looking seriously at long-standing homiletic identities and proposing a new identity that incorporates the best aspects of these older ones. To that end, let us outline what is to come.

Chapter 1 will examine the current cultural landscape that marks the world into which preachers speak. We will briefly explore some of the significant shifts occurring in culture in an effort to discern the challenges and opportunities facing the preacher today. We will then identify two significant cultural changes that particularly affect the preaching/hearing situation in our cultural moment: a renewed sense of the epistemological significance of the imagination and an emerging imperative to take orality seriously in light of transformations in communication patterns.

Chapter 2 will explore the significance of metaphor, including how metaphor can be understood to shape identity and how identity shapes the living of life. To consider the suggestion of a new metaphor for homiletic identity, we need to see why and how metaphor is pervasive in everyday living. The argument will be made that we all live by metaphors. In this light, metaphors are understood to work at the level of conceptual thought. If metaphors are perceived as paradigmatic concepts, then it is these concepts that subversively form us, becoming the concepts by which we live.[3] If this is true, then changing one's dominant metaphor of identity, whether personal or vocational, suggests the concomitant possibility of changing an established conceptual system that influences how a person thinks, feels, and acts. Accordingly, whatever metaphor of identity is associated with a particular vocation has the potential to define the practice of that vocation.

Chapters 3 and 4 will examine two pervasive metaphors of homiletic identity that have been particularly important for Christian preaching: The Preacher as Teacher and The Preacher as Herald. Chapter 3, which will

---

3. See Lakoff and Johnson, *Metaphors We Live By*, 1.

explore The Preacher as Teacher, will pay particular attention to the role of rhetoric in preaching as proposed by Augustine. It will then consider how the metaphor of The Preacher as Teacher evolved during modernity to reflect the rational, propositional discourse of its time. Chapter 4, focused on The Preacher as Herald, will explore how Karl Barth understood homiletic identity to pivot around the central issue of revelation, and how this understanding led to Barth's reluctance to embrace the rhetorical tradition of Augustine.

These two identities share understandings about the work of the preacher at some points but make rival claims at others. These differences illuminate different theological instincts and assumptions about what a preacher is to accomplish through a sermon. The Preacher as Teacher tends to place an overemphasis on the human agency of the preacher, whereas The Preacher as Herald tends to place the significance and relevance of preaching on God's divine agency at the expense of any real human contribution.

Is there a homiletic identity that can avoid the weaknesses of these identities while still honoring their strengths? Is there a homiletic identity that can encourage the preacher to speak into an emerging oral culture? Is there an identity that trusts an epistemology that takes the imagination seriously? Is there an identity that can push us to preach with the rhetorical wit of Augustine, while situating ourselves in the robust trinitarian thought of Barth? How do we keep from making preaching a completely human event at the expense of God's agency and vice versa? In other words, how do we emphasize the primary work of God in preaching while at the same time not eclipsing human participation? In short, is there an identity that can represent a synthesis of the best of The Preacher as Teacher and The Preacher as Herald?

Chapter 5 will offer for consideration the homiletic identity of The Preacher as Artist. This homiletic identity presupposes that artistry is fundamental to the practice of Christian preaching. It is proposed as an identity that takes seriously the idea of human and divine agency working in harmony without confusion, grounded within the doctrines of the Trinity and the Incarnation as developed primarily in the trinitarian thought of T. F. Torrance and J. B. Torrance. With a proper understanding of the *vicarious humanity of Christ*, in which Jesus Christ is understood to perform the double ministry of representing God to humanity and humanity to God, we see that through the power of the Holy Spirit, our humanity has been redeemed and thus set free to offer the things of creation back to God, with "added value" and with gratitude.

A presupposition of this thesis is that preachers need an identity that honors the creative and redemptive work that Jesus Christ has done and is doing to bring us into deep communion with the Father through the Holy Spirit. Preachers need an identity that will encourage them to use all of the best resources with which God has endowed humanity in creation and redemption. This thesis also presupposes that Christian proclamation needs to locate itself and learn what it can from the current cultural context. In this way, we will see the preacher as one who plants seeds in the soil of grace. This makes possible the tending of a countercultural crop that gives witness to the promises of the kingdom of God. This tending will require faith, patience, discernment, and risk as Christian preachers find ways to embrace an identity that encourages them to speak into reality "a pure and generous word."[4]

4. A phrase taken from the poem "A Task" by Czeslaw Milosz. See Milosz, *The Collected Poems*, 231.

Acknowledgments

A Task

In fear and trembling, I think I would fulfill my life
Only if I brought myself to make a public confession
Revealing a sham, my own and of my epoch:
We were permitted to shriek in the tongue of dwarfs and demons
But pure and generous words were forbidden
Under so stiff a penalty that whoever dared to pronounce one
Considered himself as a lost man.[1]

In the spirit of this poem by Czeslaw Milosz, I think I would fulfill the task of this book only if I brought myself to make a public thanksgiving, attempting to express a gratitude that is difficult to put into words. This project has been a significant part of my life for longer than I had anticipated, planned, or hoped. But the result has widened my circle of conversation partners and friends, and has allowed me to discover wisdom that is more valuable than gold. This project has taught me the value of friendship, humility, and the joys of participating in a community that is willing not only to critique, but also to encourage.

The interdisciplinary nature of this work is a result of a liberal arts education that formed me for a life of learning. I am grateful for the learning communities of Northwestern College, Western Theological Seminary, and Hope College, whose faculties and students both inspired and equipped me to explore and practice the ideas in this work. To the faculty who became

---

1. Milosz, *The Collected Poems*, 231.

friends and who unhesitatingly gave of their time, opened their office doors and even their homes, and who were willing to offer wisdom and counsel without reservation, I am grateful. I think particularly of my first academic advisor, Michael Kugler, and others from Northwestern College, including Karen Barker, Dave and Jody Nonnemacher, and of course, John and Kathy Brogan. I have in mind also my professors from Western Theological Seminary, John Hesselink, Leanne Van Dyk, the late Jim Cook, Jim Brownson, Tom Boogart, and the best pastor I have ever had, Matt Floding. I owe a special thanks to Tim Brown, without whom this project would never have been imagined, and who more than anyone I know embodies the title of this work. From Hope College I am grateful for my faculty who have been nothing less than a source of constant encouragement, especially Jeff Polet, Carol Simon, Jeff Tyler, Steven Bouma-Prediger, Curtis Gruenler, David Cunningham, Charlotte VanOven Witvliet, Jim Boelkins, Fred Johnson, Marc Baer, Jim Herrick, and my conversation conspirator Mark Husbands. To those who work closest with me every day in the soil of Hope, and have prayed with me through the ups and downs of this journey, I can't say thank you enough. I think of Paul Boersma, Lori Bouwman, Dan and Grace Claus, Nancy Smith, and Paul Chamness. I am especially grateful for Jim Bultman, Hope's former president, who has taught me more about leadership than anyone, and whose faith and patience have allowed me the opportunity to finish this project. Without him I would never have enjoyed the joy of preaching Hope.

To those who graciously allowed me to discuss with them my work and furthered it through their own comments and concerns, I am grateful. I thank the members of the Institute for Theology, Imagination and the Arts, as well as John Witvliet and the Calvin Institute for Christian Worship and the Bast Preaching Committee of Western Theological Seminary. I thank the members of The Big Chill and the Friday Night Prayer Group (aka the best prayer group ever). I would be remiss if I did not thank by name Kurt and Leah Dykstra, Keith and Becky Starkenburg, Michael and Nelleke Wooten, Karsten and Gretchen Rumohr Voskuil, Mark and Becky Husbands, Tim and Nancy Brown, Matt and Marcia Floding, Todd and Rachel Billings, and Dave and Betty Jo Bast. Also, to all the members of The Project, especially Brian Keepers, Jon Sherrill, and the best young preacher I know, Jon Brown. Included in my thanks are members of The Dead Preachers Society for allowing me to test my ideas with you and on you. Your feet are beautiful! I am also grateful for Eugene and Jan Peterson, who encouraged me to write, and whose friendship has been one of the great joys of my life. It is their generosity that made this book a possibility, and it is their hospitality that showed me how to walk the narrow path into the high country, where the air is thin.

To those who have been directly involved in this project, I owe a special work of thanks. For the careful reading and editing of Nicole Brace, Amanda Bieri, Grace Claus, and Chikara Saito I am in your debt. I am also indebted to Tee Gatewood, whose friendship has been like that of a brother, and whose faith and determined persistence to encourage me every day in writing and revision are the reason I have the opportunity to write these words of thanks. I am grateful for my advisor Trevor Hart, whose thoughtful reading and willingness to show "grace upon grace" have been a model for me of a faithful scholar who embodies what he professes. His is the rare gift of wisdom and revelation. I also am in debt to Clayton Schmit, whose belief and enthusiasm about this work made its publication possible, as well as to Mark Labberton and Fuller Theological Seminary for endorsing this book for its Lloyed John Ogilvie Institute of Preaching Series. Thank you.

And finally, I would fail to fulfill my task if I did not thank my family. To Peter and Elka, who have not only taught me how to ski, they have taught me how to enjoy life. To my sister Jill, who is more loyal than I deserve, and who is more beautiful than she knows. To my father and mother, big Dave and little Arlene, who gave me everything I could have ever hoped for in life, especially the confidence and the encouragement to follow my passions. They, more than anyone, have given me a picture of how to love. To my son Trygve David Johnson Jr., or New Trygve, whose birth came as this project was finishing, and whose smile is a contagious gift of grace. I also thank my daughter Ella Arlene Karis, who knows nothing of this book, but who embodies the hope of why it was is written. And finally to my beloved, Kristen Deede Johnson, who is grace without edges, and who is for me the home I had barely dared hoped existed. It is with reverence for your love and friendship that I dedicate this to you.

1

Preaching in Twilight

...the Owl of Minerva first takes flight with twilight closing in.—G. W. F. HEGEL

INTRODUCTION: AWARENESS FOR FAITHFULNESS

The identity of the preacher cannot be understood in a vacuum. To reflect on the identity of the preacher and the act of preaching requires reflection on the culture in which preaching takes place. If we are to understand the promise and perils for the preacher in our time, we must not only pay attention to the Scriptures the preacher seeks to illuminate, the skills required to speak well, or the theological foundations for such speaking; we must also pay particular attention to the cultural context that impacts how people understand or hear such preaching. That assumption is what this chapter wishes to explore. As we begin this journey, I want to locate the preacher within our cultural moment, trace some significant cultural shifts, and then suggest that these shifts may open up particular opportunities for Christian proclamation. Though some lament these shifts as a loss that puts the identity of the preacher in peril, I see instead an invitation to reclaim the artful work of Christian proclamation that may call forth the need for a renewed engagement with not the "how" but the "who" of preaching. Indeed, if we preachers have the discernment to astutely reflect upon the cultural shifts that are taking place, it may encourage us to reconsider the assumptions that shape what I call *homiletic identities*.

It is impossible to trace and isolate all of the currents pulling at the preacher within our cultural moment. The scope of this reflection is more

1

modest. In this chapter, we will begin with an exploration of the commonly held assumption that modernity is waning by looking at the broad brush-strokes of modernity and postmodernity. Our concern is with how each one's tacit assumptions impact and relate to the identity of the preacher so that we might begin to see how cultural forces impact the practice of preaching. We will then focus in more detail on two examples of how our cultural situation could affect preaching by exploring how a renewed emphasis on both imagination and orality encourages the art of Christian proclamation.

The difficulty, however, in attempting to describe any cultural moment is that the lenses one looks through are colored by one's own experiences, prejudices, and traditions to such a degree that one can never claim to have complete objective integrity. I claim no such integrity, nor do I claim that what I identify represents the full scope of perspective. What I do suggest, however, is that recognizing that our culture is in the midst of shifting to different ways of thinking, knowing, and hearing encourages us to consider what it means to be a faithful preacher in our particular cultural context. Awareness of our cultural moment allows for an opportunity to be more faithful to Jesus Christ and his way of preaching in our particular pulpits. Specifically, I want to claim that two conditions of today's shifting culture— the recovery of imagination and the renewed importance of orality—have an impact on the work of Christian preaching.

BETWEEN THE TIMES: CAUGHT IN A PARADIGM SHIFT

Preachers today enter the pulpit at a complex moment in human history. In this context of cultural change, preachers need to practice what John Stott calls *double listening*[1]—meaning that the task of the preacher is to listen to the Word with a humble reverence, anxious to understand it, and resolved to believe and obey what we come to learn and understand. At the same time, we preachers listen to the world with critical alertness, anxious to understand it just as intimately, and resolved not necessarily to believe and obey it, but to sympathize with it and to seek grace to discover how the gospel relates to the world. What I take Stott to mean is that the Christian preacher has to learn how to translate a gospel that is for the world, but not of it.

What does it mean to preach a gospel that is culturally engaged, but not co-opted? If we listen to the modern world, it is clear we are living in an age that is more ethnically and culturally fluid than any in past history; as the technologies of mass media and mass travel make it possible to move

1. Stott, *Contemporary Christian Thinker*, 28.

around the globe with relative ease, we have more exposure to new people, new ideas, and new assumptions of what it means to say that God so loved the world. In this context of fluid crossing of borders and boundaries, visible and invisible, the normativity and relevance of the dominant institutions and practices of the past are being openly challenged. This context means that preachers need to have the dexterity to speak into many different kinds of situations with fresh sensitivities. In such a diverse environment, the future ethos of Christianity may not feel as Western as it has in the past. Specifically, Protestantism in the West and its preachers may soon find themselves as a minority in the church's future.[2] Indeed, in the future it may matter little if one's identity is Lutheran, Presbyterian, Anglican, Baptist, or Catholic. What has been called the Protestant Era—referring to a synthesis of faith and Enlightenment—may be coming to an end, or at the very least evolving into a new Christian movement. As a result of these ecclesial, global, and technological changes, a number of preachers find themselves caught between times. Some are on the defensive, as they desperately try to hold onto norms and practices that no longer seem to be as trusted while a new culture begins to emerge.

Some historians of the church, such as Robert E. Webber, suggest that the cognitive dissonance experienced by these preachers is caused in part by a paradigm shift from modern to postmodern culture.[3] Webber argues that the value of having a historical perspective on culture lies in its ability to help us understand the past contextually, appreciate the variety and diversity of the great models of the past, and deal with times of transition in an intelligent way. Webber focuses on five eras in Western church history and the primary means used to interpret the Christian faith in each (see Table 1). For our purposes, we are most concerned with what Webber identifies as the cultural transition from modernity to postmodernity and its potential impact on contemporary preaching.

Ancient	Medieval	Reformation	Modern	Postmodern
Mystery, Community, Symbol	*Institutional*	*Word, Systematic & Analytical, Verbal, Individualistic*	*Reason*	*Mystery, Community, Symbol*

Table 1. Paradigms of Christian History.[4]

2. See Jenkins, *New Christendom*.

3. See Webber, *Ancient-Future Faith*.

4. Ibid., 34.

Though most scholars agree that we are in the midst of a cultural shift, many suggest that it may not be as decisive or clean a break from modernity as Webber would have us believe. For example, Jean-François Lyotard declares that postmodernity is merely a continuing possibility arising out of the modern. Calling postmodernism "the condition of knowledge in the most highly developed societies," he prefers to describe it as "undoubtedly a part of the modern rather than an age following upon and supplanting the modern."[5] Sociologist of religion Craig Gay argues that we are not so much in a postmodern world as in an age of "hyper-modernity."[6] Theologian Garrett Green agrees. Rather than simply describing the contemporary cultural situation as postmodern, Green suggests that a more modest metaphor of description for our cultural moment would be to speak of ours as the hour of *twilight*, suggesting that modernity has not simply vanished but rather survives in a condition of profound transition.[7]

Looking Back: Modernity

To describe this age of *twilight*, let us look back on the dominant features of the modern age. For the last two hundred years, being called "modern" was a compliment. It was a term that carried the hope of a progressive humanity, the triumph of reason over superstition, the cutting edge of scientific revolution, and new rational methods of inquiry.

Stephen Toulmin notes that modernity was birthed in the Renaissance, as human reason in both science and philosophy reigned supreme, and was crowned in Enlightenment culture.[8] Modern Western culture was sustained by great confidence in the human mind's ability to question ideologies and explain all of life. Human progress was seen as the inevitable outcome of asking the right questions and finding the right answers. The patron saint of modernity, René Descartes, inspired a new progressive credo for modern humanity: *Cogito ergo sum* ("I think, therefore I am").[9] Descartes' theory signaled a major change in Western epistemology in that it located the source of meaning in human subjectivity (the act of the "I think") rather

5. Lyotard, *Postmodern Condition*, 79.

6. Gay, *Way of (Modern) World*, 18.

7. Green draws this twilight imagery from Hegel: "When philosophy paints its gray on gray, a form of life has grown old, and with gray on gray it cannot be rejuvenated but merely recognized. The Owl of Minerva begins her flight only at the coming of twilight" (Hegel, *Vorlesungen uber Rechtsphtsphilosophie*, quoted in Green, *Theology, Hermeneutics and Imagination*, 1).

8. See Toulmin, *Cosmopolis*, 22–30.

9. See Descartes, *Discourse on Method*, 53.

than in the objective world of reality or transcendent being. Thus, he argued for an analysis of knowledge that carried one back to the primitive elements in experience that were, in principle, available to reflective thinkers in any culture and at all times. This modern move had a reassuring, overarching sense of rational coherence. It offered a vision of an ideal rationality that could access universal moral maxims that would frame and solve society's ills and was open to all reflective, self-critical thinkers. Webber describes this modern vision with the following words: reason, systematic and analytical, verbal, and individualistic (see Table 1).

In modernity, people looked for a set of absolute and universal principles by which to understand the world. Modernity involved not only the philosophical world of ideas, but also economics, technology, and social factors. With optimism, modernity saw science and technology as instruments of reason and progress and believed it could order social life in such a way that social ills and conflict could ultimately be eradicated. Obviously, these modern dynamics influenced Christianity and the church.

Though Enlightenment's rationality gave human optimism a secure place, it also tended to subdue the intuitive and spiritual dimensions of Christian experience. Webber writes of the "dead end-street of modernity, which proudly thinks the human mind is the final arbiter of truth."[10] Andrew Walker identifies some of modernity's sociological characteristics and their impact on Christianity: "functional rationality," which involved domination of the clock and money; "structural pluralism," which moved the Christian faith out of the public arena and into the private sphere; and "cultural pluralism," by which a Christian distinctive was lost.[11] Walker claims that functional rationality caused society to lose the Christian story through "gospel amnesia." Modernity replaced the gospel with its own story that science and the technology it produced were all important.

Lesslie Newbigin's withering analysis of modernity's impact on Christianity similarly argues that modernity privatized the Christian faith, taking it out of the arena of public truth, and that we need to bring it back into focus.[12] He urges Christians to see modern Western culture for what it has become. Newbigin writes, "Its paganism, having been born out of the rejection of Christianity, is far more resistant to the gospel than the pre-Christian paganism with which cross cultural missions have been familiar."[13] Rather than thinking we live in a secular society, Newbigin argues that we must see that it is a pagan society. He warns that the traditional church is in

10. Webber, *Ancient-Future Faith*, 34.
11. Walker, *Telling the Story*, 103–37.
12. Newbigin, *Foolishness to the Greeks*.
13. Ibid., 20.

much greater peril than it realizes. In light of these concerns, Western culture needs a homiletic movement that is determined more by content of faith than context of culture even as it pays attention to shifting cultural dynamics.

Looking Ahead: Postmodernity?

As suggested above, it is not yet exactly clear into what modernity is emerging. Despite the confusion we are using the term postmodern to describe our current cultural situation. Modernity's ever-ambitious faith in human progress and its commitment to an overarching set of truths that give meaning to life have begun to disintegrate. There seems to be a growing awareness of the limitations of a rationality, and the science it encouraged, after the brutalities of two world wars all but shattered notions of a utopian view of human progress. Indeed, there is a mounting witness that the sharpness of modernity has been dulled. As Stephen Toulmin observes:

> Rather than our being free to assume that the tide of Modernity still flows strongly, and that its momentum will carry us into a new and better world, our present position is less comfortable. What looked in the 19th century like an irresistible river has disappeared in the sand, and we seem to have run aground. Far from extrapolating confidently into the social and cultural future, we are now stranded and uncertain of our location. The very project of Modernity thus seems to have lost momentum, and we need to fashion a successor program.[14]

Instead of modernity's one "big story," which was perceived to be true for everyone, postmodernity is marked by the claim that anything can be true for anyone—truth is what you make it or interpret it to be out of your own experience or perspective. It is also marked by suspicion toward authoritative answers and absolute truths. This postmodern approach to life is hungry for experience and prioritizes intuition and pragmatism. It is a mind-set or a worldview that glories in personal choice, discovery (including spiritual searching), and a new sense of belonging to a global village. The influence of postmodernity's pluralism and relativism can be seen almost everywhere in Western society. In architecture, art, intellectual life, literature, and popular culture, anything goes—if it feels good.[15] Some observers see an increasingly ominous build up of pressures as postmodernity takes hold.

14. See Toulmin, *Cosmopolis*, 3.
15. See Harvey, *Condition of Postmodernity*.

It is important to clarify what we mean by postmodernity. Green distinguishes between two senses of postmodern.[16] The first he calls *descriptive postmodernism*. This is simply a depiction of the "non-foundationalist" situation that increasingly characterizes our cultural moment. If modernity is defined by the Enlightenment appeal to universal norms to which (in principle) we have access through the right use of reason, postmodernity can be defined in negative terms as the rejection of that possibility. Green notes that modernist thinkers, like Ludwig Feuerbach, attempted to ground human knowledge and experience of the world in certain incorrigible foundational truths or experiences.[17] In this way, Feuerbach sought to show that the human person rather than God is the center and source of truth and knowledge. As Feuerbach writes, "there is no distinction between the predicates of the divine and human nature, and, consequently, no distinction between the divine and human subject."[18] If we define the modern in this positivistic way, Green argues, the postmodern departs from these kinds of foundationalist assertions.

This descriptive use of the term "postmodern" neither celebrates nor vilifies; it simply points to the cultural-historical fact that we seem to have rejected a foundationalist certainty in universal categories that transcend traditions, cultures, and languages. In this sense, to describe our situation as postmodern is simply to take note of the fact that fewer people today are willing to accept the "modernist" axiom that there are universal, trans-cultural, and trans-historical norms of truth and morals, to which we have access through reason. The "sacred canopy" has been lifted, and with it, its foundational assumptions.[19]

Green notes that "postmodern" may refer to another cultural dynamic as well. Green calls this *doctrinaire* or *normative postmodernism*, and it is especially flourishing among continental philosophers and their followers who deny that texts have any determinate meaning of the kind that modernist hermeneutics presupposes.[20] Green suggests that this kind of normative postmodernism is a philosophical doctrine that is responding to the intellectual postmodern situation in the descriptive sense, by arguing that the axioms of foundationalism are to be attacked or even all-out rejected.[21]

16. Green, *Theology, Hermeneutics, and Imagination*, 8–11.

17. Ibid., 13–18.

18. Feuerbach, *Essence of Christianity*, xxxvii.

19. See Berger, *Sacred Canopy*.

20. For examples of contemporary breeds of this form of postmodernity see Derrida, *Margins of Philosophy*; Derrida, *Writing and Difference*; and Lyotard, *Postmodern Condition*.

21. See Gay, *Way of (Modern) World*, 237ff.

This sense of postmodernism has more of an agenda than the former sense, hence Green's use of the term "normative" in association with it.

Overall, because of the different ways in which it has been used and its amorphous diversity, the term postmodernity is difficult to describe. We might say that postmodern*ity* reflects the constellation of our cultural milieu in late modernity, or that it is the air we breathe within culture, whereas postmodern*ism* refers to a critical system of thought or set of doctrines and assumptions.[22] The point is that together these assumptions create a new way of thinking, learning, hearing, and living. It is also worth noting that it is not that modern foundationalism is gone altogether, but that Western culture's fundamental assumptions are morphing or evolving into a new kind of modern suspicion about what we can and cannot know.

Homiletics scholar Thomas Troeger notes that this cultural paradigm shift is impacting the mind-set and challenging the assumptions of the preacher today. He writes that "modern preaching sought to bring recognized authorities into harmony with each other, while postmodern preaching works under the suspicion of all authority that now pervades our culture."[23] Preachers today, according to Fred Craddock, go about their work in a world transitioning from a hermeneutics of confidence to one of doubt, while preachers themselves are moving from having a voice of cultural authority to being those "without authority."[24] The self-assured sermon is giving way to something new, the precise form of which is not yet plain to see. Preachers today preach at twilight—caught between the dusk of one age and the dawn of another—in the twilight where the proverbial owl "takes flight."

Many preachers whose assumptions are wed to modernity often feel particular tension in the face of modernity's dusk. Preachers are caught between the times, suffering the loss of the assurances of a passing age, where sermons were well conditioned to demonstrate faith's credibility and rationality, and they are now left anxious about what is being put in its place.

It is impossible to predict what the dawn will bring. Whether preachers should lament this situation or rejoice remains an open question for each preacher, but to ignore the reality of this twilight is not a viable option. Neither pastoral naivety about such cultural dynamics, nor spiritual retreat and fortification is a wise way to serve the church. In the effort to preach the gospel faithfully, it is wise to understand the cultural moment in which one is speaking. People today are living in the age of "twilight," an age

22. For more on defining the terms postmodernism and postmodernity, see Harvey, *Condition of Postmodernity*, 3–9, 113–20.

23. Troeger, *Imagining a Sermon*, 122.

24. See Craddock, *As One Without Authority*.

where mass suspicion of old foundations has conditioned us to perceive and experience the world in new ways. Modernity clearly did not discover the proper ordering of human society, and utopian dreams of what rationalism alone can achieve have been shattered by the realities of increased cultural alienation, poverty, addictions, and violence. In short, the confidence of modernity has given way to an increased sense of humility and to suspicion of knowledge and authority.

Whatever the tensions one experiences, I want to suggest that gospel proclamation in our cultural moment has many opportunities for the preacher who is discerning. The contemporary mind-set should be explored and understood. Much promise is contained in the patterns of thought that are encouraging preachers to move from focusing on the individual to recognizing the role of the community of faith; from trusting rational certainty alone to favoring an intellectual encounter of revelation within human experience; from the dualism of mind and matter, private and public, reason and imagination, to a holistic approach to life and the gospel that calls for synthesis and integration. Instead of viewing the universe as a machine, as it was in modernity, postmodernity shows an openness to mystery, wonder, and transcendence, which provides a significant opportunity for the gospel to be preached. Rather than the rational being dominant, there has been a move toward the intuitive and more emphasis on the role of imagination. Indeed, postmodernity contains many insights for the preacher today, but of particular importance is the sense that the epistemology of postmodern people is shaped by their yearning for experience; genuine relationships; holism in worship and lived life; mystery, wonder, and awe in personal spirituality; and local stories that help make sense of their own stories in light of the story of the triune God of grace.

The cultural moment of modernity has changed and this change is significant for preachers. It requires that we be aware of how people are thinking, feeling, and acting in this age of twilight. We need to recognize how this culture has shaped people to hear, or not to hear, the gospel that preachers are privileged to proclaim. This book argues that if preachers reflect on our cultural moment, they will find some surprising resources that may help them reshape a homiletic practice. For example, one of the surprises that preachers ignore at their own peril is how the "hermeneutics of suspicion," a phrase credited to Paul Ricoeur, celebrates, or, at the very least, gives a legitimate place to the recovery of the imagination.[25] Another critical example is the way in which people receive information; in postmodern culture there appears to be a return to orality. We will explore both of these examples to further describe the shift from modernity to postmodernity.

25. Ricoeur, "The Critique of Religion," 205.

More importantly, we will describe and explore these examples to better understand the ways that preachers can and should understand their identity in this era of twilight.

PARADIGM SHIFT IN HERMENEUTICS: RECOVERING THE IMAGINATION

The cultural transition from modernity to postmodernity has had significant implications for how reason and imagination are conceptualized. Within modern thinking, reason and imagination were viewed dichotomously, with reason valued over imagination, while more recent scholars have questioned the division between the two and suggested that imagination plays a crucial role in the use of reason. This section will explore how the modern division between reason and imagination emerged and suggest that the contemporary recovery of the imagination is important for preaching today.

In the hopes of teasing out some positive insight for homiletics in our cultural context, let us take a step back and look at the philosopher Ludwig Feuerbach as a primary example of one of modernity's beloved despisers of religion. A look at Feuerbach's thought may enable us to see something highly significant about the hermeneutics of suspicion, which might, ironically, offer preachers today a path forward in our contemporary twilight zone.

Feuerbach's *The Essence of Christianity* helped to encourage a subjective and objective division—between religion and science, faith and reason, fiction and reality—which is a mark of a modern worldview.[26] On the one pole is objectivity controlled by rationality, and on the other pole is imagination, the generator of fiction, of which religious faith is a primary example. Here Feuerbach gives us a clue to understand better the modern suspicion and critique of Christian faith. By combining the descriptive claim that imagination is the source of religion with the judgment that religious consciousness is therefore false consciousness, Feuerbach suggests that Christian faith can be nothing but an invented fiction.[27]

For a modernist such as Feuerbach, imagination has the potential to become the source of self-deception, illusion, speculation, and fantasy unless (and this is the critical point) it remains securely subservient to rationality. Reason is where reality is verified, whereas all intellectual error is guided by the imagination. In this sense, reason is the neutral tool that

26. Feuerbach, *Essence of Christianity*.

27. For more detail on Feuerbach's suspicion of religion and how it relates to the imagination, see Green, *Theology, Hermeneutics, and Imagination*, 83–107.

allows humans to critically examine and verify what is foundational—what is true or real—and what is not. Feuerbach understands the imagination to be a dangerous distraction, or a threat, to reason's critically objective endeavor. Thus, the hermeneutics of suspicion is controlled by the following assumption: religion is the product of imagination; therefore, religious claims are untrue or untrustworthy.

Feuerbach's assumption that the imagination is at odds with rationality has plagued the Christian pulpit. If faith is a product of the imagination, and the imagination is the source of self-delusion, then the preacher is suspected of propagating fiction. When this occurs the preacher is placed in a position of defending the presupposition of preaching itself. For many preachers, this modern critique of religion as a product of the imagination was (and continues to be) persuasive. As a result, preachers tried to mirror the rational age by out-rationalizing the despisers of religion. And in so doing, many modern preachers bought into the assumption that the imagination is somehow set over-against rationality. They believed that the imagination was to be viewed with suspicion, as it can be the source of fiction and fantasy. Thus, Christian proclamation privileged positivistic certitude over the imaginative. Preachers, in other words, did not want to be perceived as irrational. However, this created a challenge for the modern preacher: how to bridge the gap between the idea of reality grounded in objective scientific observation and a faith grounded in the texts of a supposedly revealed God? It was easy to fall into the assumption that it must be one or the other, reason or the imagination, without considering that this polarization does not necessarily have to be a binary relationship.

In the "twilight" of postmodernity, this polarization no longer seems as obvious. Postmodernity is suspicious of the belief that reason can extrapolate universal maxims by looking at a mechanistic world in its finitude. Instead, this season of *twilight* assumes a world that operates with an energizing force that pushes past finitude to inspire the process of personal, social, cultural, and institutional change. It takes seriously the role of experience and perspective as a way to challenge the assumption of the neutrality of reason. In this sense, postmodernity is not a set of practices as much as it is an attitude of hyper-suspicion that critiques even the most basic assumptions of modernity, including the schism between faith and reason. This shift from a mechanistic worldview to an open and dynamic worldview raises the possibility that reality as we experience it is not grounded in one single unifying theory, but is characterized by a "web of relationships," none of which, on its own, is the key to unlocking the door of the universe.

Postmodernity, then, is less a unified doctrine than an attitude that accepts that all perspectives of truth, or all visions of reality, are grounded in faith in something. It must be noted, however, that this attitude is con-comitant with the belief that one person, or one community, has authority to speak only for that person and has no universal value.[28] This relativistic or pragmatic view of truth consequently encourages a pluralistic mind-set, or the notion that there are many ways to understand and access truth, not just one.[29]

What is significant for those who preach in today's hour of twilight is that as soon as the preacher realizes that the culture has made a postmodern turn, one of the first assumptions left behind is the modern confidence that there is trustworthy access to a "reality" against which imagination might be judged true or false. In such a context, the imagination is not perceived as undermining the reality of the world, as much as seen as supporting it.

Postmodern attitudes are open to the idea that imagination may be the necessary means by which we can actually apprehend "reality." The imagina-tion is seen not so much in opposition to or distinct from rationality—or even as one particular function of the mind—but rather as a particular "flexibility which can invigorate all mental functions."[30] This imaginative "flexibility" is seen as central to our human capacity to apprehend and orga-nize—to tidy and untidy—meaning.[31]

Ricoeur, for example, argues that the imagination is central to our capacity to think of possibilities, as it performs a "prospective and explor-ative function" in our mental life.[32] It is by means of the imagination that we make ourselves see the possible worlds and selves we might inhabit or become. This leads to formulations that "the real is the realization of one of

28. For an example of this postmodern mind-set at work see Rorty, *Objectivity, Relativism and Truth?*, especially the chapter "Solidarity and Objectivity?" However, in fairness it should be noted a scholar like Michael Polanyi, for example, might es-chew absolute universal claims of a sort which ignore the "personal coefficient" in all knowledge (including "scientific" knowledge), while yet insisting upon the "universal intent" of one's truth claims. For more on Polanyi's theory of knowledge see Clark, *Divine Revelation*, 77–144.

29. The perspective of this book is not in keeping with this Rortian view of truth or pluralism. Instead, it represents the idea that the imagination may be a means by which we understand reality as we experience it. To hold such a view does not exclude the possibility of a revealed authority or truth. Polanyi's notion of universal intent (i.e., I may believe that, as far as I can tell, something is universally true, and present it for consideration as such) prevents a collapse into "perspectivism."

30. Egan, *Imagination*. For an excellent narrative of "a very short history of the imagination," see chapter 1, pp. 9–43.

31. See Richard Kearney's summary of how meaning is made in the context of post-modernity in Kearney, *Wake of Imagination*, 397.

32. Ricoeur, *History and Truth*, 126.

many possibilities."[33] In other words, imagination is an intentional act of the mind that is the genesis of creativity, novelty, and originality. In this sense, it is understood to be what ties all perception, memory, emotional thinking, and rational thinking together. It is not distinct from rationality but is rather a capacity that greatly enriches rational thinking. What imagination does with reality is the reality we live by.

We might articulate this understanding of imagination another way, by borrowing a phrase from Gerard Manley Hopkins, who conceives of the imagination as the "inscape" of rationality.[34] Hopkins himself defines "inscape" as "the individual essence or quality of a thing; the uniqueness of an observed object, scene, event, etc. . . . 'Inscape' is what I above all aim at in poetry."[35] With the imagination understood to be rationality's "inscape," we can see how the capacity to conceive of possible worlds—which is essential in a vocation that speaks of the kingdom of God—enables the preacher to plumb the heights and depths of alternative realities as described in Scripture. Thus, the work of biblical interpretation sees itself as an imaginative work that encourages the preacher to explore beyond what is conventionally represented or can be formally extrapolated from what seems to be reality. The notion of "inscape" helps to obliterate a false and destructive dichotomizing of imagination and rationality, and suggests an enriched and expanded notion of rationality. In this sense, the poet Wallace Stevens said it well as he wrote of the imagination, "I am the necessary angel of the earth / Since, in my sight, you see the world again."[36]

The influence of this newfound "angel of the earth" is nowhere more evident than in recent philosophy of science. One might summarize by saying that the history of science is the history of scientific faith in paradigms of the imagination.[37] For example, through such influential scientific revolutionaries as Copernicus, Galileo, Newton, and Einstein, we have been converted to seeing reality through the lenses of their imaginative models of the cosmos. Their paradigms have diffused into popular culture to provide powerful metaphors that shape our epistemology, poetry, politics, and even our theology. Green describes this as the "paradigmatic imagination" at work. He writes, "The discovery that imagination plays a crucial role in scientific theory and practice calls into question familiar dichotomies between what counts as subjective and objective, theory and fact, interpretation and observation, forcing a fundamental rethinking of the relationship between

33. See Halling, "Imaginative Constituent," 140.

34. Egan, *Imagination*, 42–43.

35. Hopkins, quoted in MacKenzie, *Reader's Guide*, 232.

36. Quoted as the epigraph of Kearney, *Wake of Imagination*.

37. See Kuhn, *Structure of Scientific Revolutions*, 158.

science and religion. No longer can theology view science as typifying the "other" way of thinking; on the contrary, attention to imagination can clarify the nature of theology by showing significant parallels to the natural sciences."[38] As the scientific world embraces the imagination to discern and describe reality, it mirrors the postmodern quest to abandon modern dichotomies between the objective and subjective and fact and illusion.

As shocking as it may sound to the modern preacher, the wisdom of our postmodern moment supports Feuerbach's notion that religion—including Christianity—*is* very much a product of human imagination. Christianity is a result of the Holy Spirit working through the particularity of the imagination to birth us from above and into the kingdom of God. Contemporary theologians depart from Feuerbach by maintaining that simply because religion is a product of the imagination does not itself make it untrustworthy or untrue. The imagination can, in its own way, be just as reliable a foundation as other accepted hermeneutical standards, such as analytic reasoning.[39]

This opens a new possibility for the imagination's role for Christian preaching. Such a positive view of the imagination can enrich our interpretation of the Bible. For example, Green offers an account of Scripture as a text through which God forms, enables, and stimulates Christian imagination to see our relationship with God: "The Christian claim that the Bible is inspired by God means that it is the instrument of revelation, the means by which God makes himself known in the present life of believers. This claim can be stated more precisely by saying that Scripture embodies the paradigm through which Christians view the world in its essential relation to God, the images by which God informs the imagination of believers."[40]

Green articulates a critical point for preaching in what he calls the "faithful imagination."[41] Considering the possibilities of the imagination to shape a hermeneutical paradigm for Christian preaching may encourage preachers to rethink some old assumptions about how we read, prepare, and preach sermons grounded in Scripture. This will be done in the next few chapters as we look at two traditional identities of the preacher and ask what, if any, false dichotomies have limited the proclamation of the gospel and the Christian life.

38. Green, *Imagining God*, 45.

39. This argument is made with care by Trevor Hart in *Faith Thinking*, 23–69. Here Hart claims that there are different degrees of certainty. The physicist has a different kind of discernment than a theologian. One type of discernment does not necessarily discount the other. Not every claim has to have the same standard of certitude—indeed not every claim can.

40. Green, *Imagining God*, 108.

41. Ibid., 187.

In the twilight of modernity, the Christian pulpit needs a homiletic identity that can encourage a performance of preaching that takes seriously an enriched understanding of imagination for Christian proclamation. In other words, I am suggesting that what may be needed for preaching in this hour of twilight is not a new technique to be mastered, but a new identity that appreciates the imagination's role in interpreting and performing the Scriptures in ways that will edify the church in the days ahead. Christian preaching suited to faithfulness in the twilight of modernity must begin by taking the biblical text with renewed seriousness—that is, by appropriating the scriptural paradigm as the place where God makes Godself available to human imagination. This task is not an onerous one imposed upon us as the consequence of sin; it is the hermeneutical consequence of living in a divinely created world in which the human spirit yearns for God by virtue of grace rather than nature. When Christian preaching attends to its proper task of describing and clarifying the grammar of the Scripture, the "homiletic imagination" may heuristically discover within its own resources a source of cultural suspicion potentially and actually more radical than that advocated by any of the secular "masters of suspicion."

PARADIGM SHIFT IN COMMUNICATION: RECOVERING ORALITY

In the first part of this chapter, we repeated the common claim that we live in a culture caught in the transition from modern to postmodern. Second, we claimed that with this transition has come a renewed appreciation for the role imagination plays in discerning how to interpret not only texts but also the reality toward which these texts point, which has significance for preaching today. In this third part of the chapter, it is our task to think about recent changes in communication and how they bear upon the preacher. This section will focus primarily on the work of Walter Ong, who argues that the Western world has undergone a significant shift in communication and that our current cultural moment is recovering the communication patterns of orality. In *Orality and Literacy: The Technologizing of the Word*, Ong traces three main periods in the history of communication.[42] We will briefly introduce his argument and listen to his critics with the goal of better understanding the way our shifting culture can both communicate and receive descriptions of reality. The recovery of orality identified by Ong leads

---

42. Ong, *Orality and Literacy*. It is worth noting that while Ong's historical typology may be overly simplistic, ignoring the complexity of human experience in history, it is still a helpful foil for us to consider in the attempt to understand our own cultural moment. I am seeking only to make modest claims using Ong's thought as a helpful guide.

us into the heart of the challenge and opportunity of postmodernity for the Christian preacher.

Primary Orality

Ong begins his communication typology by suggesting that primary orality occurred among people who were not writers and whose communion was given primarily through spoken and heard words. In this era, words were "sounds" from within a person's "interior consciousness," and these sounded-out words were events in themselves. Hence, the Hebrew word *dabar* means both "word" and "event." The ear was primary to communication because only sound mattered. There was no backup for memory if people failed to hear and remember what was heard. If people could not speak or remember what they heard, the result was a failure of communication.

Printing would later aid memory by preserving words on paper and in dictionaries. Prior to such help, people possessed a small vocabulary and used words carefully so that truths could be remembered. To recall something important, speakers had to "think memorable thoughts." Many techniques were developed to help people remember, such as mnemonics, linguistic rhythms, and phrase repetitions, but the most obvious and far-reaching technique was the use of story. The "stitching together" of stories, as Ong calls it, was a fundamental way of ensuring that truths were passed on from generation to generation. Because primary orality required speakers and listeners to be physically present, the telling of stories was inevitably also responsible for nurturing community experience and identity.

Ong prefers to call these primitive societies *oral-aural* rather than illiterate because he refuses to concede that the lack of widespread reading skills is a disadvantage. Oral-aural cultures, or cultures of primary orality, have strong social bonds precisely because their interactions are connected by the immediacy of sound rather than being mediated in print. Cultures governed by primary orality are incapable of ornate syntax and abstraction, but they are rich with a communication culture marked by personal interaction. Indeed, without artificial amplification, we need to be fairly close to each other in order to hear each other speak. In contrast, the emergence of cultures of literacy meant that over time much of communication became less dependent on interpersonal interaction. In short, such communication was not interactive but isolated. Ong admits that the submissive character of listening tends to lead oral societies toward authoritarian forms of social institutions. Every organization of the "sensorium" has its limitations, but Ong insists on using primitive societies as a standard for all others.[43] This

43. Ong uses the term "sensorium" to denote the way socialization involves building

is because he believes that listening honors human dignity in a way that seeing, which objectifies and fragments, does not.

By giving primacy to the story of how oral culture was supplanted by writing, Ong opens our eyes to consider a different way of understanding human history—through changes in communication rather than political transitions. Ong helpfully outlines some characteristic differences between oral and written cultures and gives a detailed analysis of the psychodynamics of oral culture.[44] He also calls us to an understanding of sound that forms our relationship and response to the *viva vox Dei* (the living voice of God).

It is important for preachers to be aware of the significant role orality played in Jesus' ministry, as well as in much of Scripture itself. Jesus did not write a book, and most of what is written down in the Bible was most likely first spoken aloud for a listening audience. Of course, there were written manuscripts, especially those that compose what Christians now refer to as the Old Testament, which were crucial for even how Jesus understood himself to be fulfilling his own ministry. Jesus began his public ministry by unrolling the "scroll" and reading it aloud (Luke 4:17). However, Jesus' own preaching ministry is marked by the characteristics of primary orality as described by Ong. Jesus revealed and communicated memorable images and lessons through the techniques of a primarily oral culture. At the center of Jesus' discipling were sounded-out words that created a community of the ear. From the first, the Christ of historic Christianity was profoundly oral.[45]

Writing of similar dynamics, Walker argues that primary orality was profoundly significant for the birth of the Christian faith because oral culture was the most conducive for the creation of community. For example, the reliance on voice for communication encouraged immediacy in communication, and resulted in a cohesion of techniques, especially the use of story, that enabled people to recall and pass on the testimony of Jesus Christ. Walker wonders what would have happened to the gospel in other communication cultures, writing: "If the gospel had come into existence in an electronic culture, it is difficult to see how it could have survived intact. Its texuality—for we must assume that the gospel events would have been written down—would have been subject to the manipulation and infinite

---

patterns of relationship among the senses. He assumes that the organizational structure of the senses that results from socialization can never be democratic or egalitarian. One sense always rules the others. Consequently, cultures, or movements in history, can be compared according to the senses they privilege. He argues that cultures specialize in one of the senses because a hierarchical organization of our perceptual skills makes the act of knowing more productive.

44. Ong, *Orality and Literacy*, 31–56.

45. See also Babin, *New Era*, 19.

maneuverability of word processing."[46] Film would have allowed even more
distortion of gospel truth, as "film can be manipulated by script, camera,
and editor. This pales into insignificance, however, with the advent of digital
recording and the new special effects this makes possible."[47] For Walker, all
of this adds up to show "just how crucial oral culture was for establishing
the gospel."[48]

Building further on these ideas, one could argue that the idea that we
are present to each other in sound helps us to understand God's relationship
to us. For Ong, hearing connects us with another person in an immediate
and inward way while paradoxically preserving some distance between us.
The sense of hearing, then, can point to the way God is simultaneously with
us and beyond us. Put another way, the voice of God reveals God's inner-
most purpose without exposing God to our objectifying gaze. Sound is the
medium that best carries a revelatory message because it delivers something
external without putting us in control of its source. Of course, hearing is not
always so benign. Hearing can be used for spying and eavesdropping, activities that aim at mastery and control. Listening, in its theological guise, needs
to be learned. It is a moral skill, related to the virtue of patience. For Ong,
the sacramental theology of his Roman Catholic faith is instructive for practicing the faithful habits of intimate and loving hearing. We are enabled to
listen to each other only if we learn to listen to God. Thus, the spoken word
elevates our merely physical presence to each other into something deeply
spiritual. Ong's perspective could be summed up in the Pauline phrase that
faith comes through hearing (*Fides ex auditu;* Rom 10:17).

Writing and Print

According to Ong, a second era of communication was initiated by the
writing down of the phonetic alphabet into words that could be read. In
contrast to oral speech, which welled up from unconsciousness, writing involved artificial "context-free language." Communication was now possible
through the eye and not the ear. Though this process took centuries and
began with primitive symbols, it evolved into more complex and diverse
languages that could be written down. The point Ong wants to press is that
this communication practice, because it could happen without sound, was
a paradigm shift.

Gutenberg's invention of the printing press in the 1450s had a profound influence on human culture because, for the first time, individuals

46. Walker, *Telling the Story*, 94.
47. Ibid.
48. Ibid., 95.

expressed themselves on paper for mass distribution. No longer was the story read through stained glass windows by the masses; rather, the words of the Bible could be located on a page. Writing became indispensable. Words became precise "things" that could be recorded in indexes, dictionaries, and lists, and science became possible through exact verbalization. The eye was now primary instead of the ear. No physical relationship was necessary between speakers and hearers; individual readers picked up and put down words on paper within their private worlds. Community was no longer essential for communication.

What happens with a change of communication culture is a change in the way we think. Ong contrasts the right-brain thinking of aural-orality with the left-brain cerebral thinking associated with writing and print. With print, doctrinal catechesis could have a logical order and could be memorized from texts with greatly extended vocabularies. Ong makes the judgment that this led to a "more cerebral form of faith . . . but one day we woke up to the fact that, for the majority of people, the living reality of faith had fled."[49]

To connect this with preaching, preachers in a print-literary world have their tacit consciousness fashioned by the linear message of print. The primary medium of print affects how preachers understand reason, discern truth, and attempt to communicate. Ong writes: "Without writing the literate mind would not and could not think as it does, not only when engaged in writing but even when it is composing its thoughts in oral form. More than any other single invention, writing has transformed human consciousness."[50]

Through writing, the mind learns to think in linear patterns. This new mental mode of thinking fostered by the alphabet changed the ways humans, and in turn preachers, think and relate to the world. This may be why those centuries marked by phonetic literacy have favored the chain of inference as the mark of logic and rationality. Likewise, sermons composed in the print-literary era of communication have favored linear and rational forms of thought. This is still in evidence today, although, if Ong's argument is correct, our culture has moved into a third communication era.

Secondary Orality

The third communication era identified by Ong, secondary orality, is marked by the advent of the electronics revolution. Ong argues that "the

49. Ibid., 99.
50. Ong, *Orality and Literacy*, 28.

electronic transformation of verbal expression has both deepened the commitment of the word to space initiated by writing and intensified by print and has brought consciousness to a new age of secondary orality."[51] Comparing secondary orality with primary orality, Ong stresses that secondary orality is "both remarkably like and remarkably unlike primary orality."[52]

The electronics revolution has opened up new possibilities for group listening and preaching, where head and heart, word and image can merge into one experience. Secondary orality has brought a new way of learning, combining both the right brain and the left brain. Michael Quicke summarizes the differences between the three communication eras as seen in the table below.

Primary Orality	Writing and Print	Secondary Orality
Before writing, but also affected a majority of the population before print	*Alphabetic letter-press, invention of print (1450s)*	*Since 1985, electronic revolution*
Aural/oral way of thinking	*Literate way of thinking*	*New ways of thinking*
Ear: thought relates to sound	*Eye: thought relates to sight*	*Ear and eye: thought relates to sight and sound*
Mono: right brain	*Mono: left brain*	*Stereo: right and left brain, image, beat, and visualization*
Story: memorable, mnemonics, rhythms, repetitions	*Ideas: conceptual, abstract, analytic, explanation, linear, one way*	*Narrative, story and ideas: symbolic, image, experiential, modulation, participation, intuitive, holistic, two-way*
Language: mobile, warm, personally interactive	*Language: inhuman, passive, unresponsive*	*Language: new self-consciously informal style*
Community: group-minded because no alternative	*Individual: private world of print*	*Community: self-conscious global village, spectacle*

Table 2. Characteristics of Ong's Three Areas of Communication[53]

51. Ibid., 135.
52. Ibid., 136.
53. Quicke, *360-Degree Preaching*, 81.

It is particularly important to notice the reemergence of narrative in the era of secondary orality. This classical method of acquiring knowledge was eclipsed in the West with the rise of modernity in the seventeenth century. This was significant for preachers because it meant that the work of interpreting Scripture was dedicated to identifying the ideas that could appeal to reason through ordered proposition. Rather than trusting the Biblical story itself, the preacher had to find the ideas behind the story. As Hans Frei comments in *The Eclipse of the Biblical Narrative*: "In the course of the eighteenth century it [interpretation] came to signify not so much a literary depiction that was literal, metaphorical, allegorical, or symbolic, but rather the single meaning of a grammatically and logically sound propositional statement."[54] Frei argues that during modernity, narrative was often considered an inferior way of knowing, but postmodernity has led to the recovery of the importance of the narrative of the biblical texts, not just the ideas behind the narrative.

With a renewed attention to narrative, words appear to work differently in our culture. For example, Jolyon Mitchell emphasizes that the use of language is now marked by "'spontaneity' and 'conversational casualness' but a spontaneity and casualness that are carefully constructed."[55] This crafted "spontaneity" appeals to all five senses. Multisensory language and story have reemerged as the preferred ways of communicating, as they involve painting pictures in words and evoking multisensory experiences.

Communication in today's electronic age is also clearly influenced by television, cell phones, and the Internet. Michael Rogness stresses this, arguing that the "electronic age" is creating a new kind of audience.[56] Television combines seeing and hearing in ways that contrast remarkably with previous eras of speaking or reading. As a visual medium, "the picture and the graphics are the heart of communication, not the words spoken."[57] Rogness argues that talking on television is not conversation, but is rather a celebration of visibility. In other words, talk on television isn't meant to be listened to. In this sense, the secondary orality that Ong associates with today's electronic age is significantly different from the primary orality of previous ages.

As much as these insights are important for understanding our cultural moment, Ong does not account for nor foresee significant new technological developments in his argument. This is part of the critique of Stephen

54. Frei, *Eclipse of Biblical Narrative*, 9.
55. Mitchell, *Visually Speaking*, 193.
56. Rogness, *Preaching*, 22–23.
57. Ibid., 15.

Webb, who suggests that Ong's interpretation of history as a series of media revolutions is flawed. Webb claims that Ong falls victim to a "nostalgia for the past" that is itself "a byproduct of the way modernity sentimentalizes everything it destroys."[58] Webb critiques Ong's attempt at futuristic predictions of secondary orality by pointing out what Ong could never have predicted. The second coming of orality is being challenged by yet another media revolution—the ubiquitous, omnipresent technological innovations of the Internet. Webb's assessment of this new, wired world of global communication is that it is in "some ways the second coming of the printing press," which once again immerses us in the written rather than the spoken word. However, I would argue that Webb's critique of Ong itself fails to take into account the significant emergence of new technologies like iPhones, iPods, and iPads, which may be giving the voice more power than ever before.

Regardless of Ong's lack of success in predicting the future, he is successful in articulating the importance of sound in our cultural moment. Ong is attentive to the fact that sound is once again shaping how we think, feel, and act. This emergence of the significance of sound through the new technologies of TV, film, and radio is a hopeful sign of a return to one of modernity's neglected senses—the ear. For Ong, sound, not paper, is the native medium of communication. Ong wants to attend to the ways in which the priority of the oral is specific to Western culture, while at the same time making universal claims on behalf of the power of sound.

This brief sketch of Ong's thought highlights that sound is once again shaping our human communication. For preachers interested in the future of Christian proclamation, Ong's study is invaluable. The future of preaching is going to be shaped by a sensorium featuring technological contours similar to those of cultures whose consciousness was formed by orality. By adapting some of the characteristics of what Ong describes as primary orality, preachers may receive insight into how preaching in today's culture of "secondary orality" may be developed.[59]

The reality that our culture has been recovering the significance of orality through electronic media and reorganizing our capacity and interest in hearing invites preachers to consider the dynamic possibilities of orality for Christian proclamation. Preaching dominated by print-based methods of communication may not be the most effective way for people to hear in this cultural moment. The culture of print is in a twilight of its own. The sounded word has returned to our ears through contemporary communication

---

58. Webb, *Divine Voice*, 37. See also 36–47.
59. Ong, *Orality and Literacy*, 136.

technologies. What might this mean for the preacher who is seeking to communicate in this culture of orality's second coming?

Working off the page of Ong, homiletics scholar Richard Jensen identifies some practical dynamics of the shift from preaching in a print-literary world to a world of oral communication and conjectures what form preaching might take in an emerging world of orality.[60] Jensen's thesis is that preaching is shaped by the communication culture of its time. He argues that there is a difference between preaching in a culture where communication is shaped by the eye and preaching in a culture where communication is achieved through the ear. In other words, the homiletic mind shaped in the print-literary world of modernity preaches differently than that of a preacher in an oral-aural culture.

To highlight the distinction, Jensen contrasts the preaching dynamics in an oral culture with preaching shaped in a print-literary culture.[61] He concludes that in a culture in which the human sensorium is shaped by the eye rather than the ear, sermons take on a literary characteristic. For example, sermons in a print-literary culture tend to be left-brained and linear, with the preacher thinking in ideas and structuring these ideas in a logical outline, expressed as propositions to be delineated in an analytic nature. In a print-literary culture, metaphors are used as illustrations to highlight the main ideas, but can be dispensed with once the listener grasps the main ideas. In contrast, according to Jensen, sermons in an oral culture are right-brained, as the preacher thinks in stories rather than abstract ideas. The stitching of stories together, use of repetition, situational rather than abstract themes, a tone of conflict, and metaphors that invite imaginative participation all mark sermons influenced by an oral culture.[62] Thus, a sermon delivered in a print-literary world is going to appeal to an individual's analytic powers of rationality and logic, whereas a sermon preached in a world of orality is going to appeal to the communal, relational powers of narrative and imagination. On the surface, this may seem to endorse the dualism between rationalism and imagination against which we have warned. Jensen himself may be open to this critique. But for our purposes, the essential point to grasp is that the shift from oral to literate culture represents a shift in human sensorium—in how we actually acquire, organize, and process information. An oral culture massages the ear. A culture of print massages the eye.[63] The rise of the print-literary culture dramatically altered

60. Jensen, *Thinking in Story*, 23–29.

61. Ibid., 40–43.

62. Ibid., 28.

63. Ong, *Presence of the Word*, 8.

human interaction with our environment, just as the rising technological culture is altering how we communicate and reason today. Making the shift from eye to ear would be wise for current preachers because they preach in a time of historical transition with significant implications for Christian proclamation.

CONCLUSION: THE CHALLENGE AND THE INVITATION

This time of cultural transition points our attention to a growing anxiety felt in Western preaching for two reasons. First, a literary culture necessarily makes certain assumptions about knowing and relating to the world that must be agreed upon for its influence and power to be secured. However, in today's shifting culture, those assumptions are not as secure. One of the key issues is how a literate clergy deals with the growing postliterate ethos of emerging world Christianity. This is a large part of the existential identity crisis facing the modern preacher. As Ong notes, print helped to create a linear approach to the task of proclamation. When this approach was applied to preaching, the goal of preaching became to teach the abstract idea of a text. The faith engendered in the hearer is "faith" that the *ideas* are true—which, when translated, means that the proposed propositions are logically or empirically verifiable. This assumption, that ideas can be logically proven, is no longer taken for granted within our culture. Second, today's preaching culture is evolving into a new species of communication inspired by technological media. Print technology is rapidly being replaced with new forms of electronic media; churches are making an adjustment to this world of electronic communication that emphasizes sound. They are integrating multimedia technologies to supplement and enhance their worship services. For example, many churches are fitting their auditoriums (not sanctuaries) with new technologies such as multimedia screens, microphones, and soundboards. Preachers are faced with the reality that in the marketplace of competitive religious consumerism, they have to pay attention not only to the right ideas, but also to the right sound. One can lament this situation, but the issue that needs to be faced in today's culture is that *how* something is heard may be just as important as *what* is heard.

Not everyone celebrates the current transition in communication. In *Amusing Ourselves to Death*, Neil Postman unapologetically laments the erosion of the print-literary influence on the American mind and its public discourse.[64] One of Postman's main critiques is that the patterns of communication encouraged and sustained by media such as television (with

---

64. Postman, *Amusing Ourselves to Death*.

its moving images, competing sounds, and virtual experience of place) are displacing those encouraged by print (characterized by the word, discursive reasoning, and the possibilities of logic). Postman's argument is not that words are good and images are bad but that the images preferred by television—as it actually exists as a social institution—are images designed to titillate and entertain. Postman's ultimate concern is for the quality of public life and the possibility of promoting serious discourse. In his estimation, without serious discourse and without the tools that allow serious discourse to happen (e.g., logical reasoning), the institution of democracy will crumble.

For anyone who is called to engage in public discourse like preaching, Postman's warning is wisely heeded. Much of what shapes our culture's idea of "serious" communication is nothing but entertainment designed to brand merchandise. While preachers need to recognize that a shift in communication is happening, they also need to acknowledge that technology, and the ways different technologies communicate information, are not neutral. When preachers get their cues from those in the popular entertainment industry, much of their proclamation can be rendered inane, shallow, or just plain ridiculous. However, while preachers need to recognize that electronic technologies of media are epistemologically loaded, there are reasons for preachers to be more optimistic than Postman acknowledges.

Postman believes that "literate" Christianity is doomed by electronic forms of communication. He suggests that preachers will no longer be able to communicate their faith in the literate manner to which most of Protestantism has been accustomed. Postman's critique, however, is problematic. First, he conflates the content of Christianity with the printed word and the form of thought created by print. However, the content of Christianity is not dependent on the written word, but the Word who became flesh—Jesus Christ. Christianity is a result of God's revelation, which is always the event of God's self-giving, and thus can never be limited or located simply on a page. In other words, preaching and its message are a work of the Holy Spirit given to us in Jesus Christ.

Second, preachers can take comfort by remembering that the world of Scripture was handed down from generation to generation for centuries prior to the development of the printing press. The church does not rise or fall by the eye, but by the ear—with the speaking of the Word. The Christian faith does not require a literate culture in order to communicate its good-news message. Interestingly, Jesus Christ, the eternal Word, chose not to write any words down himself. Jesus passed on his wisdom by word of mouth and action to his apostles, the apostles passed it to their disciples, the disciples to their families and friends, and so on. Christianity spread from person to person by way of mouth, by the telling of the story orally. Postman needs to remember that faith still comes "through what is heard, and what is heard comes through the word of Christ" (Rom 10:17). Thus, preachers need not be anxious as they preach in an emerging context of a postliterate world, even as they are attentive to and discerning about our current communication technologies. Through the power of the Holy Spirit, working in Jesus Christ, God is still able to communicate to humanity.

If we are to take Ong seriously, the shift of communication we are experiencing is not simply a matter of people favoring entertainment over serious discourse, but rather of our technologies having physically changed the human sensorium—the patterns of association that help us to think and make meaning. The point for us is not to evaluate or judge whether this is to be celebrated or lamented, but to observe that it is a real situation with which the preacher today must contend. The primary issue for the preacher is to recognize that people fundamentally hear and process information differently. It is not that sermons dressed in a logical suit are necessarily bad, but that many of our most important ideas may best be heard and understood when communicated through narrative and story rather than in logical outlines subdivided into many points.[65] This is indeed similar to how Jesus himself preached. Jesus, working out of a largely oral culture and tradition, spoke in ways that appealed to the imagination of the hearer. Could it be that what is the matter with preaching today is that we have lost the way that Jesus, God's spoken Word in the flesh, embodies a broader artistic and aesthetic understanding for gospel proclamation?

In a time of transition and twilight, when a print era is fading into an electronic era, it may be that the thinking and speaking modes of oral cultures invite us to consider some possibilities for homiletic practice. The question before us is this: given that today's preacher is caught at twilight between a modern and postmodern world, given that the hermeneutics of suspicion has helped to reclaim the significance of the imagination, and given that the communication culture is recovering the importance of sound and forms of preaching that emphasize orality, what would be a helpful and faithful "homiletic identity"? More specifically, would a metaphor that encouraged preachers to operate with the broader identity of an artist help them to follow the artist Jesus as they find themselves situated in an era that is marked by a renewed interest in both the imagination and the experience of an oral communication? To begin this consideration, we first need to examine the role and power metaphors have in shaping the ways we think, live, and act in the world.

65. Jensen, *Thinking in Story*, 38–39.

2

Metaphor and Identity

Metaphors are very strange because when you put two things together it's a way of discovering meanings which haven't been discovered before.—WALKER PERCY

INTRODUCTION: SEEING AND SEEING AS

The word metaphor comes from the Greek word *metaphora*, derived from *meta*, meaning "over," and *pherein*, meaning "to carry." It refers to a particular set of linguistic and thought processes whereby aspects of one object are "carried over" or transferred to another object, so that we speak of the second object as in relationship with the first. In this way, metaphor is the witness of language to the interconnectedness of all things visible and invisible. A metaphor often takes a word that is commonly used to refer to a thing or an action that we experience by our five senses and then uses it to refer to something that is beyond the reach of those immediate senses.

It is commonly accepted that a *rock* refers to a hard mass of minerals that can be held and weighed, seen and thrown. It is an object a person can feel, see, taste, and touch—it is something on which people stub their toes or which people throw through a window. Rock: there is no ambiguity in the word; it stays the same no matter what. Or does it? Is a rock always perceived as merely an association of mineral grains calcified by pressure and time? Is a rock *always* a physical rock or can it take on and give new meaning when connected to something else? We will return to these questions below as we explore the power and significance of metaphor.

27

When words are put together in relationship and combined as metaphor, they expand and explode into life. As metaphor, words have the ability to shape our perception, our experience, and consequently, our performance. They do this because they inform our values, our imagination, even our feelings. This is possible because metaphors can make us participants in creating meaning as we enter into the relationship between words and objects. We can no longer understand the word by looking it up in the dictionary, for it is no longer just itself; it is alive and inviting us to participate in a new meaning through its re-description of reality. We never see or understand the world the same again after a metaphor—in fact, it may be that without metaphors we cannot see or understand the world at all. This chapter is interested in this "may be." It is interested in how metaphors work and how they subversively shape how we see, experience, and perform life. In this chapter I want to suggest that we live and move by metaphor—that is, in tacit associations of one thing relating to another. I want to claim that metaphor shapes the way in which we see and understand ourselves; it shapes our relationships, roles, and even our identities. More specifically, I want to argue that metaphors of homiletic identity create an association between preachers and the task of preaching that decisively shapes the work preachers do and the way they try to communicate the good news about Jesus Christ.

To that end, this chapter will serve to advance the argument that homiletic identity is shaped by the metaphors associated with the preacher and that a new homiletic identity is needed for our cultural moment. First, we will make this argument by offering a description of metaphor with a clarification of terms; second, we will identify two basic theories of metaphor and offer reasons for adopting the interactionist position; and, third, we will discuss how this theory of metaphor relates to identity formation and offer a brief conclusion assessing how metaphors applied to homiletic identity can shape the performance of preaching.

Our goal will be to gain an appreciation of how metaphor creates concepts and how those concepts direct the perception, experience, and performance of our lives. Following the lead of thinkers such as I. A. Richards, Max Black, Paul Ricoeur, and especially George Lakoff and Mark Johnson (among others), this chapter claims that metaphors have the power to untidy and reorganize the perceptions that form the experience of our reality. We will explore how metaphor "invents" in both senses of the word—that "what it creates, it discovers; and what it finds, it invents."[1]

---

1. Ricoeur, *Rule of Metaphor*, 239.

CLARIFYING TERMS

To begin, let us pull up a chair at a roundtable discussion focused on the exploration of the significance of metaphor. This conversation has a history that stretches deep into the very origins of Western philosophy, and has over time gathered the attention of an impressive and eclectic inter-disciplinary group of thinkers. Philosophers and theologians, scientists and historians, artists and anthropologists, linguists and liturgists come to this table to seriously converse about the power of metaphor. These theorists do not represent a unified voice or perspective. Their views of human language, epistemology, imagination, and philosophical activity are as diverse as the fields they represent. It may at first be daunting to appreciate the delicate complexities represented by these theorists, especially if we do not first understand the vocabulary. The theorists involved freely use a variety of terms without explanation. To begin, let us identify some of the key terms in the discussion on metaphor, which will serve as a vocabulary that may help us enjoy the conversation around the table.

Metaphor

As stated above, metaphor refers to a particular set of intellectual and imaginative processes whereby aspects of one object are "carried over" or transferred to another object, so that the second object is spoken, or thought of, as if it were the first.[2] Various types of metaphor exist and the number of "objects" involved can vary, but the general procedure of "transference" remains the same no matter what type we examine.

    Aristotle's definition of metaphor is still the most quoted definition. Metaphor, according to Aristotle, is simply "the application of a strange term."[3] When we speak of the "hands" of the clock or the "mouth" of a river, Aristotle suggested, we use a term in a way other than its most obvious or literal sense. Aristotle's definition includes some features that are not disputed, such as the claim that metaphor involves a "transfer" or new relationship. Nearly every definition of metaphor includes concepts like these. I. A. Richards, for example, suggests that "when we use a metaphor we have two thoughts of different things active together and supported by a single

2. See Lakoff and Johnson, *Metaphors We Live By*. They argue that metaphorical processes are pre-linguistic and maybe even "pre-conceptual" (in the sense that we make or notice the connections before we think them through consciously). Hence, the way in which a metaphor functions "subconsciously" to shape self-perception and sense of priorities, etc., whether or not it is actually articulated and analyzed.

3. Aristotle, *Poetics*, 82.

work, or a phrase whose meaning is a resultant of their interaction."[4] Max Black expresses the same notion in this definition: "A memorable metaphor has the power to bring two separate domains into cognitive and emotional relation by using language directly appropriate to the one as a lens for seeing the other; the implications, suggesting and supporting values entwined with the literal use of the metaphorical expression, enable us to see a new subject matter in a new way."[5]

Or, more simply, Janet Soskice asserts that: "metaphor is that figure of speech whereby we speak about one thing in terms which are seen to be suggestive of another."[6] More memorable are Nelson Goodman's witty definitions: a metaphor, writes Goodman, involves "teaching an old word new tricks"; a metaphor is "a calculated category mistake"; metaphors are "an affair between a predicate with a past and an object that yields while protesting."[7] Metaphors, however, serve more than simply decorating language so that ideas are more interesting to ponder. Metaphors are pervasive and we could not understand the world without them. In the largest scope of our thinking, speaking, and praying, the coalescence of metaphors is utterly necessary.[8] Mutual metaphors both help make sense of and correct each other. This leads us to consider how the use of some metaphors shape our perceptions of reality.

Root Metaphors: Models, Paradigms, and Moral Frameworks

While some metaphors are used occasionally and incidentally, others are used frequently and systematically. They become a prominent or even the predominant way of speaking about a given topic. Such metaphors are often called "root metaphors," or what we might call "models" or "paradigms." Black defines models as "sustained and systematic metaphors."[9] Sallie McFague describes a model as a "dominant metaphor with comprehensive, organizational potential."[10] Other terms are also used to point to the same

4. Richards, *Philosophy of Rhetoric*, quoted in McFague, *Metaphorical Theology*, 37.

5. Black, *Models and Metaphors*, 236–37.

6. Soskice, *Metaphor and Religious Language*, 15. See also similar definitions by Lakoff and Johnson, *Metaphors We Live By*, 5; and Levin, "Metaphor," 285.

7. Goodman, *Languages of Art*, 68, 69, 73.

8. See Brummer, *Personal God*, 57.

9. Black, *Models and Metaphors*, 236.

10. McFague, *Metaphorical Theology*, 39.

phenomenon, such as "metaphoric system," "paradigm," "framework," or even "parable."[11]

While some metaphors are incidental to life, others are a part of a large system of images for a given entity. These metaphors are so pervasive that we can hardly think or live without them. This is the case in almost every arena of life. For example, Lakoff and Johnson highlight that in North American culture, time is regularly described in terms of money. We speak about spending, saving, buying, wasting, investing, and budgeting time. Likewise, arguments are usually conceptualized with metaphors drawn from war: arguments are won and lost, positions are attacked, shot down, or demolished.[12] Lakoff and Johnson have argued that these models are fundamentally linked with the way we think and live: "It is important to distinguish these isolated and unsystematic cases from systematic metaphorical expressions . . . [for] systematic metaphorical concepts . . . structure our actions and thoughts . . . they are the metaphors we live by."[13]

Regardless of their other qualms, all of these theorists agree that these root metaphors or models are the essential means by which we understand and enlarge our perception of the world, and at the same time they offer us the power to change it. Essentially, metaphors that become models offer us a fresh way to see the world, a way we grasp only through the indirectness of a metaphor's association, an association that suggests both "is" and "is not."[14] The metaphors that are commonly used to enlarge our world of perception are the ones that become root metaphors or models.

It is this understanding of the extension of metaphor as a model, paradigm, or framework that is most compelling when we think of its impact on daily life. The self-conscious use of models, with both their benefits and their risks, is a common phenomenon in most fields of study. Among other things, what this means is that when poets and preachers think via metaphor, it no longer needs to be perceived as an intellectually deviant activity. Such metaphoric thinking is widely accepted as necessary in all creative, orderly, and constructive thought. "What we do not know," writes McFague, "we must simulate through models of what we do know."[15] Before we apply this enriched terminology of metaphor to daily life, this chapter shall

---

11. These are terms often distinguished by theorists of metaphor, but they all in some way refer to fundamental thought patterns that are reflected in systems of metaphors. The term "root metaphor" was introduced by Stephen C. Pepper in *World Hypothesis*, 91.

12. See Lakoff and Johnson, *Metaphors We Live By*, 4–9.

13. Ibid., 55.

14. See Ricoeur, *The Rule of Metaphor*, 22–23.

15. McFague, *Metaphorical Theology*, 24.

consider two divergent theoretical approaches to metaphor that emerge at the roundtable conversation of those who discuss metaphor.

TWO SIDES OF THE TABLE: SUBSTITUTIONARY VS. INTERACTIONIST THEORIES

It does not take long to notice that the theorists who engage the significance of metaphor are not speaking from the same page. Rather, they have developed competing hypotheses to explain how metaphors work and how they relate to human perception and thought. Generally speaking, these hypotheses can be distilled into two broad perspectives. On one side of the table sit theorists who, in the words of Samuel Levine, "see metaphor as a secondary use of language, a departure from its basic function of describing our responses to the outside world," and on the other side of the table sit "those that see it as an essential characteristic, inherent in the nature of language itself."[16]

On the one side are those whose theories of metaphor are known as *substitutionary* or *comparative*.[17] This side understands metaphors to be "a decorative way of saying what could be said literally."[18] This group suggests that the chief use of metaphor is to "sex up" ideas or to ornament human communication and provide colorful, memorable, or artistic embellishment of language. According to Mark Johnson, this perspective maintains that "a metaphor is an elliptical simile useful for stylistic, rhetorical, and didactic purposes, but which can be translated into a literal paraphrase without any loss of cognitive content."[19] This view was developed by Aristotle who believed that by far the greatest accomplishment in philosophy was to be a master of metaphor.[20] His influence on the subject remains dominant throughout most of the history of Western thought.

Historically, this view has often implied that metaphors were secondary, unnecessary, even *deviant* forms of speech. Empiricist philosophers Thomas Hobbes and John Locke, for example, took this depreciation of metaphoric speech to new levels. Locke often mocked the use of metaphor, as well as all figurative speech in rhetoric, as the art of fallacy.[21] In the interest of crisp communication of empirical facts, Hobbes argued that metaphors

16. Levin, "Metaphor," 285.

17. See Black, "More About Metaphor," 27.

18. Soskice, *Metaphor and Religious Language*, 24.

19. Johnson, *Philosophical Perspectives*, 4.

20. Aristotle, *Poetics*, 122.

21. See Locke, *Essay Concerning Human Understanding*, II.X.34.

were unnecessary and deceiving. "Reasoning upon them," according to Hobbes, "is wandering amongst innumerable absurdities."[22] Likewise, Voltaire once scoffed, "Ardent imagination, passion, desire—frequently deceived—produced figurative style. We do not admit it into history, for too many metaphors are hurtful, not only to perspicuity, but also truth, by saying more or less than the thing itself."[23] It seems that one of the assumptions of these Enlightenment intellectuals was that a metaphor was a lie, or at least a way for the imagination to obscure the objective interpretation of reality. In light of this, it is no wonder that from the cold soil of rationalism grew Romanticism's passions as a corrective balance to such extreme positivism.

Though *substitutionary* or *comparative* views of metaphor proved dominant for centuries, recent rethinking of metaphor among philosophers of language has generated a series of theories that attempt to supersede these traditional views. This thinking has had a forceful influence on the metaphor discussion over the last century, so much so that few theorists today appear to defend the traditional view of metaphor at all. [24] Especially important among twentieth-century accounts is the development of an *interactionist* view of metaphor. Many of the key ideas in this approach were first put forward by I. A. Richards and stated most influentially by Max Black and Paul Ricoeur.[25] The *interactionist* view rests on two assumptions. First, it argues that some metaphors are irreducible, such that their meaning cannot be expressed in literal speech. As Johnson summarizes it, Black's theory "argues that there is a class of metaphors with irreducible meaning above and beyond any statement of literal similarities between two objects. . . . Cases of live, effective metaphor, then, are seen as irreducible thought process that can stretch and reorganize conceptual boundaries."[26]

Second, this view posits that "metaphor creates the similarity [rather] than . . . formulates some similarity antecedently existing."[27] This approach emphasizes that metaphor creates a "semantic innovation"—a new or otherwise unimagined meaning—in ways that would not have been possible in more literal speech. It characterizes metaphor not as incidental, but as essential to human language, hermeneutics, epistemology, communication, and creativity. This view is widely reflected among contemporary

22. Hobbes, *Leviathan*, quoted in Johnson, *Philosophical Perspective on Metaphors*, 12.

23. Voltaire, *Works*, 64.

24. See Miller, "Images and Models," 357–400.

25. Richards, *Philosophy of Rhetoric*; Black, *Models and Metaphors*, especially chapters 3 and 13; Black, "More about Metaphor"; Ricoeur, *The Rule of Metaphor*, 85–87.

26. Johnson, *The Body in the Mind*, 70.

27. Black, "Metaphor," 284–85.

theorists. Richards argues that we all live and speak only through an eye for resemblances, whose meanings are a result of the tensive "interaction."[28] Ricoeur adds to this insight by declaring that metaphor's "most important theme . . . is the rhetorical process by which discourse unleashes the power that certain fictions have to redescribe reality," which does not produce a new reality except by creating rifts in an old description of reality's order.[29] Johnson's own theory is based on the thesis that "metaphors are sometimes creative in giving rise to structure within our experience"; or, as he writes, "speech is creative in its metaphorical aspect, by virtue of metaphor's power to restructure our conceptual framework."[30]

To summarize thus far, the theories and descriptions of metaphor that have been briefly described here are representative of a diverse field of study. For the rest of this chapter, let us sit on the *interactionist* side of the table and think about some of the implications of that perspective. We are sitting on this side of the table because, as suggested earlier, some metaphors are irreducible. Not every experience or thought is best engaged through didactic or literal speech. This is an important dynamic to understand if one's vocation is to speak about God. If it is the case that some metaphors are irreducible, it then makes sense that the metaphors one chooses for the identity of a preacher share sympathy with the belief that metaphors are at times the clearest way to articulate complexities.[31] The second reason we are selecting this theory is that most of the contemporary scholarship is being contributed from this theoretical conversation. As these ideas are being pressed forward into new areas of study, they may hold the best promise and possibility for how to help preachers think about their identity in the twilight of modernity. Finally, by choosing to investigate this perspective more deeply, this conversation about metaphor allows us to probe how metaphor is involved in our everyday conceptual thinking and acting in the world. To that end, let us focus more directly on recent scholarship that will enable us to appreciate the possible significance of metaphor's confluence of thought and action in our lives.

28. Richards, *Philosophy of Rhetoric*, 89.

29. Ricoeur, *Rule of Metaphor*, 7, 22–23. See also Ricoeur, "Problem of the Will," 283.

30. Johnson, *Body in the Mind*, 98; see also Johnson and Erickson, "New Theory of Metaphor," 292.

31. See Ortony, "Metaphor," 480.

CONNECTING METAPHOR TO IDENTITY FORMATION

This section is dedicated to showing how, according to recent philosophical studies of metaphor, metaphor permeates daily life—in perception, experience, and performance in reality.

Metaphor Has the Power to Shape Perception

Metaphors create perceptions of reality

To understand how metaphors are significant in creating our perceptions of reality, it is important for us to reemphasize the relationship between metaphors, paradigms, and models. According to recent scholarship, we are able to make sense of daily life by the perceptions made possible by the metaphors we live by. While some metaphors are used occasionally, others are used systematically. As suggested earlier, these metaphors are known as "root metaphors," or what we might call "models" or "paradigms." Lakoff and Johnson have argued metaphors, when they work at the level of paradigms or models, are the fundamental means by which we perceive the world. Essentially, metaphors that become models offer us a unique way to discern the world. The metaphors that become commonly used to help us see our world of perception are the ones that become root metaphors. It is this understanding of the extension of metaphor as a model, paradigm, or framework that is most compelling when we think of the impact of metaphor on the perceptions that make up our reality.

Models, in an organic, consistent, and comprehensive manner, give us a way of thinking and feeling about the unknown in terms of the known. Or, as Black suggests, a model gives us a "grid," "screen," or "filter" which helps us organize our thoughts about a less familiar subject by means of seeing it in terms of a more familiar one.[32] Models are necessary for they give us something about which to think when we do not know what to think, or a way of talking when we do not know how to talk. But they also carry a real danger, according to Black, for they exclude other ways of thinking and talking, and in so doing can easily become literalized or identified as the one and only way of understanding a subject. This danger is more prevalent with models that act as root metaphors because models have a wider range and are more permanent; they tend to object to competition in ways that metaphors used merely as figures of speech do not. Metaphors that become models do not welcome conflation, and even in the case of models of the

---

32. See Black, *Models and Metaphors,* chapters 3 and 13.

same type there is often great resistance to it. This is due in part to the literalization of models, and it is probably their greatest risk, while at the same time their greatest strength.

Arguably, no one has done more to champion the pervasive power of metaphors that work as paradigms to shape our human perception than Thomas S. Kuhn in *The Structure of Scientific Revolutions*.[33] While challenging traditional assumptions, he puts forward an argument that sheds light on some significant features of scientific thinking and research that have been misunderstood or overlooked in one way or other. Kuhn raises the idea that perhaps science "does not develop by the accumulation of individual discoveries and inventions,"[34] but instead through a change of scientific "paradigm." This concept of "paradigm" as the means for scientific revolution has been the point of greatest interest in the subsequent conversation.[35]

Kuhn shows how "paradigms" in science serve as ideal types that show forth a coherent nexus of relations that become a normative model for understanding a human endeavor or object of knowledge.[36] For example, light is conceptualized in terms of waves. Atoms and molecules are conceived to function like billiard balls. Understood as a double helix, DNA is often compared to a ladder. In each case, a single metaphor has given rise to a whole pattern of scientific thinking and theorizing that functions as a controlling paradigm or model for scientific discovery. In other words, the prominence of various scientific theories in physics, chemistry, and the social sciences depends in part on the descriptive accuracy and imaginative power of a single metaphor that functions as a normative paradigm or model.

Metaphors as extensions into models can influence how we see reality as they limit or expand our ability to perceive the world in certain creative ways. This is the function of metaphor that is most highly regarded as a way of helping us creatively see new insights about the world. The creative act of seeing a problem or a project, whether it is the solution to a mathematical puzzle, the writing of a poem, or the understanding of the dynamics of macroeconomics, is a selection, combination, and synthesis of the already familiar into new wholes. This does not involve creating *ex nihilo*, but using

---

33. Kuhn, *Structure of Scientific Revolutions*.

34. Ibid., 2.

35. Many of the early responses to Kuhn's theory are collected in Lakatos and Musgrave, eds., *Criticism and Growth*. Another anthology is Gary Gutting, ed., *Paradigms and Revolutions*. The volume edited by Frederick Suppe, *The Structure of Scientific Theories*, surveys the broader movement in philosophy of science as well as the debate surrounding Kuhn.

36. Kuhn, *Structure of Scientific Revolutions*, 129.

what has been given or discovered to see in new ways.[37] The power and glory of metaphor, according to McFague, is its capacity to invent meaning as well as to police meaning, to give us a new "what is," while at the same time to restrict what "is not."[38] All of this is to say, we use metaphors in order to see and make sense of reality. The crucial point is that metaphors help us see or perceive the ordinary associations of existence in new ways.

Metaphors use imagination to discover and "redescribe" reality

A second significant way metaphor impacts our perceptions of reality is the way in which metaphor exercises the imagination. Ricoeur, by combining a semantic theory of metaphor with a psychological theory of imagination and feeling, explains how metaphors use the imagination. He defines this semantic theory as "an inquiry into the capacity of metaphor to provide untranslatable information and, accordingly, into metaphor's claim to yield some true insight about reality."[39] Ricoeur weds this theory to a concept of imagination and feeling, asserting that metaphors, along with what he calls truth value (or ontological claims), are partly constituted by images and feelings.[40]

Ricoeur identifies three critical steps for appreciating metaphor's dependence on the imagination. He draws "specifically on Kant's concept of productive imagination as schematizing a synthetic operation."[41] In the first step, imagination is the "seeing" which directs the shift in logical distance. The role of the imagination is to provide *insight* into likeness. Ricoeur calls this act of thinking/seeing, "the instantaneous grasping of the combinatory possibilities."[42]

The second step involves the "pictorial" dimension. It is this step that constitutes the *figurative* DNA of metaphor. This suggests that the first function of the imagination is an imaginative leap and the second is a picture

---

37. For example, Arthur Koestler's critical study, *The Act of Creation*, gives hundreds of examples of breakthroughs in various fields—especially science—made because of the ability of the human mind, when freed from conventional paradigms, to "see" new similarities that were formally blocked. He notes that placing a similarity that has not been seen before into previously unrelated matrices of thought is the essence of discovery—and this is metaphor's most obvious and brilliant distinction. See Koestler, *Act of Creation*, 199–200, 119–21.

38. McFague, *Metaphorical Theology*, 34.

39. Ricoeur, "Metaphorical Process," 143.

40. Ibid., 144.

41. Ricoeur, *Rule of Metaphor*, 147.

42. Ibid., 148. See also Johnson, *Philosophical Perspectives on Metaphor*, 40.

of the semantic innovation. Thus, according to Ricoeur, imagining "is the concrete milieu in which and through which we see similarities. To imagine, then, is *not* to have a mental picture of something, but to display relations in a depicting mode."[43] Ricoeur ties his metaphoric understanding of imagining to the Wittgensteinian duck of "seeing as" (the famous duck/rabbit gestalt), even though Wittgenstein himself did not extend his analysis beyond the field of perception.[44] It is here, again in the imagination, that our perceptions begin to organize language into ways that redescribe reality.[45]

The third step in the evolving function of imagination is the moment of suspension, or "the moment of negativity brought by the image in the metaphorical process."[46] This crucial step renders possible a remaking of reality. Ricoeur claims that "a metaphor may be seen as a model for changing our way of looking at things, of perceiving the world."[47] This involves a suspension of the ordinary and an invasion of the extraordinarily new. However, the ordinary is not destroyed but is held in tension with the new. The contrast between the daily routines of ordinary life and the possibility of a new world created and redescribed by metaphor is crucially important for understanding the pervasive impact metaphor plays in daily life.

Overall, Ricoeur is arguing that metaphors serve as "heuristic fictions" whose meanings may occupy a privileged position in ontological discourse.[48] The case is not merely that a metaphor expresses one subject

43. Ricoeur, "Metaphorical Process," 150.

44. See Wittgenstein, *Philosophical Investigations*, 194.

45. Ibid. Ricoeur locates the second stage of his theory of imagination on the borderline between the geography of psychology and pure semantics. The metaphorical meaning thus compels an exploration of the boundary between the verbal and the nonverbal.

46. Ibid.

47. Ibid., 152.

48. See Johnson, *Body in the Mind*, 139. Here Johnson argues that any adequate

as like or unlike another, but that metaphor creates—in the tension of duality—a judgment between a literal, conventional interpretation (which self-destructs) and an extended, new interpretation, which is recognized as a plausible ontological condition. That is to say, through metaphor, the imagination is used to *redescribe* our reality in order to discover or *disclose a new* possibility of reality, and this possibility at the same time points beyond ordinary reality. This is a weighty assertion, resting on the imagination's capacity in metaphor to both create a literal meaning and subvert and extend that meaning through a "heuristic" transformation.[49]

Metaphor Has the Power to Shape Experience

Metaphors can shape experience because they are pervasive in everyday life

Nearly every recent work on metaphor sees metaphoric speech as a pervasive feature of almost all types of spoken and written communication. In other words, it is almost impossible to communicate without metaphor. Several theorists go so far as to say that all human thought and experience is fundamentally metaphorical.[50] For example, in aesthetics, Timothy Binkley maintains that there is no pure core of literal meaning, and, therefore, there is no reason to treat the literal as an ideal against which metaphor is to be measured.[51] In sociology, R. H. Brown insists that all knowledge is metaphorical.[52] In rhetoric, Gerald W. Casenave claims that metaphor is fundamentally a world-structuring discourse.[53] In philosophy of language, Ted Cohen points to the aesthetic, cognitive, ethical, and intimate values of metaphor.[54] Philosopher S. I. Hayakawa suggests that language changes and grows through metaphor,[55] and Paul deMan asserts that metaphor can

---

account of meaning and rationality must give a central place to the embodied and imaginative structures of understanding by which we grasp the world.

49. Ricoeur, "Metaphorical Process," 152–53. Metaphors, according to Ricoeur, operate as "heuristic instruments," which can create a "new language" for scientific theories.

50. For example, Mary Hesse argues that all language is metaphorical in "The Cognitive Claims of Metaphor," 1–16.

51. Binkley, "Truth and Probity," 136–53.

52. Brown, *Society as Text*, 97–117

53. See Casenave, "Taking Metaphor Seriously," 19–25.

54. Cohen, "Metaphor," 3–12.

55. Hayakawa, *Language and Thought*, 108–12.

be seen as operating in the shaping and extending of our understanding.[56] From this perspective, metaphor's role in science is a case of unacknowledged implication, an apparent but unmentioned internal practice. Ian Barbour argues that both science and religion are erected upon hypothetical root metaphors about the nature of the world and human experience.[57] In this light, both science and religion use metaphors to convey ideas about the known, and thus their fruitful discoveries and insights are grown in metaphorical soil. The voices insisting on the primary pervasiveness of metaphor are legion, coming from philosophy, the natural sciences, the social sciences, and the humanities.[58] This is important because it suggests that metaphors are not just the provenance of poets, but are significant, in one form or another, for both language and thought patterns in daily life.

Even common prepositions often function as metaphors. Consider how often the terms "in," "on," "upon," or "into" are used with respect to something that has no literal spatial boundaries. A cup can be set "on" a table. But a prohibition can be imposed "on" a corporation. Water can be poured "into" a fishbowl. But a person can be baptized "into" the church or ordained "into" the ministry. Tables and fishbowls have definable spatial boundaries; corporations and churches do not. Yet corporations and churches are thought about in terms of spatial boundaries.[59] The simple use of spatial prepositions as metaphors suggests that metaphor pervades even the most mundane human experience.

Metaphors interpret experience

All formal disciplines that require one to describe abstract concepts and ideas, or articulate new discovery, rely, in no small way, on the use of metaphor for interpretation. Kenneth Burke points out that "abstraction" means "drawing from," or the drawing out of similar strains and motifs from dissimilar situations.[60] In other words, the principal tasks of conceptual thought—analysis, classification, and synthesis—all depend on this process of "drawing out" similarities from dissimilarities.[61] When we practice interpretation, that is, when we analyze, classify, and synthesize a series of events,

56. DeMan, "Epistemology of Metaphor," 13–30.

57. See Barbour, *Myth, Models, and Paradigms.* For a similar work and argument, see MacCormac, *Metaphor and Myth.*

58. See Dunne, *Search for God.*

59. See Goldingay, *Models for Scripture,* 8.

60. Burke, *Permanence and Change,* 137.

61. Ibid., 141.

structures, objects, etc., we suppress the ways in which they are dissimilar because we have discovered significant similarities among them. What we find to be significant arises from our own limited perspective; metaphorical thinking—which is to say, all thinking—is intrinsically a matter of one's perspective, and that perspective is a result of lenses of interpretation. We say "this" is like "that," but we realize that it is also *not* like that, and that other ways of linking the similarities and dissimilarities are possible. Thus, it is possible to have more than one metaphor or even to change existing metaphors depending on one's interpretation.

This understanding of interpretation is particularly important in the experience of communication on both sides of the effort. Effective communication by means of metaphors requires an imaginative speaker, but also an active and perceptive listener who can do the work of interpretation. "The effect of metaphor," observe Mary Gerhart and Alvin Russell, "is largely dependent on the knowledge state of the reader."[62] Like irony, sarcasm, and hyperbole, metaphor requires a listener or reader to recognize and interpret it as such. New or striking metaphors require additional time and effort to comprehend.[63] Some metaphors, especially the most pervasive, commonplace metaphors, are understood effortlessly. Others require contemplation or spontaneous insight.[64]

Many metaphors go unrecognized and unappreciated in our daily practice of interpretation. As Donald Davidson observes, "Many of us need help if we are to see what the author of a metaphor wanted us to see and what a more sensitive or educated reader grasps." Davidson goes on to suggest that "the legitimate function of so called paraphrase is to make the lazy or ignorant reader have a vision like that of a skilled critic."[65] Until we become skilled users of language, we need paraphrases, overt similes, and patient critics to help us sense the power and potential of metaphoric speech. Just as a music appreciation course can enable students to interpret the power and presence of a Bach fugue or the delicate inner logic of a Chopin nocturne, so too can careful instruction in the power of metaphor make a Hebrew psalm, a Victorian hymn, or a eucharistic prayer come to life with new meaning and significance.[66]

62. Gerhart and Russell, "Cognitive Effect of Metaphor," 121.

63. See Ortony, "Metaphor," 479.

64. Paul Ricoeur argues, "a metaphor does not exist in itself, but in and through an interpretation" (*Interpretation Theory*, 50).

65. Davidson, "What Metaphors Mean," 48.

66. Part of the work of Christian discipleship in catechesis, according to liturgical scholar John Witvliet, is to point to the pervasiveness and power of metaphoric experience in the activity of worship. See Witvliet, "Metaphor in Liturgical Studies," 28–30.

Metaphor Has the Power to Shape Performance

*We perform our metaphors through the intimate
connection between thinking and acting*

Metaphor has long been treated simply as a matter of rhetorical device, merely a deceptive figure of speech. But twentieth-century reflection, beginning with Richards,[67] and more recently with Lakoff and Johnson,[68] has a more positive and constructive view of metaphor as fundamental to the way we think and speak. Lakoff and Johnson press further by suggesting that metaphor is also intimately related to how we act. We approach an argument differently, they observe as an example, because we think of it and talk about it in warlike metaphors. In other words, something similar pertains in all spheres of action and experience when we conceptualize something metaphorically.

Ricoeur also suggests that metaphor is essential not only to the process of human cognition but also to human behavior. He maintains that "conceptualization cannot reach meaning directly or create meaning out of itself *ex nihilo;* it cannot dispense with the detour of mediation through figurative structures [e.g., metaphor]. This detour is intrinsic to the very working of concepts that inform human behavior."[69] If metaphors are seen as paradigmatic concepts, then it is these concepts that are the very things that direct our actions. As Lakoff and Johnson write, "If we are right in suggesting that our conceptual system is largely metaphorical, then the way we think, what we experience, and what we do every day is very much a matter of metaphor."[70] Significantly, the claim being put forward here is that the concepts or images created by metaphor have the potential to shape the roles we perform in life.

Metaphor shapes our actions in life because it puts into tensional or interactive relationship words and the objects to which those words refer, thereby structuring our world and our selves in it. In Lakoff and Johnson's example, Argument Is War, our conceptual system of argument is partially structured, understood, performed, and talked about in terms of war.[71]

67. Richards, *Philosophy of Rhetoric*, 94.

68. See Lakoff and Johnson, *Metaphors We Live By*, 3.

69. Ricoeur, *Dialogues*, 23.

70. Lakoff and Johnson, *Metaphors We Live By*, 3.

71. The capitalization is a stylistic technique used by Lakoff and Johnson in *Metaphors We Live By*, and a device I will use in later chapters to consider different metaphors

The crucial point is that "because we conceive of things in that way—we act according to the way we conceive of things."[72] In short, we *perform* our metaphors.

Metaphors not only create concepts but also impact our affective experience

Metaphors as interpretive, explanatory devices share structural charac-teristics with scientific models, but because models can also emerge from existential experience, they have affective dimensions in the same way po-etic metaphors do. If we consider how extended metaphors, models, and paradigms manifest priorities within a Christian tradition, we see that they organize networks of images and therefore contribute to a kind of system-atic thought, or a comprehensive way of envisioning reality. This envision-ing implicitly raises questions of truth and reference, particularly if making ontological claims such as "Christ is Lord." As metaphors control the ways people envision both human and divine reality, we cannot avoid exploring how this affectively impacts human experience. What kind of Lord is this Christ? How we understand the metaphoric association impacts how we feel about the status of this particular faith claim.

Ricoeur argues that "imagination and feeling are not extrinsic to the emergence of the metaphorical sense."[73] In other words, metaphors not only reflect acts of cognitive comparison, they also stimulate emotion. For ex-ample, identifying Jesus Christ as the "light of the world" or the "lamb of God" not only makes a statement about who "Christ" is ontologically, it also suggests an affective emotion that is quite different from one that might arise from the claim that "Christ is the master and commander." Both ex-amples conjure particular feelings within us. Successful metaphors are able to make an apt comparison and create an *ethos* or milieu that is appropriate for the subject.

Working from Ricoeur's imagination theory, Rodney Kennedy argues that the metaphors preachers use in a sermon have an affective shape on the hearer's perception of a preacher's character. As a preacher uses metaphors to construct a different reality for his or her audience, the focus is on the *invitation* to participate with him or her. It is an invitation to intimacy and a shared view of reality, and when participated in, begins the creation of an emotional bond between the speaker and the listener that shapes the

for homiletic identity.

72. Lakoff and Johnson, *Metaphors We Live By*, 5.

73. Ricoeur, "The Metaphorical Process," 246.

invisible character of the community. In this way, Kennedy argues, "metaphor forms community and affective intimacy between the preacher and the congregation."[74] As significant as this is, our aim is to go beyond this, to explore not just the power of metaphor used in the relationship others have to the pulpit, but its prior "power" to shape the preacher's own sense of his task and how to approach it.

Metaphors can shape patterns of behavior

As discussed above, Kuhn shows how "paradigms" in science function as ideal types that reveal a coherent nexus of relations that become normative models for understanding a human endeavor or object of knowledge. A paradigm, argues Kuhn, organizes and "determines larger areas of [our] experience,"[75] and it can give rise to a whole pattern of scientific thinking and theorizing that serves as a controlling framework for research and discovery. In other words, the prominence of various theories in science (physics, chemistry, the social sciences) is dependent in part on the descriptive accuracy and imaginative power of a single root metaphor, model, or paradigm. Kuhn's thesis of models and paradigms can also be employed to think about the patterns that shape our actions and history outside of science.

For example, competing historiographical patterns use different metaphors or paradigms for thinking about historical change. Consider how Karl Marx uses the Hegelian dialectic to argue that all history can be reduced to economic competition between the powerful *bourgeois* and the working *proletariat*. Or note how many Christians continue to debate about what was the "high-point" or "driving force" in the development of worship: liturgies, rites of initiation, daily prayer, or eucharistic practice. One's interpretation depends on one's paradigm. It is in this light that Kuhn radically suggests that if one can successfully change an operating paradigm or model, one can not only understand history—one can change it. As Kuhn writes, "Scientific Revolutions are here taken to be those non-cumulative development episodes in which an older paradigm is replaced in whole or in part by an incompatible new one."[76] This new conceptual model, once established in the mind, assesses the "what is" of reality. It follows that revolutions in science, history, religion, or personal life are born not by the slow evolutionary accumulation of information over time, but by sudden and often unpredictably jarring paradigm shifts. These shifts can create new

74. Kennedy, *Creative Power of Metaphor*, 105.

75. Ibid., 129.

76. Kuhn, *Structure of Scientific Revolutions*, 93.

commitments that impact not only a discipline, but "group commitments" of shared values, meaning, and loyalty.[77]

In this sense of "group commitment," models also have a pervasive influence on the way we conceive moral ethics. For example, Trevor Hart argues that Charles Taylor's account of identity in *Sources of the Self* overlaps with the extension of metaphor developed by Lakoff and Johnson.[78] Taylor's basic claim, according to Hart, is that human selfhood is constituted by a continuous attempt to make sense of our lives. He argues that such sense-making is contingent on our inhabiting "inescapable frameworks," or imaginative constructs which alone can finally account for our moral reactions and responses in the world. These frameworks are both "experience-constituted and (duly) experience-constitutive." Hart maintains that Taylor's "inescapable frameworks" function as imaginative inventions that inherently make sense only when "articulated in ontological terms."[79] We are given a "sense" of these ontological distinctions as frameworks—as a "pattern tacitly known which structures our moral experience" and gives us a "sense of the good."[80] Hart argues that Taylor's "tacit sense" does not lead us to lounge in a room of relativity, but instead may show us the path that leads into a larger world where we are compelled to reconsider the deepest structures of human nature—and, indeed, all reality.[81] What this suggests is that the visions of the good that guide our moral practices are not arbitrary frameworks, but are particular metaphors that shape our ontological beliefs and in turn our practices.

CONCLUSION: REDESCRIBING A ROCK

These samplings from the metaphor distillery are not exhaustive, nor are they intended to be. Interested tasters could sample many more drams, but these quick shots offer a varied tasting to help us appreciate the complex and subtle influence of metaphor in our daily lives. These samplings highlight the power and glory of our ability to discover and create meaning through metaphor and highlight how meaning shapes our behavior. It is with this palate of appreciation developed that we will consider how metaphor may

77. Ibid., 184. Kuhn himself draws this connection. In a postscript discussing how paradigms are the constellation of our group commitments,

78. Hart, "Creative Imagination," 1–13. See also Taylor, *Sources of the Self*, especially part 1.

79. Hart, "Creative Imaginaiton," 9–10.

80. Ibid., 10.

81. Ibid., 11.

shape the event and performance of Christian proclamation. In our brief time at the metaphoric roundtable discussion, we examined metaphor's quality of unifying witness as it acts as a linguistic sign to the interconnectedness of things visible and invisible. Metaphors can take a word that is commonly used, link it to a thing or action that we experience by means of our five senses, and then use it to refer to something that is beyond the reach of our immediate senses. This chapter began by asserting that it is commonly accepted that a *rock* refers to a hard mass of minerals that one can empirically feel, see, taste, and touch. The word contains no ambiguity. A rock remains unchanged.

And then one day Jesus looked at his disciple Simon and said, "You are a *rock.*" Jesus gave Simon a new name—a fresh identity. By means of the miracle of metaphor, the word took the man with it, and was launched, surprisingly, into another realm of meaning altogether. Simon has been Rock (*Petros—Peter*) ever since. One can only imagine how this new self-description functioned as a revolution in Simon's understanding of his identity. From that moment, his life was forever framed by this metaphoric association. To this day we still wrestle with the connections and implications springing from that simple metaphor. In a similar way, it may be wise to wrestle with the simple metaphors that we apply to the homiletic identity of the Christian preacher.

Suggesting the importance of metaphor to homiletics is not an original idea.[82] However, the significance of metaphor for the pulpit has traditionally been limited to discussions concerning talk of God and has focused on the reliability of human language to describe God in proclamation. This book attempts to take the relationship between homiletics and metaphor in a different direction. As previously discussed, certain root metaphors become models—systematic images that shape a sense of meaning and expectation of reality—that have the power to mold our conceptual thought and, in turn, direct our behavior. This project explores how established root metaphors of homiletic identity influence the way in which preachers think and perform in the pulpit and how these metaphors of identity betray particular theological assumptions about the nature of revelation in the divine drama of Christian worship. As part of the divine drama of Christian worship, these metaphors of homiletic identity influence not only a preacher's method of preparation, sermon content, and performance of delivery, but they also possess a commissive force that shapes the attitudes and expectations of those who listen to the preaching. As Wittgenstein writes, "A *picture* held us

---

82. See, for example, Buttrick, *Homiletic*, 113–25; Kennedy, *Creative Power of Metaphor*; Long, *Preaching*; and Troeger, *Creating Fresh Images*.

captive. And we could not get outside it."[83] This is true in the church, as both preachers and congregations find it difficult to get outside governing images of the preacher that condition how they value and what they expect of the sermon. The task of this book is to explore the conceptual models that shape homiletical acts and then, in a Kuhnian sense, to offer a new paradigm or model by articulating a new metaphor for homiletic identity.

Competing homiletic identities exist, but the vast majority cluster around two pervasive root metaphors. The first is The Preacher as Teacher—operating within the Augustinian legacy of relying on rhetoric as a means of teaching Christian faith; the second is The Preacher as Herald—championed by Karl Barth, whose strong emphasis on revelation completely severed rhetoric from homiletic consideration. These two metaphors of identity agree at some points regarding the purpose of preaching, but at other points rival each other, thereby illuminating different theological suppositions about who a preacher is and what a preacher is expected to accomplish through a sermon. By exploring these models, we can begin to overhear a historical conversation within homiletic theory, and we can assess their respective theological strengths and weaknesses. In the end, I will suggest another "as" be added to this conversation: The Preacher as Liturgical Artist. I will propose that this root metaphor has the power to pull into its inescapable framework the best of both the previous metaphors, while at the same time avoiding some of their dangers, which will free the Christian preacher to speak with a fresh imagination and creativity that are reminiscent of Jesus' own preaching.

83. Wittgenstein, *Philosophical Investigations*, 115.

3

The Preacher as Teacher

He who teaches should avoid all words that do not teach.—AUGUSTINE

INTRODUCTION: GUARDING THE DEPOSIT

In chapter 2, we explored the significance of metaphor as we considered its potential to shape a person's framework of perception. We understand and make sense of the world by thinking, often implicitly, with complex metaphoric relationships. Metaphors weave a tacit web of relations between *this* and *that*, which guide the way we perceive, feel, and act in the world. These implied metaphors are not a matter of mere words; they are a force shaping how we live. By applying this insight to metaphors associated with identity, whether chosen or given, personal or professional, we can see how metaphors shape the ways in which identities are lived and experienced. More specifically, if we apply this argument to identities given to the Christian preacher (hereafter referred to as homiletic identities), we can trace a nexus of relationships and theological assumptions in a given identity that encourage certain homiletic practices and reveal presuppositions related to proclamation.

In the next two chapters, we will explore how the metaphors associated with two traditional homiletic identities have shaped the practice of preaching. We will investigate how a given metaphor applied to a homiletic identity shapes who a preacher is to be and what particular entailments that metaphor has for the preacher. In this chapter we will focus on The Preacher as Teacher (*didache*) and in the next chapter we will turn to The Preacher as Herald (*kerygma*). Both of these identities have long traditions in homiletic history; consequently, both have considerably influenced assumptions of what a preacher is to accomplish in the pulpit. Though on the surface they may seem closely related, each is guided by subtle but significant differences of theological emphasis. We will argue that The Preacher as Teacher places a burden of responsibility on the human agency of the preacher to communicate the "right" Biblical ideas, while The Preacher as Herald places particular importance on divine agency in proclaiming the gospel, at the potential risk of underestimating the nature and significance of the human contribution.

Since the flowering of classical culture, there has been a close link between education and virtue that exalted the role of thinkers and teachers. Following his teacher, Plato suggested that philosophers should rule the ideal state. While he was less ambitious in this regard, Aristotle himself suggested, "the true aim of education is the attainment of happiness through perfect virtue."[1] This assumption that truth is connected to happiness and virtue also underlies the church's exaltation of the role of teachers within the society of the blessed. As in the world, teachers in the church perform basic tasks that can be summarized as follows:

1. A teacher is one whose occupation or vocation is to teach.

2. A teacher causes others to know something.

3. A teacher guides the studies and development of students.

4. A teacher imparts knowledge.

5. A teacher instructs by example.

6. A teacher forms habits and practices of learning.

In the modern pulpit, The Preacher as Teacher is one of the normative homiletic identities. The Preacher as Teacher is a homiletic identity that understands the event of preaching as an act of catechesis.[2] That is, the preacher's goal is to offer sermons that give clear and persuasive instruction on the meaning of Scripture, the doctrines of the church, and the ethical implications of both for Christian living.[3] Christian preachers who are shaped by this metaphor serve as an instructional aid for the baptized. As a result,

1. Aristotle, *Nicomachean Ethics,* X,VIII.

2. See Gatch, "Basic Christian Education," 79–108.

3. For definitions of the preacher as teacher, see John H. Westerhoff's description in "Teaching and Preaching," 467–69. See also Allen, "Preacher as Teacher," 29–46; Allen, *Teaching Sermon,* 13–16; Williamson and Allen, *Teaching Minister,* 26–46; and Williamson and Allen, *Vital Church,* 78–80.

the sermon is designed to help the listener grasp and assimilate the main ideas of a scriptural text, doctrine, or creed into an assenting belief that shapes daily life. In this sense, according to Ronald Allen, The Preacher as Teacher understands himself or herself to be an authoritative agent for the intellectual and moral formation of the Christian church.[4] The preacher assumes that what people need or are looking for when they come to church is more knowledge, both theoretical and practical. The purpose of this identity can be conceived as a bridge spanning a gulf, where the freight of biblical and theological wisdom can be passed over the expansive distance between pulpit and pew. The preacher and congregation who operate with this homiletic identity expect a sermon to clearly communicate ideas extracted from the Bible and church doctrine in such a way that it will enable congregants to integrate these ideas into daily living.[5] The end goal is always to teach the Bible or Christian doctrine.[6]

In what follows in this chapter, we will identify the ancient source of The Preacher as Teacher and then explore a modern example to demonstrate how this homiletic identity has more recently shaped the purpose, content, language, and form of sermons. We will next highlight the cultural context of this identity in modernity to investigate its influence before analyzing some of the entailments of this model. At the conclusion of the chapter, we will discuss both the promise and the perils of this identity for today's preacher.

THE PREACHER AS TEACHER

It may be argued that The Preacher as Teacher is a homiletic identity whose roots go as far back as synagogue worship, where the teacher, or rabbi, was one who gave an "exposition" and "application" of Biblical texts to the lives of the hearers.[7] Jaroslav Pelikan notes that in the Hebrew synagogue tradition, rabbis provided "an exposition of the text that compared and contrasted earlier interpretations and then *applied* the text to the hearers."[8] In this sense, the rabbi is the communal teacher of law and tradition applied to practical living. John H. Westerhoff argues that in the early church this

---

4. Allen, *Preaching and Practical Ministry*, 33.

5. Williamson and Allen, *Teaching Minister*, 42.

6. Williamson and Allen, *Vital Church*, 79.

7. See Worley, *Preaching and Teaching*, 57–61. See also Turner, "History of Preaching," 186. For a detailed study of ancient Jewish preaching, see Osborn, *Folly of God*.

8. Pelikan, *Jesus through the Centuries*, 12.

rabbinic model is linked to the Greek word *didache*.[9] Preaching that can be considered *didache* is dedicated to aiding in understanding the meaning of Scripture and the doctrinal and ethical implications of the Christian faith. In this sense, the preacher is charged with the responsibility of intellectual, moral, and spiritual formation through the act of instruction.

Within the Christian tradition, no one has done more to encourage this identity than Augustine of Hippo (354–430), who defines and describes it in his classic work *On Christian Doctrine*.[10] Augustine, influenced by the rhetorical approach of Cicero, believed that the calling of the Christian preacher was to explain Scripture in a way that "teaches, delights, and persuades" the hearer toward the ultimate end of life, which is the love of God.[11]

By looking at Augustine, we will be able to understand a primary source for the metaphor of The Preacher as Teacher in its original context, which will then enable us to see how it has been adapted for use today. Moreover, this will also allow us to see how metaphors of identity can change in focus and meaning within different cultural contexts. For example, the ancient and modern castings of a metaphor differ in accordance with changes in the wider cultural and intellectual milieu. We will see how a metaphor with considerable strength, such as Augustine's, can be weakened in a different cultural context. To accomplish this, we will look at how Augustine understands this homiletic identity in *On Christian Doctrine*, especially book 4 where he lays out in more detail who the preacher is and what the preacher is to accomplish. After probing some aspects of Augustine's thought, we will go on to see how the contemporary articulation of this metaphor has been impacted by modernity.

CLASSIC ROOTS: AUGUSTINE

The first goal of this section is to observe Augustine as an authoritative source of The Preacher as Teacher. Second, we will suggest that one of the primary assumptions of Augustine's metaphor for the preacher suggests the significance of rhetoric. We will suggest that this image assumes the neutrality of rhetoric, as well as to observe that one of the primary purposes of rhetoric is to encourage the eloquence needed for persuasion. This tension raises questions about the relationship between the preacher or the

9. See Westerhoff, "Teaching and Preaching," 468–69.

10. Augustine, *On Christian Doctrine*. For more on the long influence of this book, see, for example, the fine collection of essays and extensive bibliography in Arnold and Bright, eds., *De Doctrina Christiana*.

11. Augustine, *On Christian Doctrine*, 4.12.27.

human agent and God in the act of preaching. We will suggest that although Augustine is able to hold together both divine and human agency within preaching, The Preacher as Teacher as an identity has the potential to place the burden of persuasion on human skill. We will conclude that one significant shortcoming of this identity is that when it becomes unmoored from an emphasis on teaching Scripture and doctrine, it may be replaced with a pragmatic rhetorical emphasis on persuasion.

Augustine was a man of words—a teacher of the book.[12] Peter Brown notes that in the oldest surviving portrait of Augustine, we see him sitting with his eyes fixed on a book.[13] This observation offers an insight into how Augustine understood his vocational identity. He believed that teaching and persuading others to the truth found in Holy Scripture was his essential calling for the church. Telford Work suggests that Augustine understood the teaching of Scripture for the church as "intended by God and empowered by the Holy Spirit to build communal and personal virtue and to accomplish personal salvation."[14] Indeed, as a preacher Augustine became focused on understanding and teaching salvation in a way that was "perfectly adjusted to stir the hearts of all the learners."[15]

Augustine was arguably one of the greatest and most prolific Christian preachers we know in late antiquity. It is believed that Augustine preached nearly 8,000 times over a period of thirty-nine years, and that an estimated one in fourteen sermons have come down to us. George Lawless notes that roughly 568 authentic sermons have been preserved, along with more than 200 *Commentaries on the Psalms*, 124 *Tractates on the Gospel of John*, and 10 *Tractates on the First Letter of John*, making more than 900 authentic sermons.[16] As Lawless writes, "Together with those of John Chrysostom, Augustine's sermons constitute more than one-half the homiletic material which has survived from the patristic age."[17]

Aside from the quantity and quality of the sermons that have survived, one of the most lasting influences Augustine has had on Christian proclamation, and more specifically, on the homiletic identity of the preacher, comes from his classic treatise on the subject, *On Christian Doctrine*. It is

12. For excellent summaries of Augustine as a preacher, see Brown, *Augustine of Hippo*, 244 and Lawless, "Augustine of Hippo," 13–14. See also Old, *Reading and Preaching*, 344–98 and, most importantly, Meer, *Augustine the Bishop*.

13. See Brown, *Augustine Of Hippo*, 256.

14. Work, *Living and Active*, 307.

15. Brown, *Augustine of Hippo*, 257.

16. See Lawless, "Augustine of Hippo," 15. For an excellent overview and summary of these sermons, see Old, *Reading and Preaching*, 346–82.

17. Lawless, "Augustine of Hippo," 15.

one of the first texts on homiletics for teaching preaching in the Christian church.[18] As a former professor of rhetoric in service of the state, Augustine was perhaps better prepared than many within the church of the fourth century to write an instructional book for the Christian preacher.[19]

Augustine wrote the four books that make up *On Christian Doctrine* between A.D. 396 and 426. These four books, according to Steven Oberhelman, represent "Augustine's views at the end of a lifetime of Christian study and preaching."[20] The fruits of his reflections are recorded in books 1–3, which are a general discussion of what it is that motivates the Christian exegete, or more simply what the preacher seeks to learn in Scripture, and consequently how the preacher should go about interpreting Scripture. "There are two things necessary to the treatment of the Scriptures," says Augustine, as he opens book 1 of *On Christian Doctrine*, "a way of discovering those things which are to be understood, and a way of *teaching* what we have learned.[21] For Augustine, Christian preaching exists between the poles of interpretation and communication. In book 4, Augustine turns to the question of how to preach—that is how best to express or communicate the message of Scripture.

Here, Augustine uses the image of teaching to underscore the task of preaching.[22] According to Augustine, the purpose of the preacher was to make plain the central truths of Holy Scripture in a manner that persuades the hearer toward the ultimate end of life, which is the love of God.[23]

Augustine understands the preacher's main task to be first an exegete of Scripture and then a communicator or instructor of the knowledge discerned through the hermeneutic work of exegesis. Hence, it may be argued that *On Christian Doctrine* was written to teach preachers what and how to teach Holy Scripture. Indeed, some scholars think that the English translation of the title of *On Christian Doctrine* ought to more accurately reflect the book's emphasis on teaching Scripture. For example, Hughes Oliphant Old argues, "the title of this most influential book might be translated into English as *On the Art of Christian Teaching* instead of *On the Art of Christian*

---

18. For this historical argument see Edwards, *History of Preaching*, 106.

19. The literature on Augustine's life is vast. Among the most helpful in regard to biographical material and general interpretation are the following: Bonner, *St. Augustine of Hippo*; Brown, *Augustine of Hippo*; and Meer, *Augustine the Bishop*.

20. See Oberhelman, *Rhetoric and Homiletics*, 153.

21. Augustine, *On Christian Doctrine*, 1.1; emphasis added.

22. Kennedy, *Classical Rhetoric*, 157.

23. Augustine, *On Christian Doctrine*, 4.12.27.

Doctrine, as in this case the Latin word 'doctrina' means *teaching* rather than doctrine."[24]

Properly understood, the title alone suggests that *teaching* Scripture is the primary purpose of the Christian preacher. According to Augustine, the preacher's primary purpose is to discern and understand the content of Scripture and then find the appropriate language, style, and forms to teach and persuade the hearer to belief in the content.[25] This act of transmission of scriptural and doctrinal content from pulpit to pew is a primary entailment that shapes this tradition for the identity of the preacher, which consequently shapes the purpose, language, and form of the sermon.[26]

Augustine defined The Preacher as Teacher.[27] That being said, this was not the only image Augustine used in reference to the preacher. Lawless notes that Augustine uses a variety of images to describe the Christian preacher.[28] He observes over fifty images for the preacher from Augustine's sermons alone.[29] Lawless captures well Augustine's fondness for finding images to capture the particular work of preaching. It is interesting, however, that Lawless fails to take note of what may be Augustine's most used image or homiletic identity for the Christian preacher. This may be due to the way that some metaphors function in a dominant or normative way by comparison with others.

To better understand the degree to which Augustine identifies preaching with teaching, and the preacher with a teacher, let us look at two examples from Augustine's book dedicated to exploring the task of preaching.

> Thus the expositor and *teacher* of the Divine Scripture, the defender of right faith and the enemy of error, should both *teach* the good and extirpate the evil. And in this labor of words, he should conciliate those who are opposed, arouse those who are remiss, and *teach* those ignorant of his subject what is occurring and what they should expect.[30]

24. Old, *Reading and Preaching*, 386. See also Augustine, *Teaching Christianity*, 98.

25. Augustine, *On Christian Doctrine*, 1.1. "There are two things on which all interpretation of scripture depends: the process of discovering what we need to learn, and the process of presenting what we have learnt."

26. We will explore these four marks of the sermon of The Preacher as Teacher in the modern example of John Broadus later in this chapter.

27. The identity of preacher as teacher is arguably one of the longest lasting legacies of Augustine because of the influence of *On Christian Doctrine* on preachers. For more on this legacy, see Schaublin, "De Doctrina Christiana," 47–61; see also Amos, "Augustine," 23–32.

28. Lawless, "Augustine of Hippo," 18–22.

29. Ibid., 18.

30. Augustine, *On Christian Doctrine*, 4.4.6; emphasis added.

Does the Apostle contradict himself when he says that men are
made *teachers* by the operation of the Holy Spirit and at the
same time tells them what and how they should *teach*? Or is it
to be understood that the office of men in *teaching* even these
teachers should not cease even with the generosity of the Holy
Spirit assisting?[31]

In these and many other examples, the term *teacher* or *teaching* is applied interchangeably to the identity of the preacher and the task of preaching.[32] Augustine saw no clear distinctive between the two roles. To preach
was to teach Scripture and to teach Scripture was to preach.

This homiletic identity is properly understood as one whose task it is to
give "instruction" and "expose" the meaning of the Scriptures and the doctrines of the church—to teach people the "truth."[33] Augustine seems to believe that the image best suited to accomplish this end is a preacher who sees
oneself in the position of a teacher whose exegetical instruction of Scripture
is guided by the discerning application of classical rhetoric. For Augustine,
rhetoric is viewed as a neutral tool that enables clearer instruction.

The Neutrality of Rhetoric

In book 4 of *On Christian Doctrine*, Augustine sets out broad Ciceronian
principles of rhetoric and transposes them toward homiletic ends. To
best achieve the purpose of teaching Scripture, Augustine suggests that
preaching ought to utilize the principles of classical rhetoric for Christian
instruction. In Augustine's day rhetoric was considered an aid to teaching
because it identified principles of effective modes of communication and
speech, needed to persuade listeners.[34] Indeed, the mastery of rhetoric was
considered the "highest achievement" of any citizen of classical culture.[35]
Therefore, Augustine, whose selected metaphor of homiletic identity sought
to teach the truth of Scripture, did not hesitate to apply the use of rhetoric
toward this end.

31. Ibid., 4.15.32; emphasis added.

32. For other examples, see ibid., 4.16.33; 4.10.24; 4.15.32.

33. See Atkinson Rose, *Sharing The Word*, 14–15. Here Atkinson Rose argues that
the tradition of preaching Augustine inspired is a homiletic tradition marked by words
commonly associated with teaching—such as *convince, inform, explain, communicate*.

34. See the excellent "General Introduction" in Bizzell and Herzberg, eds., *Rhetorical Tradition*, 1–2.

35. Carol Harrison makes this argument in "The Rhetoric of Scripture and Preaching," 215.

One could read *On Christian Doctrine* as a treatise that distills Augustine's wisdom from a lifetime of reflecting on his classical training within the context of Christian preaching.[36] Augustine realizes that knowledge is not enough for successful preaching. The preacher also needs knowledge of how to best communicate in a way that makes Scripture persuasive. With such a concern, Augustine views the use of classical rhetoric, the vocation of his past, as an essential tool for Christian preaching, the vocation of his present. Indeed, according to Harrison, his discussion of preaching "proceeds almost entirely within the frame of classical rhetoric, in order to evaluate its aims, practices, rules and their usefulness for the Christian preacher."[37] It may be argued that *On Christian Doctrine*, or at least book 4, was written with an eye toward merging two cities: the city of man, where the people spoke with an eloquence learned from classical culture, and the city of God, where citizens learned to speak with the eloquence of Scripture.

This emphasis is historically insightful as it takes place in the context of the church still wrestling with how to assimilate a secular culture that was baptized as "Christian" under the reign of Constantine.[38] The application of rhetoric—or the art of persuasion—was viewed with caution within the early church. Rhetoric was suspect for many Christians because it was considered to be primarily a tool to persuade others to pagan philosophy, values, and a worldview seen as antithetical to the Christian faith. The early Christian church, forced to carve out an identity in a world saturated in the eloquence of pagan wisdom, sometimes viewed anything that represented secular culture as a threat to the identity and practice of the church. One could say that "worldly" association tainted rhetoric for many Christians and inspired them to fortify themselves against any form of engagement with such "worldly" matters.[39] Peter Brown comments, "Christian rejection of the classics was met by a pagan 'fundamentalism'; the conservatives crudely 'divinized' their traditional literature, the classics were treated as a gift of the gods to men. Christians for their part would play in with this reaction by 'diabolizing' the same literature. Many, indeed wanted to end this tension by denying culture altogether."[40] Thus, it is not surprising that the early Christian church was reluctant to operate with a view of rhetoric

---

36. See Amos, "Augustine and the Education of the Early Medieval Preacher," 23.

37. Harrison, "Rhetoric," 215.

38. For an articulation of the challenges this new culturally and politically sanctioned status posed for the work of Christian preaching, see Dunn-Wilson, *Mirror for the Church*, 62–73.

39. See Cameron, *Christianity*, 7.

40. Brown, *Augustine of Hippo*, 265.

as merely a neutral device that could be employed with any subject matter, especially the subjects associated with preaching. [41]

The suspicion towards rhetoric was openly challenged when Christianity was adopted as the new civil religion of the Roman Empire under the reigns of Constantine and Theodosius I. With Constantine's conversion to Christianity and the subsequent Christianization of the Roman Empire, many things once denounced as a secularizing influence soon began to be baptized into Christian service.[42] Indeed, as Christianity gradually became sanctioned as the norm for culture, preachers had a new challenge. Christian preachers, once on the margins of society and political power, now began to find themselves among the authorities responsible for the spiritual welfare of a new kind of Christian society and culture. The Christian preacher was now responsible for edifying, equipping, and teaching a Christian society. Consequently, the preacher was now expected to give a mostly pagan and largely pluralistic culture a newly articulated vision and purpose for work, marriage, life, and death. George Kennedy notes that many Christians of this time pragmatically began to adapt the use of rhetoric to meet this new challenge:

> We need not charge such thoughtful Christians as Gregory or Chrysostom with pandering to the mob, but they were concerned with moving the hearts of their audience and inspiring their lives, and the devices of sophistic rhetoric had become the cues to which their audiences responded and by which their purposes could be best accomplished. This trend is in many ways a victory for classical rhetoric. Ambitious young Christians now did not hesitate to study in the schools of rhetoric, and as the fourth century advanced, the Christian communities were less and less a simple company of simple folk content with the message of the gospel.[43]

As Christian preachers began to take public ownership for conditions of society after years of social marginalization and even persecution, they began to learn the fine arts of classical antiquity with great effectiveness. It

---

41. See for example, Tertullian's suspicions in "Prescriptions Against the Heretics," 36. "What has Jerusalem to do with Athens, the Church with the Academy, the Christian with the heretic? Our principles come from the Porch of Solomon . . . I have no use for a Stoic or a Platonic, or a dialectic Christianity. After Jesus Christ we have no need of speculation, after the Gospel no need of research. When we come to believe, we have no desire to believe anything else; for we begin by believing that there is nothing else which we have to believe."

42. See Roberts, *Jeweled Style*, 122–47.

43. Kennedy, *Classical Rhetoric*, 145–46.

is in such a context that we need to remember Augustine's encouragement for the preacher to use classical rhetoric. Arguably, there was no one more suited to teach the classical high art in the fourth century than the Bishop of Hippo, given his experience with rhetoric prior to his conversion.

No doubt Augustine must have been aware of the need for a mediator between a secular and a sacred style of rhetoric. Augustine attempts to integrate his secular past into the vocation of preaching in *On Christian Doctrine*. He does so by "baptizing" his rhetorical training into the service of Christ. In book 4 of *On Christian Doctrine*, we see Augustine attempting to put rhetoric toward Christian ends, as he tries to tune a secular instrument for sacred sound.

Augustine accomplishes this synthesis, not because of his status and authority as a secular rhetorician, nor because he is a trusted bishop, but because he honestly does not see a problem in doing so. Augustine pursues a unique synthesis by asking a rhetorical question: why do the pagans get to brandish their rhetorical artillery while Christians, who posses real truth (that is, knowledge of the triune God through revelation), stand unarmed and outwitted by their attacks?[44] Augustine sees no contradiction in using the best communication tools available for teaching Christian truth. To Augustine's mind, classical rhetoric was as neutral as mathematics or as impartial as a hammer, and as such could be an instrument to build up or tear down depending upon one's intention. Augustine writes:

> By means of the art of rhetoric both truth and falsehood are urged; who would say that truth should stand in the person of its defenders unarmed against lying, so that they who wish to urge falsehoods may know how to make their listeners benevolent, or attentive, or docile in their presentation, while the defenders of truth are ignorant of that art? . . . while the faculty of eloquence, which is of great value in urging either evil or justice, is in itself indifferent, why should it not be obtained for the uses of the good in the service of truth if the evil usurp it for the winning of perverse and vain causes in defense of iniquity and error?[45]

Augustine understands the rules of rhetoric to be "indifferent." If rhetoric is used toward good ends—such as instructing Christians in Scripture—then rhetoric is good. Or conversely, if rhetoric is used in the hands of those who "urge falsehoods," then it can be considered bad. Moreover, if falsehoods and heresies had to be refuted, how better to fight falsehood than with its propagators' own favorite weapon? For Augustine, what makes all

44. Augustine, *On Christian Doctrine*, 4.2.3.
45. Ibid.

THE PREACHER AS TEACHER   59

the difference is intention, or to what end rhetoric is put to use. Augustine sees no problem with using rhetoric for Christian teaching, provided that its pagan ends were subjected to the ends of Christian truth.[46]

If rhetoric could be used for the purpose of glorifying God and making known the gospel hidden to humanity, why not exploit it? In Augustine's view, rhetoric is to the pulpit what a key is to a locked door: "Of what use is a gold key," writes Augustine, "if it will not open what we wish? Or what objection is there to a wooden one which will, when we seek nothing except to open what is closed?"[47] From Augustine's perspective, if the preacher is given a key to help unlock the door to reveal truth, why not use it?

Persuasion as the End of Teaching

Augustine believes rhetoric could be used, but only with caution, for this secular tool if unchecked is susceptible to causing the words of the preacher to be loved more than the message of the Scripture itself.[48] Still, Augustine believes rhetoric to be an invaluable tool in making the Scripture message clear and eloquent; and eloquence, if nothing else, helps persuade. Thus, the better the preacher can grasp the tools of rhetoric, the better one will serve as "the defender of right faith and the enemy of error."[49]

To this end, Augustine restates broad Ciceronian principles and transposes them into homiletic advice for the preacher.[50] Though he never mentions Cicero by name, he often salutes the one he calls the "author of Roman eloquence."[51] It is the echo of Cicero we hear when Augustine suggests the job of the Christian preacher is to teach, to delight, and to persuade: "To teach is a necessity, to delight is a beauty, and to persuade is a victory."[52] Augustine employs Cicero's conception of these three offices of rhetoric (teaching, delighting, and persuading)[53] along with the three levels of style of rhetoric (subdued, moderate, and grand styles) to communicate the overarching calling and responsibility of the preacher. He then fuses these categories, associating teaching with conveying "small things" in a "subdued style," delighting with "moderate things" in a "temperate" style, and

46. Harrison, "Rhetoric," 226.
47. Augustine, *On Christian Doctrine*, 4.11.26.
48. See Roberts, *Jeweled Style*, 130.
49. Augustine, *On Christian Doctrine*, 4.4.6.
50. See Eskridge, *Influence of Cicero*.
51. Augustine, *On Christian Doctrine*, 4.12.27.
52. Ibid.
53. Ibid.

persuading, or moving to action, with "great things" in a "grand" style. Augustine goes on to address standard Ciceronian considerations of audience, diction, rhythm, and style to help the preacher navigate the various realms of formal rhetoric and Christian proclamation.[54] Augustine's concern is not simply what the preacher says, but how he says it.

It should be noted that this new synthesis between rhetoric and Christian teaching was merged with an eye toward not only disseminating knowledge of Scripture, but persuading the listener to its truth.[55]

This is a progression of which the preacher should be conscious, according to Augustine. One teaches in a delightful way in order to persuade the hearer. "Of what use are the first two," says Augustine, "if the third does not follow?"[56] At times Augustine is quick to point out that persuasion is not essential to the overall objective of Christian preaching. Indeed, Augustine suggests that there is a delight and persuasiveness to truth itself that is beyond mere rhetorical adornment. Yet at other times, Augustine seems to contradict himself. He does not, for example, explain how the power of truth to persuade in and of itself is to be distinguished from the speaker's use of rhetoric to make the truth attractive. Sometimes Augustine insists that persuasion is not simply a matter of truth, but depends upon the effect of eloquence.[57]

The teacher is successful if at the end of the sermon the listener has not only received the right information, but has been persuaded to apply what was taught in response to the sermon.

God or Teacher: Divine or Human Persuasion?

This emphasis on the use of rhetoric for persuasion raises important questions for the legacy of The Preacher as Teacher. Is the test for successful teaching merely persuasion? If the preacher uses rhetorical techniques with an aim toward persuasion, and the hearer is not persuaded, does that mean that the sermon failed? Does persuasiveness defined in this way become a matter of style rather than the integrity of substance? Who is ultimately responsible for persuasion? Does the burden of persuasion rest on the shoulders of the preacher's ability alone? Where does the work of the Holy Spirit fit into the homiletic equation? Is teaching Scripture nothing more than the mastery of exegetical method and rhetorical skill, so that a sermon is

54. Oberhelman, *Rhetoric and Homiletics*, 126.

55. Augustine, *On Christian Doctrine*, 4.13.29.

56. Ibid., 4.12.28.

57. Ibid., 4.25.55.

clear, delightful, and persuasive? Is anything else going on? Augustine is not blind to these questions, but chooses to emphasize that the preacher give attention to both human and divine agency. However, this emphasis comes rather late in his reflection on preaching, and he gives it only small attention, which suggests that one of the temptations of the homiletic identity Augustine inspires is that it can overemphasize the human at the expense of the divine will in preaching.

Augustine himself, however, is not guilty of this oversight. At the end of *On Christian Doctrine*, Augustine encourages the preacher not to worry, for it is God speaking through the human preacher in and through the power of the Holy Spirit. [58] The preacher, according to Augustine, ought to take comfort that the effectiveness of preaching does not rest squarely on human gifts alone, but on the work of the Spirit teaching through biblical instruction. As long as the preacher's instruction is grounded in Scripture, God's grace will be preeminent.

Why then take the time to learn and study rhetoric, or take care to work at how a sermon comes across? Augustine suggests that learning classic rhetoric and the studious application of its rules are of value if the triune God gives his Holy Spirit to its end. Augustine believes that God's grace is working before the preacher works. The triune God can save us without human help and is not dependent on preachers, but when the Holy Spirit anoints the work of the preacher, then preaching is a means of grace that brings us into communion with God. Above all, Augustine's ideal preacher is dependent entirely on the work of the Holy Spirit speaking through the Scriptures that are being taught. Thus, the Holy Spirit is the source of the preacher's "ability" to teach, delight, and persuade.

Augustine expresses a "both/and" understanding of God's role in human preaching: the preacher is responsible for persuasion by use of all skill available, and the Triune God, working through the Spirit, is also responsible for persuasion. It seems Augustine wants to root the identity of the preacher in grace and the ongoing work of the Spirit, while at the same time not minimizing the responsibility of the human work of the preacher. In other words, Augustine does not suggest that because God is responsible for persuasion, the preacher no longer needs to apply oneself to acquiring skill and knowledge for preaching: "If anyone says, however, that if teachers are made by the Holy Spirit they do not need to be taught by men what they should say or how they should say it, he should also say that we should not pray because the Lord says, 'for your Father knoweth what is needful for

58. Ibid., 4.15.32.

you, before you ask him' or that the Apostle Paul should not have taught Timothy and Titus what or how they should teach others."[59]

The preacher should do all that he or she humanly can do in interpretation and oration, as well as be expectant that God will bring the message he chooses. Preachers should do their best and expect God to do his. Preachers are to work out how to best understand and teach the knowledge necessary for "salvation." After careful preparation, however, Augustine urges the preacher to trust that God will fulfill his promise to say and do what needs saying and doing in any given sermon. Augustine rests in the grace that the triune God speaks through the preacher's sermon.

It seems that Augustine is content to hold this tension together. He does not offer us a fully developed theology of who is doing what and when while preaching. He decides instead to leave the tension tight, maybe with the knowledge that only with a tight string can you strike the right chord. Thus, the classic source of the metaphor of preacher as a teacher encourages a call to human action but always with a posture of dependence on God.

It may be for this reason that Augustine writes at the end of *On Christian Doctrine* that prayer is at the heart of the preacher's work. Summarizing Augustine's teaching on preaching, Old writes, "Christian preaching must be borne of prayer."[60] In prayer, the preacher lives in the tension between the economy of human speech and the divine speech of the Holy Spirit, "And he should not doubt that he is able to do these things, if he is at all able and to the extent that he is able, more through the piety of his prayers than through the skill of his oratory, so that praying for himself and for those who whom he is to address, he is a petitioner before he is a speaker."[61] For Augustine, prayer is a crucial aspect of the preacher's work, as it assumes the posture that reminds him or her that no matter how skilled or accomplished one becomes in the skills of human rhetoric, ultimately it is God who informs the heart.

As long as the priority of God's grace is central to the preacher's identity and practice, this metaphor is useful. For example, this homiletic identity encourages a commitment to teach the Scriptures with careful exegesis and winsome words. It is an identity that encourages the preacher to take what is useful in culture, such as rhetoric, and use it toward Christian ends. And it is an identity that calls the preacher to walk the tightrope between human responsibility and divine sovereignty.

---

59. Ibid., 4.16.33.

60. Old, *Reading and Preaching*, 396.

61. Augustine, *On Christian Doctrine*, 4.15.32.

However, within these strengths are also potential seeds of danger. What happens, for example, to the practice of preaching if the cultural and ecclesial conditions change the meaning of The Preacher as Teacher? How would the preacher respond if the context of the church and culture that informs this identity no longer values catechesis, but rather prioritizes personal choice? What might happen if the preacher no longer views teaching Scripture and doctrine with the same priority as using the pulpit to teach about politics, culture, and psychology? If, for whatever reason, the preacher loses his or her primary commitment to teaching Holy Scripture and doctrine, yet is still encouraged to use whatever tool or strategy necessary for persuasion, then would not the burden of persuasion shift away from God and onto the shoulders of the human preacher? Would the preacher then become pressured to pursue a "pragmatic homiletic," inspired more by what "works," defined more by the fads and fashions of culture than what is faithful to Scripture and doctrine? These are questions that we must explore as we understand the identity of The Preacher as Teacher in today's cultural context.

What follows contains the argument that, although Augustine's identity of the preacher has survived, it has been reshaped by the cultural conditions surrounding modernity's emphasis on rationality and individualism.

THE CONTEXT OF MODERNITY

The Preacher as Teacher is a reliable and time-tested identity for any preacher to adopt as a metaphor to shape his or her homiletic art. In the tradition of Augustine, The Preacher as Teacher follows the advice of classic rhetoricians to be holistic in the speech act: to enlighten the mind, touch the heart, and move the will. However, this holistic emphasis of The Preacher as Teacher was altered to fit the cultural emphasis of modernity. As suggested earlier, the ancient and modern casting of a metaphor can change in accordance with differing cultural and intellectual milieux.

Shifting cultural understandings can alter metaphoric assumptions of meaning as new ideas and experiences come to be associated with the relationship between *this* and *that*. Because conceptual meanings are shaped by these tacit relationships, new emphases in culture can result in a shift in the practices associated with a particular metaphor. Augustine's pre-critical world was shaped by a vastly different culture than the world shaped by the cultural assumptions of modernity. To understand how The Preacher as

Teacher is understood and practiced in today's shifting culture, we first need to appreciate the metaphor's place at the end of modernity.[62]

In this next section, we will argue that the metaphor of The Preacher as Teacher has lost Augustine's holy tension by placing emphasis on a truth rooted in natural reason over Scripture, and using rhetoric to communicate this limited epistemology. We will use the work of John A. Broadus as an example of how The Preacher as Teacher's sermon practice reflects a "rational rhetoric" for the pulpit.

The Teacher Exalts Rationality

During the modern period, the cultural context of The Preacher as Teacher experienced something of a paradigm shift that impacted how a preacher shaped by this identity understood and practiced communication. This shift helps us to understand how rational assumptions of truth became so ingrained in the cultural thinking of the church in the time of modernity.[63] As a consequence of an understanding of truth as propositional ideas, The Preacher as Teacher adapted its sermons to exalt reason and reflect a "rational rhetoric" bent towards the appeal of individual choice.

The modern period grew out of the religious wars of Western Europe that significantly eroded the moral authority of the church. This was a historical period marked by great intellectual investigation, critique, and rigor that inspired revolutions in science, politics, and religion. This period of "The Enlightenment" championed the innate and universal endowments of human reason that were adjudged to be capable of providing humanity with the knowledge of nature, morality, and religion necessary for individual and societal welfare.

A main source of this modern outlook was the new paradigm inspired by Isaac Newton (1642–1727) and Immanuel Kant (1724–1804), among others. Newton encouraged the view that the natural universe is a grand cosmic machine of interacting causes and effects, precisely measurable and predictable according to mathematical laws. This mechanistic view of the universe was an effect of the modern period's emphasis on rationality. Reason was to be the primary means to accomplish both individual and social transformation. Kant formulated the oft-quoted definition of the

---

62. This argument has been informed by a diverse reading of theologians, philosophers, and cultural critics. See for example, Lash, *Holiness, Speech, and Silence*; Cavanaugh, *Theopolitical Imagination*; Clapp, *Peculiar People*, 16–17; and Hauerwas, *Wilderness Wanderings*.

63. Craig M. Gay makes this argument in *The Way of the (Modern) World*, 1–28.

philosophy that gave the modern period its name. His 1784 essay "What is Enlightenment?" starts out with the declaration: "Enlightenment is man's release from his self-incurred tutelage. Tutelage is man's inability to make use of his understanding without direction from another. Self-incurred is this tutelage when its cause lies not in lack of reason but in lack of resolution and courage to use it without direction from another. Sapere aude! Have courage to use your own reason!—that is the motto of enlightenment."[64]

The overall ideal of the Enlightenment was rational self-determinism. With this understanding of rational autonomy in a mechanistic world, knowledge could be known quite apart from dependence on special revelation from God, Scripture, or church. Claims of ultimate meaning that relied on such foundations as supernatural revelation or miraculous interventions as described in Scripture and fortified by church doctrine were considered highly questionable. Within this perspective, common sense was bound to ask whether religious authority had any empirical "truth," worth directing one's faith. Mark Noll notes that this emphasis on the individual's reason threatened the traditional authority of the preacher because it led to the celebration of universal common sense as the guide to moral life.[65] Reason, not Scripture, was considered the new authority over moral life.

Thus began a cultural move away from locating moral authority in external sources like the Scriptures and church doctrines. In their place, the individual's reason became the sovereign moral authority of society.[66] Proponents of the use of reason believed it to be a neutral tool that could be used to discern the natural laws that would govern a people newly emancipated from the chains of the church's superstitions, Scriptures, and doctrines. Modernity also nurtured the assumption that God had endowed humanity with natural reason that made self-evident certain inalienable rights of the individual. Stephen Toulmin suggests that in modernity, meaning was limited by empirical ideals of rational intelligibility, which "emphasized regularity and intellectual order and above all stability."[67]

Samuel Wells argues that the modern turn toward the "self" as a new source of ethical reflection was a paradigm that fundamentally changed the church's witness and, as a consequence, its proclamation:

64. Kant, *Foundations*, 85.

65. See Noll, *Scandal*, 43–49.

66. This authoritative transition did not become widespread all at once. Its effects were subtle, but began to be significantly felt by preachers by the beginning of the nineteenth century. See Hunter, *American Evangelicalism*, 28.

67. Toulmin, *Return to Reason*, 43.

The seeds of salvation were now regarded as lying within the self, in the moral law written on every heart; those seeds were no longer assumed to lie outside the self, in the possession of one institution, the Church. The drama of the universe ceased to be God's unfathomable force of life, death, and judgment, and the Church's negotiation of them through the preaching of the Biblical narrative and the ministration of the sacraments. Now the center of attention was the human individual, the new self, and the drama was humanity's struggle to know and command its environment.[68]

Wells suggests that this emphasis on the "self" as a source of authority had an overarching influence on the construction of a coherent account of an individual's sense of truth. Putting faith in autonomous reason as a neutral source of revelation signaled a shift in how truth was to be taught. No longer was "truth" the primary property of the church. No longer could "rational" people blindly appeal to the sacred Scriptures or church doctrine as the sole genesis of truth. The modern turn to "self" meant that truth could be determined through autonomous reason. Both the credibility and necessity of supernaturally (God-to-human) inspired Scriptures, narratives, doctrines, and institutions were challenged by modernity's rational, often anti-dogmatic modes of critique. Hans Frei suggests that this led to the belief that "truth" was no longer located in the biblical narrative, but in the ideas inspired and verified by human reason. He argues that this functional rationality caused the biblical narrative to be "eclipsed" by the story of human reason, the autonomy of the individual, and blind belief in human progress inspired by scientific knowledge.[69] When it comes to preaching, "truth" was no longer to be located in and learned from the voice of the preacher teaching Scripture and doctrine, unless the preacher could adapt himself to the modern age.

It is not that preachers had to cease teaching Scripture altogether, it is that they had to make Scripture mirror or collaborate with the new truths being discovered through modern practices like science. As Christian Smith observes: "The Bible would reveal God's moral law and certain natural truths; science, for its part, would confirm the teachings of the Bible and expand human understanding beyond what the Bible revealed. Together, the Bible and science were expected to render a rational validation of the veracity of Christianity and lay the foundation for a healthy national moral

68. Wells, *Improvisation*, 26–27.
69. See Frei, *Eclipse of Biblical Narrative*, 111–12, 118.

and social order."[70] Thus, the person and practice of the preacher had to be reborn with a modern sensibility that could combine teaching the common-sense realism of Scripture with the empirical realism of science. Modernity imposed such constraints on the culture—and consequently on the world-views of individuals in modern society—that it made it almost impossible to resist.

Paul Scott Wilson identifies five significant influences this fusion had on the practice of the traditional identity of the preacher.[71] First, the human elements of the text gradually become the focus of meaning in the text, while theological meaning became secondary. Human experience became the primary focus rather than the acts of God. Second, natural explanations of events, including miracles, tend to be sought over supernatural ones. Third, the interpretive focus shifts from the biblical text itself to the vast un-charted historical events and territory behind the biblical texts. Fourth, the authority of the Bible is questioned in new ways as history offers competing claims for the literal sense of the text. As a result, the ability of Scripture to govern faith and morals for the church is undermined while different ways are sought to shore up scriptural authority. And finally, the grammatical and historical senses of biblical texts become distinguished from each other as historical method gains a cultural hold on the preacher. In light of a culture that understood truth to be verifiable, the goal of preaching could no longer be to *teach* the literal and figurative references of meaning that occurred in historical events of Scripture that could not be verified.

The effect of these changes was that The Preacher as Teacher began to reflect the spirit of the age, making "truth" a propositional idea that could be dislocated from Scripture. If truth was to be located in rationality, then preaching had to make appeals to universal reason. Therefore the preacher began to develop a reflex for apologetic sermons, arguing in deductive points, themes, and main ideas that were abstractly designed to persuade the hearer through "logically sound propositional" language.[72] Homiletic scholar Richard Eslinger describes the sermon practices of the preacher "as a spatial kind of activity in which the preacher constructed sermons from static themes and propositions."[73] Eugene L. Lowry writes that preach-ing under this modern assumption of "stable and ordered" rationality trained the preacher to "immediately set about to order ideas" dressed in

70. Smith, *American Evangelicalism*, 3.

71. Wilson, *God Sense*, 50–51.

72. See Buttrick, "Interpretation and Preaching," 46–58.

73. Eslinger, *Web of Preaching*, 15.

propositional prose when sitting down to begin sermon preparation.[74] The work of interpreting Scripture was dedicated to identifying the ideas that could appeal to reason through ordered propositions.

David Buttrick argues that the modern preacher, in search of this logical propositional statement, approaches Scripture the way one might mine for gold in a mountain.[75] The mountain is viewed as an obstacle to be blown apart, cleared away, and reduced in order to discover, remove, and grasp the golden nugget buried deep in its core. For the preacher, the golden nugget is the propositional *idea* buried in the text that can be extracted only by applying natural reason. Buttrick calls this a "hermeneutic of distillation," meaning that the preacher reads Scripture to glean its natural propositional or eternal themes that can be distilled into rationally organized outlines.[76]

Hence, in modernity, The Preacher as Teacher came to the Scriptures with an interest in extracting particular verifiable *ideas* from the text that could be distilled into propositional statements in a sermon. To satisfy this requirement of ordering rational ideas, the preacher began to assume that "sermon building" involved fitting together an assortment of scriptural ideas or themes into a logical order in order to justify the Scripture's truth to a rational audience.[77] The sermon became a place to hear an argument controlled by propositional ideas. In a culture that valued rationalism, it made perfect sense for the preacher to adhere to strict rules of logical argumentation that were controlled by propositional statements and outlines. Similar to the way Augustine married Greek rhetoric to preaching, modern preachers began to merge modern assumptions of rationality to preaching. The preacher began to mirror the exaltation of reason as an authoritative arbiter of truth.

There was no better tool for this modern "sermon building" than the classical wisdom of rhetoric. Craig Loscalzo argues that the burgeoning psychological and philosophical ideas of modernity greatly influenced the recovery of rhetoric during modernity. He writes, "The eighteenth century was characterized by intense intellectual fervor, marked by an avid interest in the classics. Empirical sciences flourished, and the study of human nature made its way onto the intellectual stage. Thinkers began asking questions about the origins and functions of language and how humans, from an

---

74. Lowry, *Doing Time in the Pulpit*, 12.

75. Buttrick, *Homiletic*, 264.

76. Ibid., 276.

77. Lowry, *Homiletical Plot*, 13.

anthropologic basis, were communicating beings. The stage was set for the revaluation of rhetoric as a tool for such studies."[78]

Rhetoric was understood to be an effective tool for preparing Christian preachers in both the defense and presentation of the Christian faith. Like preaching, rhetoric emphasized the purposeful use of oral discourse with stress on intent and effect. The appeal to master rhetoric was natural for the preacher because it had always been one of its entailments. In modernity, as the church was faced with the loss of its presumed authoritative status, the preacher saw once again the importance of using classical rhetoric as a means to persuade the hearer through ordered and rational arguments for the truths of Scripture.

However, rhetoric was more than just an aid to the preacher. Classical rhetoric was seen as sharing in the celebration of the "self" that marked the modern period, as its rules and laws were discerned not through Scripture but by applying natural reason to experience. Modernity respected the communication of propositional *ideas* spoken with clarity and force. Rhetoric was thus valued as a natural handmaiden for the preacher to communicate the rational truths located in these ideas. Teaching rational *ideas* became the purpose of preaching. Truth is best grasped and communicated in propositional forms that appealed to natural reason.

MODERN EXAMPLE: JOHN BROADUS

In North America, there was arguably no greater champion of the importance of rhetoric's place in the modern pulpit than John A. Broadus. During the nineteenth century, Broadus wrote of the importance of using all of the available tools for teaching the Scriptures in his homiletic text *On the Preparation and Delivery of Sermons*.[79] This book has become a classic as it was used throughout the United States in the late nineteenth century and the first half of the twentieth century as a primary textbook for homiletics classes in colleges and seminaries. Thus it is an excellent resource for us to understand how the preacher was viewed and encouraged in modernity.

Like Augustine, Broadus understood the identity of the Christian preacher to be chiefly a teacher, whose job it was to teach the Scriptures through clear instruction and practical application.[80] He believed that it was through Scripture that a preacher was to interpret the doctrines of the church, as well as discover the ethical implications of faithful discipleship

78. Loscalzo, "Rhetoric," 411.

79. Ibid.

80. See Old, *Reading and Preaching*, 6:727.

in Christ.[81] Broadus understood The Preacher as Teacher not only to be a welcome identity, but a necessary one for all who seek to abide and grow in Christian faith, and it reinforced the challenge for preachers to hone their rhetorical skills.[82]

For Broadus, rhetoric provided the basic tools necessary for persuasion, what might be called a "homiletical rhetoric" as characteristic of the Augustinian tradition.[83] As with Augustine, in the wrong hands rhetoric was understood to be a neutral tool that could be used for destruction, or in the right hands could be an invaluable aid to construct persuasive messages for moral instruction. *On the Preparation and Delivery of Sermons* is as much an instruction in classical rhetoric as it is a text in how to preach. Broadus relies heavily on the classical wisdom of Aristotle, Cicero, and Quintilian. In following Cicero's exhortation, Broadus argues, "All who preach eminently well . . . will be found, with scarcely an exception, to have labored much to acquire skill."[84] Such skill, according to Broadus, is the province of rhetoric adapted to teaching the Scriptures.

The metaphor of The Preacher as Teacher makes assumptions that shape the practice of a preacher's work in the pulpit. It is significant to note that the set of norms of the preacher established by Broadus has been reformulated with each subsequent revision of his classic text, but the core concerns that have shaped the preacher to accommodate the modern ear are still apparent.[85] To explain the precise assumptions of the preacher's identity, let us look at the preacher's purpose, language, and form, as represented by Broadus. We will also look at a few contemporary voices that have followed and applied Broadus' wisdom for today's pulpit.

The Teacher's Purpose

According to Broadus, the purpose of the preacher is to give sound instruction of Scripture that also persuades the hearer towards faith in Jesus Christ.[86] This homiletic identity envisions the preacher as the authorita-

81. See Broadus's sermon, "How The Gospel Makes Men Holy," in *Sermons and Addresses*, 97–109.

82. See Stanfield, ed., *Favorite Sermons*, 12. Also, Robertson, *Life and Letters*, 22.

83. Broadus and Stanfield, *On the Preparation*, 24.

84. Ibid.

85. Broadus's text is still used today, but has gone through several additions since his death, most recently in 1979, by Vernon L. Stanfield. I am using this text, rather than the original editions.

86. For an example of this see Broadus's sermon, "Worship," in *Sermons and*

tive voice in a community of faith whose "main duty is tell people what to believe and why they should believe it."[87] The preacher should aim to "to teach God's word . . . his very purpose is teaching and exhorting [the people] out of the Word of God."[88] Indeed, says Broadus, "teaching is the preacher's chief business . . . to teach people the truth . . . is the preacher's great means of doing good."[89]

Therefore the preacher is a bridge that spans between God's revealed truth in the Bible and the congregation listening in the pew. In this way, the preacher's purpose is to mediate between the two worlds, finding the ideas buried in the text and then speak a word in a way that allows these ideas to be grasped by the rationality of the hearer. The goal of the teacher is to get the message across the great divide from the pulpit to the pew so effectively and winsomely that it is understood, believed, felt, and acted upon.

One description of the preacher's purpose is the word *transmit*, where the preacher's goal is to transmit the sermon's truth or message to the congregation. Other words often associated with this model of preaching are *convince, inform, explain,* and *communicate.* In this light, the preacher's purpose is to receive the message or truth and pass it along to the hearer. The preacher is the mediator between the Word of God, the Bible, on the one hand, and the congregation, on the other.

Roy Pearson, a contemporary proponent of this traditional model, identifies the preacher's task as wanting the congregation "to understand what he is saying as he understands it himself and to interpret his words, as he himself interprets them."[90] Such an understanding of the purpose of preaching presupposes a gap between the pulpit and the pew. This gap is fundamental to the roles assigned to the preacher and the congregation. The preacher is the sender, the communicator, and the authority with a message or truth to transmit by means of the sermon to the gathered hearers. The hearers consist of the recipients. Although they are often described as actively participating in the process, their chief task is to give assent to the sermon's message. This transmission of information is only the first half of the purpose. The second half is to speak the information in such a way that it changes the listeners' belief and/or behavior.

In this light, the ultimate purpose of The Preacher as Teacher is not merely to transmit, inform, explain, or communicate Scripture, but also to

---

Addresses, 1–25.

87. Broadus and Stanfield, *On the Preparation,* 30.

88. Ibid., 24.

89. Ibid., 62.

90. Pearson, *Preacher,* 162.

persuade the hearer to some acceptance of a belief. The preacher seeks to give instruction to the effect that a person is changed. New knowledge must lead to new action. Implicit in this purpose is the assumption that truth, spoken in a clear, ordered, and winsome way, will have a persuasive effect on rational beings.

Thus, the responsibility of the preacher is to press the point upon the mind and conscience of the hearer.[91] In defining good teaching, Broadus declares, "There must be a powerful impulse upon the will; the hearers must feel smitten, stirred, moved to, or at least towards, some action or determination to act."[92] This belief is also echoed in a plea he frequently made to his students: "A good sermon is a good thing, but the verdict is the thing. Gentlemen, when you preach, strike for a verdict."[93]

One of the methods the teaching preacher used to strike for an immediate "verdict" was making a direct appeal, typically at the end of the sermon.[94] The use of direct appeal invites the hearer to translate the lesson of a sermon into a personal application. The sermon of the preacher does not simply express the meaning of a text, he wants to drive that meaning home by offering a challenge or call to action. It is not enough to have knowledge, that knowledge must alter behavior. This is a model that takes seriously Jesus' words in the Sermon on the Mount: "Everyone who hears these words of mine and acts on them will be like a wise man who built his house on rock" (Matt 7:24). The preacher wants to persuade the listener to make a spiritual commitment and to make better decisions based on the truth of a sermon. This emphasis on persuasion can lead to the use of whatever rhetorical technique will be most helpful.

Yet such appeals reinforce the burden of the human agency of both the preacher and the hearer. The subtle message reinforced by the aim of persuasion is that we each have the rational capacity to decide and change ourselves. Persuasion is about inspiring individual choice. As such, the use of rhetoric is a human skill that, if used correctly, does not require the work of God's grace.

The preacher is expected not only to teach knowledge about Scripture and church doctrine, but to make an effort at persuasion through direct appeal to an individual's decision. If this direct appeal is not in place, then the preacher is assumed not to be fulfilling his or her purpose in the pulpit.

91. W. H. Whitsitt summarizes well the aim which undergirded Broadus's emphasis in his article, "John Albert Broadus," 347.

92. Broadus and Stanfield, *On the Preparation*, 20.

93. A representative example is seen in a part of the conclusion in a sermon, "Ask and It Shall Be Given You," in Stanfield, *Favorite Sermons*, 9.

94. Stanfield, *Favorite Sermons*, 10.

The Teacher's Language

The Preacher as Teacher's traditional understanding of the purpose and content of a sermon is inextricably linked with presuppositions about language. Broadus insists that "clearness or perspicuity" is of utmost importance in preaching.[95] In fact, he calls perspicuity "the most important property of style," and teaches that all preachers have a responsibility to attain it on behalf of their listeners: "A preacher is more solemnly bound than any other person, to make his language perspicuous. This is very important in wording a law, in writing a title-deed, or a physician's prescription, but still more important in proclaiming the word of God, words of eternal life."[96]

The goal of such clarity is to aid the transmission of information and the persuasion of the hearer to some action or ascent. The preacher, according to Broadus, "must strive to render it not merely possible that the people should understand us but impossible that they should misunderstand."[97] The words and phrases the preacher uses, therefore, should "exactly express [their] thought."[98] The general rule is that "terms ought to be precise . . . so that the expression and the idea exactly correspond, neither of them containing anything which the other does not contain."[99]

Clarity of speech is the goal of The Preacher as Teacher. For any audience there may be those who are well educated and those of no education at all, and it is the responsibility of the preacher to be able to gain a hearing with them all. Broadus argued this is gained by clarity of expression.[100]

Such clarity of expression, as exemplified in this doctrinal instruction of justification, is a hallmark of the preacher's language. Hence, Broadus urges the preacher to cultivate a linguistic simplicity that makes preaching accessible to every ear. The rule guiding the sermonic language of the preacher is "that which does not contribute to perspicuity must never be introduced merely as an ornament, for this, as we have seen, belongs to poetry but not to practical and serious discourse."[101]

This is an important insight into how the role of metaphor shapes our practice and assumptions. In modernity, The Preacher as Teacher is suspicious of language that is not clear, or seen to appeal to the imagination. The

95. Broadus and Stanfield, *On the Preparation*, 240.

96. Ibid., 340.

97. Ibid., 96.

98. Ibid., 244.

99. Ibid., 246.

100. For a representative example is his explanation of justification see Broadus, *Sermons and Addresses*, 87–88.

101. Broadus and Stanfield, *On the Preparation*, 275.

language of poetry, metaphor, or even narrative invites the imagination to conjure up its own meanings and images. Such language is decorative for the idea or the truth that the preacher wants to explain. The imagination is to be used only to help illustrate the main idea. Figures of speech, such as similes and metaphors, are useful only as long as they contribute to the development of the preacher's central idea. The underlying conviction is that if language is clear, what the preacher sends will be identical to what the congregation receives. What the preacher sends and what the congregation receives should cohere in precise words that accurately present the truth to which they refer. The underlying attitude is one of confidence that preachers can choose words so that "the expression and idea exactly correspond."[102] Confidence that words can exactly convey truth, and that communication is trustworthy if language is clear, is an entailment of the preacher's use of language.

The Teacher's Form

The forms of a sermon used by The Preacher as Teacher are varied. The sermon of this identity can be similar to a lecture, with major subdivisions and minor subdivisions clearly enumerated. Another sermon of the preacher might begin with a provocative image on which the pastor and people subsequently reflect. The preacher might preach by making the sermon an extended parable. This homiletic identity is not distinguished by a single sermonic form, but by the ideas that control the form. Whatever the form, the sermon is fundamentally propositionally controlled in nature—meaning that the form of a sermon seeks to exposit the meaning of the text in as clear a form as possible, so that there will be no danger in missing the theme or main idea. For this reason, this metaphor is most often associated with deductive forms of preaching.

Deductive forms of preaching are sermons that develop from the presentation of a general truth to its division, application, and illustrated support. Deductive forms are designed to engage listeners and bring forth the insights or ideas of a biblical passage and its implications for their lives. It is a form seeking to encourage the logical organization of rational thought. This form promotes the importance placed on formulating the content or idea of the sermon into a single sentence. For the preacher, this focus sentence is helpful because it gives rational coherence and direction to the organization of the sermon. For the congregation, the focus sentence is helpful because it

102. Ibid., 244.

keeps the sermon from ambiguity because it enables the hearer more readily to grasp the intended information passing from pulpit to the pew.

The deductive form does not delay the arrival of the sermon's idea, but states it quickly so that hearers know immediately what is being talked about and why. In this way, the form of a sermon is chosen to carefully explain and unpack the main idea.[103] The idea is understood in homiletics to be the central theme of a sermon. A sermon's central idea can be derived from the biblical text, or can be taken from a lively conversation between a pressing social or personal topic and Scripture or doctrine. Although this idea will often be divided into several parts depending on the form a sermon takes, it is important, that a complete idea has been expressed in clear language by the end of every sermon.

Broadus' label for this summary idea is "the proposition." The proposition is subject (idea) and predicate. The subject answers the question, "What is the sermon about?" Together the subject and the predicate form "one complete declarative sentence, simple, clear, and cogent" which states "the gist of the sermon."[104] The importance of the proposition has consequently had an almost ironclad hold on preaching in the nineteenth and first half of the twentieth-century pulpit.

If The Preacher as Teacher's job is to communicate the rational ideas grounded in Scripture and doctrine, than corresponding forms are needed to organize them. The teacher uses forms that help organize the central idea of a sermon, like a logical outline conceived in a deductive form. The great strength of this rational rhetoric is a clarity with which ideas are presented. This method possesses linear, logical coherence and remains the safest and most efficient method of sermon preparation.[105] Its pattern of exegesis, exposition, and application is the bread-and-butter method of preaching. Hence, for the teacher, a sermon's form is typically logically ordered.

However, one of the dangers of this popular teaching form, suggests Thomas Long, is it reduces the witness of Scripture to "merely a box of ideas."[106] Fred Craddock is particularly associated with a critique of this deductive model of preaching. He argues that deductive sermons announce each point *before* it is developed, and as a consequence have a tenuous relationship between the points, encourage a hortatory tone, and can lose

103. See Robinson, *Biblical Preaching*; Cox, *Preaching*; Craddock, *As One Without Authority*; Greenhaw, "As One *With* Authority," 105–22.

104. Broadus and Stanfield, *On the Preparation*, 56.

105. Killinger, *Fundamentals of Preaching*, 53.

106. Long, *Witness of Preaching*, 28.

momentum between transitions.[107] Craddock suggests that much of preaching's wonder is experienced in a preacher's own experience of discovery in the text. This wonder may be lost on the hearer when the outcome of a sermon is presented in such a pre-determined outline.[108]

In response to the concerns of critics like Craddock, recent homiletics scholars committed to the identity of The Preacher as Teacher have been seeking to appropriate narrative and inductive sermon forms for this identity. For example, Harold Freeman, a proponent of this identity, shifts narrative from its supportive role to a different status as a sermonic form.[109] As though in answer to Broadus's concern for "a method of preaching upon the narrative portions of Scripture" that is "distinctively appropriate to narrative, while yet it is preaching,"[110] Freeman offers the biblical story-sermon form.

For Freeman, the first essential task in composing a story-sermon is no different from that of any other sermon—discerning in scriptural text the sermon's theme or propositional idea. When the biblical passage is a narrative, the preacher who is teaching the meaning of the text should begin with the intention of the biblical storyteller and then structure the sermon along the lines of the biblical story. What is imperative, says Freeman, is that the preacher "identify the point (moral) of the story," because "there's no point in telling the story unless the people get the point, and they won't get the point unless *you* get the point."[111] The purpose of the preacher is to persuade the hearer to believe the central idea argued by the end of the sermon.[112] In this inductive form of preaching, the principles of deductive instruction are still normative because the idea is still stated by the preacher and leaves no room for one's own sense of discovery or experience. Thus, it is clear that for Freeman, the story, or narrative sermon, is a strategy whereby the preacher is still attempting to transmit the right ideas to the congregation.

Another example comes from Ralph Loren Lewis and Gregg A. Lewis, homiletic scholars who identify themselves within this tradition model.[113] These scholars elevate the status of inductive forms over deductive forms of preaching. For Lewis and Lewis, the inductive process is the reverse of the deductive process. The deductive sermon begins with a statement of truth

---

107. For example, see Craddock, *As One Without Authority.*

108. Ibid., 49.

109. See Freeman, *Variety in Biblical Preaching.*

110. Ibid., 145.

111. Ibid., 137.

112. Ibid., 152.

113. See Lewis and Lewis, *Inductive Preaching.*

and then seeks to convince the congregation of its validity using illustrations and facts as proof. The movement is from the general to the particulars. The inductive sermon begins with particulars—"the narrative, dialogue, analogy, questions, parables, the concrete experiences"—and invites the congregation to think along with the preacher, "to weigh the evidence, think through the implications and then come to the conclusion *with* the preacher at the end of the sermon."[114] According to Lewis and Lewis, by the end of the inductive sermon the congregation will recognize that the sermon's concluding truth agrees with their understanding of the facts and their own life experiences. They will be ready to accept the sermon's conclusions.

Again, what situates this description of inductive forms within the model of The Preacher as Teacher is the understanding of the conclusion. Although the congregation is invited to participate in the sermon, to go on a journey through the inductive narrative, to think with and even ahead of the preacher's own thoughts, at the end of the sermon the aim is for the preacher and the congregation to arrive at the same destination. For this to happen, the preacher *tells* the hearer the simple lesson or main idea.[115] In the end, an inductive form for Lewis and Lewis is still a strategy that intends to lead the congregation to grasp the right information.

In these descriptions of narrative sermons by Freeman and inductive sermons by Lewis and Lewis, the traditional purpose of the preacher remains normative: to communicate the right scriptural and doctrinal information, in a manner that makes the truth self-evident and accessible.

From these examples, we see how the culture of modernity has shaped the practice of The Preacher as Teacher. We see that the purpose of the preacher remains committed to teaching Scripture and to using rhetoric in a way that persuades the hearer. However, modernity shifts to an emphasis on the use and appeal of reason in the content, language, and form of the sermon. The content of the sermon is shaped around a propositional idea found within a scriptural text; the language of the sermon aims at articulating that idea in as clear and succinct a way as possible; and the form of the sermon seeks to find the best way to use and order language that makes the meaning, or main idea, of the sermon impossible to miss. Thus, the content, language, and form of the preacher's sermon seeks to communicate and persuade the hearer to the preacher's preconceived conclusions by using tools such as rhetoric. This focus on a propositional approach to preaching reflects modernity as it calls upon the courage of the preacher to use his or her own reason.

114. Ibid., 43.
115. Ibid., 136.

THE UNSPOKEN LESSON

The metaphor of The Preacher as Teacher does offer constructive wisdom for any preacher. First, it encourages clear and precise thinking that is dependent upon Scripture. Second, it demands clear and disciplined speaking. Third, this identity leads to appreciation and use of rhetorical skills that have proven to be the collective wisdom for speaking with an eloquence that aids persuasion. Finally, this identity challenges the preacher to accept one's role with responsibility. This strength of this identity may, however, also be its potential weakness because this responsibility may place the burden of emphasis on human over divine agency in persuasion.

Despite these many strengths, The Preacher as Teacher entails certain assumptions that create difficulty for the metaphor today. Four entailments are important to note for our consideration: (1) belief in the neutrality of rhetoric; (2) the inherent distance between the pulpit and the pew; (3) the appeal to rationalism; and (4) the tendency towards homiletic pragmatism.

The Neutrality of Rhetoric

One of the primary entailments of The Preacher as Teacher is that rhetoric is a neutral tool. Rhetoric is understood to be a way for the preacher to help organize a sermon, make the ideas clearer to the hearer and more enjoyable to listen to, and ultimately to aid in persuading the hearer to the outcomes and actions the preacher suggests. This identity can be pragmatic, with a willingness to use whatever cultural devices, techniques, and technologies are deemed necessary to better communicate the content of a sermon. But is rhetoric neutral? Can rhetoric be adopted without concomitant ideological baggage? Is it void of theological implications? Without an awareness of the presuppositions and assumptions of the classical rhetorical tradition related to discourse, situations, and outcomes, and without appropriate theological discretion, rhetoric can result in the subversion of the message itself.

These issues are important for all Christian preachers to think through. Philip D. Kenneson, for example, has pinpointed one of the hidden presuppositions of recent church growth theories as the belief "that management and marketing techniques are themselves neutral, and so appropriating them poses no problem in principle for the Church." Kenneson points out that such a position fails to recognize that "all technique is value-laden." In other words, he questions if there is such a thing as neutrality when it comes to using tools for communication. Technologies, advertisement strategies, and communication theories have presuppositions grounded in foundational beliefs about the nature of reality. Indeed, "by framing certain ideas in particular ways these activities help constitute the very problems and conditions about which they purport to be neutral."[116] The lens through which one looks and the tools which one uses alter what is perceived. The point Kenneson illustrates is that nothing, not even rhetoric, is a neutral tool.[117]

Andrew Resner similarly argues that the work of persuasion is not a neutral aim. He reminds us that the goal of using rhetoric is to persuade the listener, "meaning, the convincing or winning over of one's hearers to one's position."[118] If persuasion is viewed as the goal of preaching, then the primary focus can become the person of the preacher, as the one using rhetoric to do the persuading. Resner notes that this may confuse the proper order of preaching. From a theological frame of reference, the main concern is to keep the power of God for salvation the focus. In other words, preaching is God's free grace, power, and providence—and it proves efficacious for the hearer's salvation. Resner says that "from this vantage point, God is the chief matter of concern, and any talk of the human preacher affecting or effecting the situation of God's activity borders on idolatry."[119] Resner also argues that it is a significant assumption that the tools used to influence another into a particular belief or act could be considered impartial. Physically forcing someone to act or believe something is not considered an unbiased task, nor should working on someone's conscience or mental beliefs. The goal of persuasion is to change someone or something. The rhetoric used for such change is doing something to another person. Thus, rhetoric is anything but a neutral tool.[120]

It is also critical for The Preacher as Teacher not to lose sight of the source of rhetoric. The early church's reticence to train preachers in rhetoric was not entirely misplaced; rather it was based upon the knowledge that rhetoric was not neutral. At times Augustine can sound as though he considered classical rhetoric a risk to faith. In Augustine's context, rhetoric represented not only unbridled ambition but also a pagan culture, since the classic texts that served as oratorical models were full of mythology. While Augustine himself had benefited from Cicero, at the end of the day he did

---

116. Kenneson, "Selling [Out] the Church," 325–26.

117. Ibid., 327.

118. Resner, *Preacher and Cross*, 137.

119. Ibid.

120. Ibid., 138.

not trust more susceptible Christians to read Cicero without coming under his seductive influence.[121]

Moreover, the assumption that the context of Christian preaching is essentially rhetorical, or analogous to classically rhetorical situations, is only partially accurate. Christian worship is not the same as a court of law or an oratorical piece. It takes place in a liturgical context that has a history, language, and practice all its own. This metaphor seems to treat the context of worship as neutral just as it treats the techniques of preaching as neutral, but the context in which most preaching takes place is anything but neutral. Christian worship is a context intended to invoke the name of the triune God, to invite participants into life with God, and to be the place where the Scriptures are preached and the sacraments faithfully administered.

This entailment of the preacher also seems to assume that a sermon's rhetorical form is neutral. It assumes that form is not nearly as significant a consideration as content. This assumption can make sermon construction formulaic, with sermons consisting of a predictable linear structure of properly ordered points used to catalog ideas. Just as content is not neutral, neither is the form chosen to communicate it: "The medium is the message."[122] The form of a sermon is part of the content that the sermon delivers. Not all rhetorical messages, especially those that emphasize rational order, can handle the mysteries of the gospel.

What is missing from the contemporary understanding of The Preacher as Teacher is a serious understanding of the merits of the creative power of language and the importance of non-rationalistic ways of engaging and discussing the world. The teacher as articulated today privileges the rational and conscious dimensions of preaching over against other means of discourse. The teacher offers preachers little to no place for ambiguity or playfulness with language. Because clarity is the goal, all poetic speech is viewed as carrying the danger of misrepresentation. Hence, in the teacher model, creativity is understood to be an amusement that keeps preachers from the real task of articulating clear ideas. This assumes that imagination is subservient to reason, and even dangerous if not controlled by a clearly stated idea. In reality, the preacher seeks tools that can shape what others think and imagine. The teacher is the expert whose task is to communicate clearly and precisely a "truth" in sermons structured by ideas and arguments controlled by the conventions of rhetoric.

121. See Brown, *Augustine*, 299.
122. See McLuhan, "Medium is the Message," 18–26.

The Distance Between Pulpit and Pew

Another of the inherent entailments of The Preacher as Teacher is an assumed distance between the pulpit and the pew. This is a consequence of the perception that the preacher is the expert with the answers, and the listener is a novice who needs knowledge and instruction. This perception creates a power gap between the preacher and those listening in the pew.

Some of the biggest voices challenging this power gap come from feminist critics who see the teacher model as favoring male experience.[123] Christine M. Smith, for example, argues that this traditional view of the preacher enforces typically gender-biased views of relationships.[124] Inspired by Carol Gilligan, she argues that male understandings of relationships encourage language that reinforces and creates distances that are institutionalized in structures of ecclesiastical hierarchy, whereas a majority of woman experience relationship by patterns of "connectedness."[125] Preaching, she asserts, is not grounded in the preacher's "special rights, powers, knowledge, and capacity to influence and transform."[126] According to Smith, this identity presupposes the preacher's separation from the congregation. She suggests that a female preacher needs an alternative identity for understanding her relationship to the people in the pew, because her fundamental instinct is of being inextricably *connected* within a web of interdependent relationships. Smith argues that by maintaining this traditional identity, women and their experiences and voice in the church, are innately discouraged from speaking.

The power gap created by this homiletic model is also critiqued from another angle. Fred Craddock notes that within this tradition, at least since the influence of modernity, the thesis of the sermon is typically expounded first and only later is it related to particular situations. This "deductive" style is a communication praxis that assumes that universal ideas first need to be explained before they can be clearly applied to personal situations. Craddock argues that such an approach is an "almost unnatural mode of communication, unless, of course one presupposes passive listeners who accept the right or authority of the speaker to state conclusions which he then applies to their faith and life."[127] An inherent bias exists in this traditional model because it assumes the authoritarian address of God's Word

---

123. For example, see Chopp, *Power to Speak;* and Atkinson Rose, *Sharing the Word.*

124. See Smith, *Weaving the Sermon.*

125. Ibid., 46.

126. Ibid.

127. Craddock, *As One Without Authority,* 54.

through the preacher and passive reception by the hearer. What is lacking in this approach to proclamation is the possibility of dialogue or communal interpretation. As Craddock notes, there is "no listening by the speaker, no contributing by the hearer."[128]

Rodney Kennedy further argues that in the wrong hands, this identity can even encourage an abusive spiritual authoritarianism that retreats into a narrow literalism controlled by the limits of pure reason, thereby ignoring serious questions that modern developments in interpretation theory have raised.[129] Literalism is a view of representation that has forgotten its own dependence on a social-historical community of discourse. If a preacher and a congregation wholeheartedly embrace this understanding of the preaching, in which the preacher is always correct, who is to say to the preacher a sermon is ever wrong?

The distance and the power differentiation suggested by this metaphor can be a difficult gap to bridge in a culture where an identity of authoritarianism is often viewed with suspicion. When this gap is combined with a kind of rational rhetoric controlled by reason that so marked modernity, it can be even more distancing.

Homiletic Constrained by Rationalism

A third entailment of The Preacher as Teacher, at least since modernity, is a preoccupation with rationalism. This metaphor encourages the use of rhetorical forms to help the hearer grasp the truth of Scripture in the form of propositional ideas. During modernity, the goal of the preacher became not only to communicate Scripture and doctrine clearly, but also to communicate the ideas thought to be contained within Scripture and doctrine. In this sense, the preacher thinks of truth as an abstraction to be grasped. In modernity, reason, like rhetoric, was exalted as universally neutral. If one applied reason to a problem, one could expect to find the self-evident answer. In this cultural context, the sermons of the preacher began to have an apologetic edge, as natural reason was thought to fit the pieces of faith together like a puzzle. With such an emphasis on rationality, the modern metaphor of The Preacher as Teacher may have inadvertently contributed to eclipsing the mystery of the biblical narrative as it conformed to organizing biblical ideas into an argumentative outline that would appeal to reason.

The rational entailment of his identity is expressed by speaking as directly and as simply as possible. A traditional sermon shaped by this

---

128. Ibid., 55.

129. Kennedy, *Creative Power of Metaphor*.

entailment has a clear outline. As Ronald J. Allen enumerates, such a sermon has five parts: Beginning, Exposition of the Biblical Text, Theological
Analysis of the Text, Application of the Interpretation of the Text to the
Situation of the Congregation, and Ending.[130] This style can be adapted to
sermons on Christian doctrines and practices as well as topical subjects.
In these cases, the "Exposition of the Text" would be replaced by "Exposition of the Doctrine, Practice, or Topic." Listening to such a sermon by
the preacher, the congregation has every opportunity to get the preacher's
point. This type of sermon is easy to prepare. The preacher must consider
what to say, but there is a standard outline of how to say it. The task of each
part of the sermon is clearly defined.

However, some preachers find this approach unimaginative, tedious,
and predictable (especially if the preacher uses it weekly). In addition, its
rational and ordered style can violate the forms of the biblical texts one is
preaching from. A psalm, for instance, with its use of poetic device, does
not always conform to the linear flow of exposition, doctrinal analysis, and
personal application.

This raises the question of whether it is wise to make standard rules,
prescriptions, and principles for preparing and delivering a sermon. Does
such an approach not suggest that if a preacher can just find the right rational technique or formula, the sermon will be a success? Even more dangerous is the subtle emphasis that the preacher rather than God is in control
of the sermon. Dietrich Ritschl argues that, "the ways in which God wants
to work cannot be systematized."[131] True proclamation, according to Ritschl,
is an act of revelation. Revelation is the action of God the Father, revealing
God the Son, through the power of God the Holy Spirit. This event happens
in the church by means of the human voice, but by definition, revelation is
always the work of God.[132] This event cannot be controlled and regulated by
human systems and thoughts. Harry Caplan suggests that a look into this
Augustinian model of preaching demonstrates this point very clearly. The
influence of classical rhetoric caused a mode of preaching known as "topical
preaching." Caplan suggests that the more widespread "topical preaching"
became, the greater the emphasis on abstract principles and ideas that separated the Scripture from the ideas being preached.[133] Through this process,
the Word began to be subservient to human words.

---

130. See Allen, *Preaching and Practical Ministry*, 32–36.

131. Ritschl, *Theology of Proclamation*, 135.

132. Ibid.

133. See Caplan, "Classical Rhetoric," 73ff. Here Caplan gives examples of what has
been done in preaching under this traditional homiletic legacy.

Richard Eslinger raises similar concerns in his analysis of this identity. He refers to this identity of The Preacher as Teacher as the "old homiletic," and characterizes it in two ways. First, the "old homiletic" is a discursive method of preaching that values sermonic points and propositions,[134] and, second, it is an "ideational approach" to preaching.[135] Eslinger emphasizes that sermons organized around propositions and ideas privilege a rationalistic approach to preaching. They also make assumptions about the nature of revelation as coming through depersonalized and abstract propositions meant to appeal to rationality.[136] The goal of the preacher is to make biblical truth accessible; therefore sermons tend to use plain, rational language in order to make the ideas in a sermon as clear, concise, and understandable as possible. In this way, the preacher of the "old homiletic" focuses on apologetic preaching. That is, preaching becomes an activity not necessarily to teach Scripture and doctrine but to logically argue the Christian faith in clear and orderly styles designed to change the hearer's mind. In this view, revelation comes to a person as ideas to be learned, not as the gift of God's own self-giving presence. This rational emphasis makes the truth of the gospel an idea to grasp, or a proposition to give assent to, and not primarily a relationship to receive or live into. The gospel becomes something to rationally "get" or "grasp" rather than "receive."

This emphasis on rationality forces a particular view of divine agency that is troublesome. It offers God a minor role in preaching. Revelation is conjured by the right use of logical proposition and rhetorical skill. Knowledge of God becomes the burden of the preacher's right appeal and application of reason. The burden of saving grace is thus in the mouth of the preacher. Revelation that is determined by a rationalistic proclamation maintains a boxed view of God that is determined by the limits of human reason. God's freedom becomes determined by human limits of rationality. Any model of homiletic identity that needs to be rational as defined in human terms is going to have a difficult time unfolding and probing the mystery of Word becoming flesh.

Fred Craddock observes that the modern identity of The Preacher as Teacher tends to value the rational and deductive dimensions of preaching more than narrative and inductive approaches.[137] Craddock suggests that a homiletic preoccupied with reason tends to want to subordinate the use of story, narrative, metaphor, and illustration as a kind of teaching aid to the more important methods of sermon development—definition, explana-

---

134. Eslinger, *New Hearing*, 11.

135. Ibid., 86.

136. Ibid., 31.

137. See Craddock, *As One Without Authority*, 3–15.

tion, restatement, and argument. In other words, the use of the imagination, stories, illustrations, similes, analogies, metaphors, allegories, anecdotes, parables, and fables are considered decorative functions serving as "supportive" or "auxiliary" to a homiletic rationality. Figures of speech and metaphor are useful only as long as they contribute to the development of the sermon's rationale or central idea, but they are not appropriate for serious discourse. Rationality, not the imagination, is the road to transforming the saving ideas.

When the sermon becomes a way to solve life's problems in thirty minutes or less and when answers are reduced to clear and concise propositional statements, preaching is in danger of becoming moralistic and treating the complexities of life as reductionistic.[138] The sermon controlled by the constraints of rationalism can be a way of limiting the homiletic practice and experience of The Preacher as Teacher. At its worst, it can lead to the entailment of a kind of homiletic pragmatism.

CONCLUSION: BEYOND A HOMILETIC PRAGMATISM

During modernity, The Preacher as Teacher began to reflect a pragmatic frame of reference for Christian teaching controlled by rationalism. Broadus's emphasis on sermons that call for the hearer to make a decision or a choice reflects the way the preacher shifted the center of Christian preaching to appeal to moral reasoning, the freedom of the will, and the natural ability to exercise moral choice to obey God. Broadus's theology of preaching was semi-Pelagian in that he taught that anyone who wanted to could make a rational decision for God if the right argument was presented to him or her. Within this understanding, salvation is actualized only through an individual decision that can be won or lost by a preacher's use of rhetorical methods and techniques

By placing primary emphasis on human agency, Broadus reflects a cultural voluntarism that encouraged making a decision for Christ.[139] This kind of subjective deployment of preaching was largely made popular by the American evangelical tradition that formed a preacher like Broadus.[140]

138. See Wardlaw, *Learning Preaching*, 269–311.

139. See Noll, *America's God*, 188–95. Here, Noll has shown that the frontier revivals of the 1770s and 1780s marked the emergence of a voluntarist, pragmatic, revivalist, individualist, and sectarian kind of Protestantism now associated by many with evangelicalism.

140. For more on the sociological conditions that encouraged this subjective religious experience in North America see Hunter, *American Evangelicalism*, 23–48.

Albeit unknowingly, much of North America's evangelical homiletic practice continues to be situated within a theology/practice split that embodies
a kind of *homiletic pragmatism*.[141] In this modern context, the Christian
teacher is driven by a separation between method and message, form and
content, and style and substance, as the mystery of the gospel is reduced to
appeal to private religious experience.[142]

This pragmatic focus of the preacher in modernity encourages the
adoption of techniques that *work* or cause the desired persuasive effects.
This emphasis on "what works" views preaching largely as a human act not
dependent on the power of God but instead on human skill and rhetorical technique.[143] In short, the term homiletic pragmatism suggests that the
metaphor of The Preacher as Teacher can lead to a homiletic practice that
enables the preacher to teach about God without relying on or acknowledg-
ing the agency and activity of God.

Homiletic pragmatism, then, is the utilitarian use of words and rhetoric based on the assumption that preaching is a matter of finding the right
presentational technique. The proper technique is seen to be done without
surrendering one's words and oneself to the presence and work of the Word
and the Spirit.[144]

This homiletic pragmatism is the result of a homiletic identity that
is not sufficiently grounded in a substantive doctrine of revelation beyond
what the preacher makes plain, simple, and persuasive to a hearer. For example, Broadus's communication strategy took on the form prescribed by
his own pragmatic effort to persuade his hearers to make a decision. His
focus was on a humanity that "decides" rather than the persons of the triune
God who act with, in, and through human activity by the divine power and
wisdom mediated and defined by the proclamation of the Word made flesh.

A contemporary example of this kind of homiletic pragmatism may
be seen in "megachurch" pastor and popular Christian writer Rick Warren. His books *The Purpose-Driven Church* and *The Purpose-Driven Life*,
originally sermons turned popular Christian literature, reflect a kind of
pragmatic entrepreneurship that places an emphasis on human ingenuity and consumer-desire over the larger providential story of the triune
God of grace.[145] Warren's self-identification as a senior teaching pastor

141. This term has not, to my knowledge, been used before.

142. Michael Pasquarello III argues that preaching in the modern context encourages a kind of practical homiletic that places its emphasis on technique. See Pasquarello,
Christian Preaching, 20.

143. Here I have learned much from Joseph Dunne, *Back to the Rough Ground*.

144. Ibid., 15–25.

145. Warren, *Purpose-Driven Church* and Warren, *Purpose-Driven Life*.

draws on the wisdom of this traditional metaphor, but adapts it to reflect a consumer-driven pragmatic gospel. Warren models a homiletic pragmatism that demonstrates that when uprooted from the church's larger theological soil, the teaching identity of the preacher can easily reduce the catechesis of the church to a prefabricated rhetorical formula created for the purpose of effecting results by means of explanation, technological use, and control.[146]

In a manner similar to Broadus' focus on rational persuasion, Warren's method privileges human agency over divine grace in constructing a practical vision of preaching that in both its conception and implementation locates its users outside of the narrative of Scripture and the trinitarian economy of grace. Warren acknowledges that this tension exists in preaching between two distinct realms: the divine and human, the theological and practical. However, his homiletic wisdom fails to show that this split is reconciled and overcome within the trinitarian wisdom of Scripture embodied in Christ and the traditional practices of the church.[147]

The result of the Christian teaching that informs Warren's purpose-driven way of configuring the divine/human relationship separates ends and means for the sake of preaching's "effectiveness" towards growth.

One consequence of this strategy is that God is designated as a means in service of the method and Christian preaching is redefined as a set of skills guided by instrumental reason and personal choice rather than a practice informed by the theological wisdom of Scripture and the traditions of the church. In other words, Warren's teaching about God has been severed from the larger story of a triune God. Indeed, evidence of trinitarian teaching and practice is conspicuously absent throughout Warren's work.[148] This absence is possible because doctrines like the Trinity, the incarnation, and the resurrection are considered difficult to make clear when the goal is persuasion to pragmatic outcomes.[149] Today, popular teaching pastors who rely on pragmatic preaching reduce the church's affirmation of the creating

146. See the excellent discussion of late modernity's technological environment in Long, *John Wesley's Moral Theology*, 1–36.

147. Warren, *Purpose-Driven Church*, 56–57.

148. Warren's hermeneutical method is fragmentary at best and presents virtually no canonical or theological interpretation of the pieces of Scripture he cites. On using Scripture, he states: "Since the verse divisions and numbers were not included in the Bible until 1560 A.D., I haven't always quoted the *entire* verse, but rather focused on the phrase that was appropriate. My model for this is Jesus and how he and the apostles quoted the Old Testament. They often just quoted a phrase to make a point" (Warren, *Purpose-Driven Life*, 325). For a study that clearly refutes the method advocated by Warren on theological grounds, see Hayes, *Echoes of Scripture*.

149. Rowan Williams comments on the danger of pragmatic reductions of God in *On Christian Theology*, 75.

and redeeming activity of the Trinity to manageable size by focusing on principles to apply, rules to follow, and things to do. By promoting the sermon as a path for self-improvement, the strategies of the preacher promote a pragmatic, or utilitarian, approach to faith. This pragmatic approach to preaching reflects a religious description offered by Christian Smith when he refers to the spiritual instincts of North American teenagers as "moralistic therapeutic deism"; such a religious understanding places the self rather than the Triune God at the center of salvation, church, history, and world.[150]

The Preacher as Teacher, as reflected by Warren, is unburdened by the past, and therefore Warren feels the freedom to create his own ecclesiastical tradition, "the purpose-driven life and Church," that has its own "canon within the canon." This canon includes a highly individualistic and pragmatic way of teaching Scripture that is separated from the history of Christian interpretation and its lived expression by the church.[151] Freed from the convictions and practices of a normative ecclesiastical guide, the preacher's scriptural interpretation is in danger of being reduced to a kind of self-help therapy text, in which the preacher can discover a universal "one size fits all" homiletic strategy. It is no wonder that in this context, the preacher finds it difficult to shape an imagination of faith around the wisdom and revelation of the triune God. The challenge of popular preachers such as Warren lies not in their passion for reaching people but rather in their failure to be sufficiently theological in their teachings about God, the church, and the world, as revealed in Scripture, and the doctrine of the triune God into which people are baptized.[152]

The Preacher as Teacher, to avoid the path of homiletic pragmatism, must receive his or her identity as a gift within the larger liturgical activity of the church's affirmation and confession of its belief in the triune God. When this metaphor is separated from the larger narratives of Scripture and the wisdom of the Christian tradition, contemporary scriptural interpretation and preaching are subject to any number of powerful but false ideologies and patterns of narcissism. Unchecked by theological wisdom, popular forms of preaching that aim for "relevance" by focusing on useful teaching methods can be easily co-opted, thereby ignoring the triune God's providential activity in the world and the church as a sign of the cosmic

150. To unpack the term "moralistic therapeutic deism," see Smith and Denton, *Soul Searching*.

151. In light of the Christian tradition, Warren fails to demonstrate why his purpose-driven account should be considered truthful. From Warren's writings, I assume his ecclesial "tradition" is constituted by Saddleback Church. See chapter 1 of *The Purpose-Driven Church*.

152. I have been challenged here by the argument in Reno, *In the Ruins of the Church*.

reconciliation accomplished through the work of Christ and the Spirit: the *missio Dei*.[153]

What is problematic about the identity of The Preacher as Teacher today is that the Christian practice of preaching is reduced to utilitarian techniques rather than seen as a work done in and through the divine agency of the Trinity. It is the preacher with ability to persuade through skillful use of reasoning and rhetoric who is thought to bring about reconciliation and redemption with God, not the Word made flesh. This Word is the risen Christ, who summons the church to wholeness and healing by following him in bearing witness to creation's true end of praising and knowing the triune God. This is the same Word who is active in and through preaching. This emphasis on the divine agency in the work of the preacher is the focus of The Preacher as Herald. As we move to the next chapter, we will explore the strengths and weaknesses of this important homiletic identity.

153. See the excellent discussion of abstract forms in Jenson, "What Is Post-Christian?," 21–31.

4

The Preacher as Herald

Behold I have put my words in your mouth.—JEREMIAH 1:9

INTRODUCTION: THE WORD PROCLAIMED AND PROCLAIMED AGAIN

A second metaphor that has significantly shaped homiletic identity in our current context is The Preacher as Herald. Within this metaphor the preacher is a messenger bound to transmit faithfully the message of the kingdom of God entrusted to him or her as a faithful minister to God the King. However significant the preacher may be, this homiletic identity calls the messenger to offer a message that does not originate in the preacher but outside or above him or her. In other words, The Preacher as Herald is an identity that reinforces the idea that the preacher is called by, sent by, and speaks for God alone. The preacher is given a word from above and serves as an evangelical instrument whereby the divinely initiated message, or *kerygma*, is proclaimed.

Unlike The Preacher as Teacher, whose intentional emphasis on instruction and the use of rhetoric assumed the efficacy of human agency, The Preacher as Herald preaches into a kind of human vacuum. In other words, one significant assumption of this metaphor is that the preacher cannot prepare hearers for the announcement of the Word of God through rhetorical strategies, as only God can accomplish and make effective the human hearing of God's Word. Thus, The Preacher as Herald is an identity that encourages a radical dependence on God to use the event of preaching as a bridge between the Word of God and the word of humanity. This bridge is made possible when the preacher grounds every sermon in the *kerygma,* the fundamental and essential center of the gospel message.

This chapter will begin with a concise exploration of this homiletic identity through a review of the distinction between teaching and preaching put forth by C. H. Dodd. We will then explain and interpret the metaphor of The Preacher as Herald as developed by Karl Barth. It is impossible to address fully this identity within this one chapter, but by engaging the identity as articulated by Karl Barth, we will understand certain theological implications of this particular metaphor. These include the trinitarian context of preaching, the preacher's participation in the eventfulness of revelation, and a rejection of apologetics and rhetoric by the preacher. Finally, we will articulate some entailments of this homiletic identity and offer corrective criticisms that point the way forward to a homiletic identity that incorporates the best of The Preacher as Teacher and The Preacher as Herald.

THE HERALD: A DISTINCTION AND AN EXAMPLE

According to the homiletic identity of The Preacher as Herald, the purpose of the preacher is to proclaim the *kerygma,* the good-and-saving news of the kingdom of God. This *kerygma* is understood to be the essential core of the gospel that, when announced, allows the Word of God to become an event in which God speaks the saving Word of God.

Through its emphasis on preaching as *kerygma,* The Preacher as Herald is clearly distinct from The Preacher as Teacher. The primary goal is not to disseminate knowledge of the Scriptures as such, but to make an announcement of God's reign. In *The Apostolic Preaching and Its Developments,* C. H. Dodd traces and highlights the distinction between preaching and teaching in the New Testament.[1] Though Dodd's book is not an apologetic for the homiletic metaphor of The Preacher as Herald, his discussion of the dissimilarities between preaching and teaching helpfully illuminates how the two models differ in emphasis and focus.

Teaching (*didaskein*), according to Dodd, refers in a majority of cases to ethical or catechetical instruction, which would include what we would call apologetics—that is, the "reasoned commendation of Christianity to persons interested but not yet convinced."[2] Preaching, on the other hand, is the public proclamation of Jesus Christ as Messiah. The meaning of the Greek word used so often by Paul (*keryssein*) emphasizes the preacher's call

1. See Dodd, *Apostolic Preaching,* especially 1–5.
2. Ibid., 4.

"to proclaim." Thus, preaching is accomplished by a *keryx*, a term that may refer to a town crier, an auctioneer, or an appointed herald. The *keryx* is one who speaks some definite news that must be made known to the public. It would not be too much to say that wherever "preaching" appears in Scripture, it always carries with it the implication of "good tidings." According to Dodd's biblical comparison in the New Testament, however, to preach the good tidings of the *kerygma* was by no means the same activity as offering moral instruction or apologetic reasons with an effort to persuade and teach. While the church sought to pass on the teachings of Jesus, it was not by apologetic instruction that it persuaded others to be disciples of Jesus. Dodd argues that this was achieved in the New Testament by the preaching of the specific announcement of the *kerygma*, the "gospel's essential kernel which communicates and effects salvation."[3]

What is the content of this specific announcement? Dodd's summary of the *kerygma* is not a single sound-bite proposition or any one rhetorical formula. The *kerygma* could be either brief or complex and intricate. Dodd observes that in the Synoptic Gospels we read of Jesus simply "preaching of the Kingdom of God" and in the Epistles we read of Paul simply "preaching Christ." In the Acts of the Apostles, both forms of expressions are often used as the apostles preach "Jesus" or "Christ" or "the Kingdom of God." Dodd argues that the content of the *kerygma* message could also be more intricate:

> The general scheme of the *kerygma* . . . begins by proclaiming that "this is that which was spoken by the prophets"; the age of fulfillment has dawned, and Christ is Lord; [the *kerygma*] then proceeds to recall the historical facts, leading up to the resurrection and exaltation of Christ and the promise of his coming in glory; and it ends with the call to repentance and the offer of forgiveness.[4]

We may understand the core message of the *kerygma* to be the announcement of the kingdom of God in Jesus Christ, who is its sovereign ruler.[5] If, then, the core message of The Preacher as Herald is grounded in this understanding, preachers need only the *kerygma* itself to fulfill their mission, which involves the testimony of the entire witness of Christ's life, death, and resurrection. This is not, according to Dodd, an effort to try to fix the *kerygma* as an irreducible formula.[6]

3. Ibid., 7.
4. Ibid., 72.
5. Ibid., 28.
6. Though some have argued otherwise. See, for example, Lucy Atkinson Rose's critique in *Sharing the Word*, 40. Rose argues that Dodd's *kerygmatic* legacy has resulted

Attention to the *kerygma* is not the exclusive privilege of this identity. For example, The Preacher as Teacher may give moral instruction based on the same core content of the *kerygma*. Therefore, the two models are not necessarily mutually exclusive. If both, then, could be articulating the same content, what is the significant difference?

We could say that what distinguishes The Preacher as Herald from The Preacher as Teacher as a homiletic identity is the theological understanding of what a sermon is supposed to accomplish. Whereas The Preacher as Teacher emphasizes the primarily didactic end of preaching, and encourages the use of rhetoric to help make instruction persuasive, The Preacher as Herald believes that the faithful proclamation of the *kerygma* will be heard only if God grasps the hearer through the event of revelation, meaning God's own speech to humanity and humanity's response to God. For The Preacher as Herald, preaching makes sense only when God is the active subject from first to last. A sermon is not made persuasive by clever or creative rhetoric, nor is the gospel heard through a reasoned apologetic for the faith. In other words, the difference between the two models is a theological distinction rooted in an understanding of revelation itself.

The Preacher as Herald assumes that when the *kerygma* is spoken, it is the revelation of the Word, Jesus Christ, who alone has the power through the Holy Spirit to make human hearing a possibility. The authority of the *kerygmatic* preacher demands that his personality and preferences be subjugated to the primacy of Jesus Christ. According to this homiletic identity, Christian preaching is not the place for political diatribe, turgid exposition of one's personal opinions, or experiences that "happened on the way to church." The focus of this metaphor is to announce both the presence and promise of Jesus Christ, who through the faithful preaching of the *kerygma* is "openly set forth before their eyes as crucified" (Gal 3:1).

When Dodd makes the distinction between Biblical preaching and teaching, he consciously and explicitly draws a contrast between the task of teaching and the call to preach the gospel. As noted above, Dodd draws attention to the role of a herald or town crier. Generally, the responsibilities of a crier or herald include but are not limited to the following:

1. A herald makes announcements.

2. A herald directs and marshals participants in an organized activity.

3. A herald is an officer with an official standing who mediates between leaders in conflict or in a common purpose.

4. A herald is a messenger.

---

in a fixed message that leaves no room for critique or adjustment.

5. A herald promotes and advocates a cause.

6. A herald precedes or foreshadows a greater subject.

This general definition of a herald was taken up and clarified with great power by Karl Barth, the modern master of thinking about general definitions in relation to Jesus and his person and work. We will now turn to Karl Barth to develop illustrate and explain the way the image of the herald shapes the task and agenda of a preacher.

MODERN MASTER: KARL BARTH

It is the heralding of Jesus Christ that is the concern and care of The Preacher as Herald. This model did not originate from any one preacher, and many worthy individuals could be highlighted in relation to it, but there was no better advocate for this metaphor during modernity than the Swiss theologian Karl Barth.

Karl Barth was a preacher's theologian. Indeed, it would be difficult to identify a modern theologian who could rival Barth's comprehensive theological vision for Christian preaching. Trevor Hart argues that Barth's "entire theological project might legitimately be described as a 'theology of proclamation.'"[7] He was concerned not only with the secondary question of how *to* preach, but with the primary theological consideration, how *can* one preach? His theological vision was itself an effort to serve the church's proclamation of the Word of God by identifying The Preacher as Herald.

The Herald Reflects Barth's Return to Scripture

Metaphors do not make sense in a vacuum. How we understand the meaning between *this* and *that* has resonance in a particular culture that influences our perception of the association.[8] This is true of The Preacher as Herald as proposed by Barth. For Barth, the image of a herald made sense for a preacher's identity as an antidote resisting modernity's influence on Christian proclamation.

Troubled by what he perceived to be modernity's limited Christian proclamation, Barth sought to develop a theology and a homiletic model for Christian proclamation that could set the church free to preach the *kerygma* of the gospel without limitation. He was fond of using the image of

---

7. Hart, *Regarding Karl Barth*, 28.

8. Lakoff and Johnson, *Metaphors We Live By*, 22.

the herald to ground his theology of proclamation, "Proclamation is human language in and through which God Himself speaks, like a King through the mouth of his herald, which moreover is meant to be heard and apprehended . . . in faith as the divine decision upon life and death, as the divine judgment and the divine acquittal, the eternal law and the eternal gospel both together."[9]

Barth developed the metaphor of the herald primarily from the apostle Paul. Paul gives us the image of a herald running ahead of the royal entourage to proclaim the King's arrival. *Kerygma* refers both to the act of proclamation (1 Cor 2:4) and also to the content of what is proclaimed (1 Cor 15:4). The Preacher as Herald proclaims only what the King authorizes. The word spoken by the preacher is a partisan word on behalf of the King. "So we are ambassadors for Christ, since God is making his appeal through us" (2 Cor 5:20). Thus, this identity anticipates that Jesus Christ himself is present in the *kerygmatic* occasion. He is present not as an empirical object, but as the saving power of the gospel. He is present not simply as the subject who is proclaimed, but as the abiding agent of proclamation. "No one has ever seen God. It is God the only son, who is close to the Father's heart, who has made him known" (John 1:18).

The image of the herald as a norm for a homiletic identity represents Barth's theological reaction to modernity's preoccupation with human experience and agency in favor of one that emphasizes our dependence on divine grace. Through the words of the preacher, God is doing the preaching, "making his appeal through us." In other words, in the act of preaching there is a voice beyond the voice of the preacher that is the very voice of God. This is the voice of the Word revealing the truth about itself as expressed in Scripture. Thus, the preacher ought not to embellish or elaborate on the kingly proclamation. The preacher ought simply to reiterate the Scriptures, to preach what he has been told to preach: "We have simply to assume the attitude of a messenger who has something to say. We have no need to build a slowly ascending ramp, for there is no height that we have to reach. NO! Something has to come down from above. And this can happen only when the Bible speaks from the very outset. We have then done what we could."[10]

---

9. Barth, *Church Dogmatics*, I/1, §3.1, 48-49, vol. 1, (52). In order to keep the format clear, and so that readers who have older editions can better follow my citations, I have given the section, paragraph and section (denoted by: §) followed by the page number from the edition cited in the bibliography, volume number in the Study Edition, and then the pagination of the older T. & T. Clark edition (published in Edinburgh) in parentheses. *Church Dogmatics* is hereafter abbreviated as *CD*.

10. Barth, *Homiletics*, 125.

The working assumption of this homiletic model is that listeners have no way of knowing God or what they need from God before they hear the *kerygma* announced. It is a theology of proclamation that assumes there is an unbridgeable gap between God and humanity. This is a theology of revelation inspired by what Barth understood as an unbridgeable dialectic between the Word of God and the Word of Man.[11]

In this sense, Barth's homiletic project for the church developed a model that would discourage any hint that proclamation could be understood or made effective through human agency. Unlike The Preacher as Teacher that emphasized the didactic purpose of preaching and the use of rhetoric to help people grasp its core ideas in a way that persuaded the affections toward the gospel, the image of The Preacher as Herald suggests that the person and work of the preacher play no role in a sermon's success.[12] Thus, Barth's homiletic was driven by his understanding of revelation as a God-to-human movement of grace through the Word preached, written, and revealed.[13]

Therefore, The Preacher as Herald, unlike The Preacher as Teacher, need not be concerned with rhetorical stratagems or oratorical ornamentation, because the Word of God makes its own way through the power of the Holy Spirit who makes the eternal Word known. In this sense, The Preacher as Herald seeks only to be a faithful vehicle, an ambassador, or a witness of the revealed Word, as exemplified by John the Baptist.[14] Indeed, John the Baptist as a witness to the Word was Barth's favored image for Christian preaching.[15] The preacher serving as a witness in the tradition of John the Baptist emphasizes that the preacher's authority is external, and rests upon something the preacher has seen and heard.[16] In this spirit, and in service to the congregation, the preacher goes to the Biblical text hoping there to be

11. See Barth, *Word of God*.

12. Barth speaks with contempt for those who try to "present the truth of God aesthetically in the form of a picture, an impression, or an aesthetic evocation of Jesus" (Barth, *Homiletics*, 48).

13. *CD* I/1, §4, 85-122, vol. 1, (88-124).

14. Barth writes that the standard of the witness is precisely the attitude "which must be the standard for dogmatics as the model of Church proclamation." The theme of theology as witness is developed in *CD* I/2, §23.2, 74-75, vol. 4, (817).

15. This claim is suggested by William Willimon, as represented by Barth's lifelong attraction to a painting of John the Baptist by German expressionist painter Matthias Grunewald, in *Conversations with Barth on Preaching*, 6. Willimon cites as the source of this idea Barth, *Karl Barth's Table Talk*, 196.

16. For more on the image of the witness as a reflection of the herald identity, see Long, *Witness of Preaching*, 42–47.

encountered by a voice, a living presence. It is from this encounter that the preacher is ordained as one who is a reliable and dependable witness.

Why did Barth come to this understanding of The Preacher as Herald? What was the theological context that shaped his need for a recovery of this Biblical imagery? Or, in other words, how did the culture that Barth was immersed in as a preacher shape his awareness of the need to emphasize this particular image as the norm homiletic identity? For our context, if we are in the twilight of modernity, how is Barth's metaphor still appropriate?

In the context of modernity, Barth found Christianity itself assaulted by ways of thinking and comprehending that claimed a beginning point in a general universal human experience that undermined any human dependence on God's revelation. Barth understood modern preaching to be too influenced by its turn away from the agent active in revelation.[17] Christian preaching had fallen captive to a world controlled by epistemological ground rules set down by Kant and expressed in positivism, emotivism, pop-psychology, and existentialism. In this development, Barth saw a creeping influence of the modern period's emphasis on human reason and autonomy on the pulpit as another way in which the church had lost any sense of dependence on God's grace. By turning away from the subject of revelation, preachers lost the sense that Christian speech is "essentially response, and not essentially a source."[18] This made preaching itself one more way that we Christians attempted to make ourselves at home in a world that is not our home.

Samuel Wells notes that amid the intellectual assaults of modernity and Christianity's dismissal from the "table" of public debates of significance, preachers in modernity typically responded in one of two ways. One was to show the reasonableness of the Christian faith. Preachers tried to find ways to make the Bible plausible. One way this was accomplished was by an appeal to the psychological experience of faith, attempting to demonstrate its existential genuineness. The second way was to demonstrate the pragmatic usefulness of Christian belief. In this vein, the church could be perceived as a community helping to order the disorder of desires of public life, by helping people behave better. Consequently, this instinct was attractive to many who sat in positions of power, and thus they saw a way to use the church for their own ends.[19]

According to Wells, these were the predominant options for those who attempted to gain a hearing for the Christian faith.

17. Hart, "Revelation," 38.
18. Ibid., 41.
19. Wells, *Improvisation*, 27.

Barth didn't choose either one of these responses. He instead emphasized the simple reiteration of the *kerygma* in the biblical text. Barth believed
this to be the best antidote to recover the witness of the church.[20] Barth
says, "Preaching is exposition, not exegesis. It follows the text but moves on
from it to the preacher's own heart and to the congregation."[21] Preaching is
biblical when it reflects a playful submission to and repetition of the Biblical
text that is a faithful exposition of what God says and is saying. Barth says,
"Christianity has always been and only been a living religion when it was
not ashamed to be in all seriousness a book-based religion."[22] In this way,
the human preacher would always be dependent on the movement of the
Word of God to humanity.

This theology began to take shape in response to an intellectually inspired spiritual crisis that overtook the young Barth when he was a pastor of
the Reformed Church in Safenwil in the canton of Aargau in north-central
Switzerland.[23] Here, in 1916 Barth began to carefully work through Paul's
epistle to the Romans, making copious notes as he went along clarifying his
ideas challenging the essential "goodness of humankind."[24] It is in his commentary on Romans that Barth began to develop his understanding of the
preacher's purpose as The Preacher as Herald.[25] This identity was antidote
to modern homiletic dedication to some kind of inner experience or *a priori*
logic of God. Instead, Barth favored Christian proclamation that would allow God to speak for Godself through the Scriptures and through preaching, heralding forth the God of grace to a world absorbed in its own misery.
For Barth, the modern emphasis on religious individualism and historical
relativism called for a recovery of an old prophetic paradigm for preaching,
one that could promote an active understanding of revelation that calls for

20. *CD* IV/1, §59.2, 242-43, vol. 21, (250). Barth believed that a sermon consists of
the preacher's careful repetition of the Biblical text in a homiletical restatement of what
the Bible says.

21. Barth, *Karl Barth Reader*, 33.

22. Ibid., 34.

23. See Bush, *Karl Barth*, 51.

24. Ibid.

25. See Barth, *Epistle To The Romans*. Though Barth does not use the term herald
here, we do see the beginning of his working his understanding of this identity out in
the opening sentences of his epistle to the Romans when he comments on the work of
Paul. Barth begins with these thoughts: "Paul, a servant of Jesus Christ, called to be an
apostle. Here is no 'genius rejoicing in his own creative ability' (Zundel). The man who
is not speaking is an emissary, bound to perform his duty; the minister of his King; a
servant, not a master. However great and important a man Paul may have been, the essential theme of his mission is not within him but above him—unapproachably distant
and unutterably strange" (27).

repentance in light of the grace of God revealed in himself in the person and work of Jesus Christ.

THE UNSPOKEN KERYGMA

Shaped by the identity of The Preacher as Herald, theologians and homileticians describe preaching as a transmission of evangelical and theological message.[26] To the traditional metaphor's emphasis on The Preacher as Teacher, this metaphor adds the eventfulness of the Word that happens only by the miracle of God's grace in revelation.

Let us unpack the theological implications of this identity using Barth as an example for this homiletic model. What are the theological foundations for this metaphor? We will suggest three: (1) Barth's trinitarian analogy; (2) Barth's emphasis on Revelation as event; and (3) Barth's rejection of apologetics and rhetoric as an appeal to natural theology. It is to these entailments that we now turn our attention to explore the metaphor of The Preacher as Herald.

The Trinitarian Pattern

Within Barth's thought, the identity of The Preacher as Herald functions within the threefold understanding of the Word of God. Barth first identified and described the threefold Word of God as: (1) the Word of God *Preached*; (2) the Word of God *Written*; and (3) the Word of God *Revealed*.[27] Revelation operates within the symbiotic unity of God's Word within a trinitarian pattern. God the revealer speaks to humanity through the revelation of Jesus Christ, and is made known to us when the revealed Word as witnessed in Scripture is preached. Even the response of the hearer to the Word is a result of God's revelation testifying to itself. It is God's one Word in three forms working as in a unity, "whether we understand it as revelation, Bible, or proclamation there is no distinction of degree or value between the three forms."[28] Appeal to these three forms of the Word of God in Barth's

---

26. For example, see Torrance, *Preaching Christ Today*, 1. In this book, Torrance explores and explains the role of Barth's homiletic project for today's preachers. He writes, "Preaching Christ is both an evangelical and theological activity, for it is the proclamation and teaching of Christ as he is actually presented to us in the Holy Scriptures. In the language of the New Testament, preaching Christ involves *kerygma* and *didache*—it is both *kerygmatic* and a *didactic* activity. It is both *evangelical* and *theological*."

27. *CD* I/1, §4, 85-122, vol. 1, (88-124).

28. *CD* I/1, §4.4, 118, vol. 1, (120).

understanding of Christian proclamation is analogous to the Trinity.[29] The revelation of Jesus Christ in Scripture, and the announcement of him as good news, works as a symbiotic unity in preaching. Each has a duality of unity inherently embodied within in a christological, or twofold, pattern where God takes upon himself human conditions. As when considering the doctrine of the Trinity itself, it is necessary to understand that these forms do not represent three separate and independent words but are actually three forms of the one Word of God.

The logic for Barth's triune analogy and the image of the preacher is modeled via a *perichoretic* guide, which "carefully distinguishes the sense in which these various realities are one from the sense in which they are yet three distinct realties, and equally carefully differentiating their human and their divine aspects."[30]

Like the Trinity itself, the revelation of the Word of God maintains a *perichoretic* unity. Thus, the three forms of the Word of God—preached, written, and revealed—cannot be separated as if they could be understood in isolation from each other. However, similar to considering the triune God, we must think in terms of "appropriations" in order to understand the work of each particular form of the Word of God. Each mode of revelation has its specific task and function in the miracle of the event of God's own self-revelation.

If we can accept Barth's three-form witness of the Word of God, and if we further accept the so-called *perichoretic* unity, then it is possible for us to see how Barth reaches his basic conclusions about the question of preaching. For Barth, preaching is the event in which God the Father graciously acts in God the Son through the Holy Spirit. As witnessed in Scripture, God acts through the Holy Sprit by leading humanity out of darkness and into the light of truth and by empowering preachers to give witness to God's self-giving revelation Jesus Christ as witnessed in Scripture. It is significant to pause and note that this trinitarian analogy emphasizes that we can worship, pray, and preach only in the ongoing event of God's objective self-revelation in Jesus Christ through the Holy Spirit. God (the Father of Jesus Christ) is acting in the Holy Spirit when the Word is preached, that is, when the assembly of the church is gathered in worship to hear and to taste Christ in word and sacrament.[31] Barth is uncompromising in his insistence that the Biblical witness must be understood in relation to Jesus Christ through God

29. *CD* I/1, §4.4, 118–19, vol. 1, (121).

30. Hart, *Regarding Karl Barth*, 32.

31. See Barth, *Homiletics*, 58–59. Barth was emphatic that preaching of the Word and the proper administration of the sacrament should never be severed. The one legitimates the other.

the Holy Spirit. In the same way and with the same certainty, it can now be said that the life and faith of the church must primarily be understood in relation to the Holy Spirit.

The preacher then becomes a vital part of this work of the Holy Spirit, as the preacher becomes a medium through which the Holy Spirit reveals the Word. When the preacher speaks, a human word is commandeered by the Holy Spirit and transforms the sermon into a revelation event in a mysterious exchange. Fundamental for Barth, says Hart, is that this event is completely the work of God and can never be "seized and subjected to a confident process of analysis by human reason, put in a box and defined, and thereby effectively tamed."[32] And yet it does in fact include a human person, not by necessity, but by gracious participation in the mission of the triune God.

It must not be forgotten that the trinitarian pattern of revelation maintains that there is only one Word of God. When the preacher speaks the Word, in that moment the Word itself speaks; it is the very content, history, and being of God encountering humanity. This provides the confidence that protects the preacher from anxiety over his or her effectiveness in the pulpit.[33] It is only in the unity of the one crucified Word in three forms that preachers can speak with confidence that the act of preaching of the Word of God is more than human reflection and speech. It is the expectation of encountering the revealed Word when the written Word is preached that frees the preacher from "compulsive worldly models of success."[34] The message of the Word "liberates" the preacher from every attempt to make the event of the Word of God happen. In the identity, the preacher is freed from the responsibility of generating a divine encounter, and is unchained from the pressure created by those who demand the latest religious fad and fashion. Christian preaching is the free and merciful decision of the will of the Father to reveal his Son through the Holy Spirit. Only then does the human word of the sermon truly become the event of the one Word in a threefold witness.

One of the strengths of this *perichoretic* unity for preachers is the recovery of an emphasis on the preaching of the Word. The epistemological order of the church begins with preaching, and the first order for faith is to hear the gospel proclaimed, as faith comes through hearing (Rom 10:17). However, working behind the human preacher, is the Spirit, proclaiming a message of the Word, making the message meaningful for those listening.

---

32. Hart, *Regarding Karl Barth*, 42.

33. For Barth's dependence on Luther see *CD* I/2, §22.1, 4, vol. 6, (747).

34. See Lewis, "Kenosis and Kerygma" in Hart, *Regarding Karl Barth*, 46.

In this sense, the Bible is not, in the primary sense, the decisive foundation for the sermon. There is a higher authority to which even the Scriptures are dependent, which is the Word behind the words, which created and brought forth all things (John 1:10).

"This other reality," says Hart, "is the event in which God acted decisively for our salvation in the life, death, and resurrection of the Jesus Christ. It is this which is the real object of preaching."[35] Knowledge of God starts with Christ, whose economy of saving faith calls forth the Scripture as a witness in due course, which leads inevitably to the herald's ministry of proclamation. Failing to draw these careful distinctions and failing to maintain the relationships of order would be fatal for the church's health, argues Hart, "It might entail, for example, either an absolutizing of Scripture as the ultimate referent of preaching (in which case it would become opaque, rather than serving as the transparent witness to the risen Christ which it is intended to be), or else a failure by the preacher to stand under the authority of the apostles and prophets (to confuse his words with theirs), and thence, rather than an absolutizing, a relativizing of the Biblical text."[36]

It is within this order of knowing that Barth conceives the preacher as someone who first seeks to hear not just what the Scriptures say in Barth's historical context, but who seeks to hear the Word behind the strange new world of the Bible. Having heard afresh the Word from the Scriptures, the preacher then stands up to relate faithfully what he or she has witnessed. This faithful listener becomes God's ambassador of the Word to the world.

In Barth's trinitarian analogy, The Preacher as Herald is an amateur trumpeter, and no matter how unskilled he may be at scales, this trumpet will sing a melody that will awaken the deepest of sleepers because it is God himself who plays the notes. "Preaching is the Word of God which he himself has spoken," says Barth, "but he makes use, according to his good pleasure, of the ministry of a man who speaks to his fellowmen, in God's name, by means of a passage of Scripture."[37] God chooses to use humans and their words, inspired by the written Word, yet, at the same time is never bound by them. The *herald* understands that God is ever free and in that freedom, God gracefully condescends to use preachers as a primary medium for revealing knowledge of the Word. When he does use human preachers it is always an event of revelation.

---

35. Hart, *Regarding Karl Barth*, 32.

36. Ibid., 32–33.

37. Barth, *Preaching of the Gospel*, 9.

Revelation As Event

As noted above, Hart suggests that Barth's "entire theological project might legitimately be described as a 'theology of proclamation.'"[38] This project was not consumed with the secondary question of how *to* preach, but on the primary, theological consideration, how *can* one preach? How do people separated from the holiness of God by their sin have any capacity to speak of God? How can a preacher speak about God confidently if he has no natural capacity to know or experience God? Barth's answer to these questions is linked to his belief in revelation as an event.

The meaning of revelation, Hart reminds us, suggests that something is "disclosed or given to be known to someone which apart from the act of revealing would remain hidden, disguised and unknown."[39] This is the fundamental issue for all God talk because God remains hidden and unknown apart from his self-revelation. In this emphasis Barth stands in the long tradition of the church which believes that to know anything or speak anything about God means that God has first given us a prior word of knowledge to speak.[40] This Word is a gift, an act of grace, that is Jesus Christ, the subject and object of revelation. With this fundamental assumption in place, a sermon is never revelatory until God Himself, through the Spirit, reveals the Word through the human word.[41] This act of revealing through preaching is never static, but always a dynamic event accomplished by the triune God.[42]

Barth's "event" language is in greater part his attempt to embody Luther's theology of justification by faith in a theology of proclamation.[43] Barth closely follows Luther's understanding of salvation not as a process but as a person, an accomplished fact, something to be gratefully acknowledged and received as a gift. There is no soteriological gradualism in Luther or in Barth, no gradual acquisition of a righteous disposition, certainly no "faith development," or any other gradualism, no sequential process. In other words, salvation is the work that God has accomplished for us in the life, death, and resurrection of Jesus Christ. And when we sinners comprehend our salvation, through faith, it is an event in which we, in a moment, wake up to the facts of what God has accomplished for us in Jesus Christ. The problem for Barth is not a vain effort to persuade the hearer to overcome

38. See Hart, *Regarding Karl Barth*, 28.

39. Hart, "Revelation," 37.

40. Ibid.

41. Barth then does differ from a classical reformed insistence that preaching itself *is* the Word of God. See David G. Buttrick's foreword in Barth, *Homiletics*, 9.

42. Hart, "Revelation," 37.

43. See Dorrien, *Barthian Revolt*, 151.

sin in the attempt to communicate the gospel; rather, the problem is human ignorance, which is a symptom of sin. Thus, the preacher's concern is epistemological; it is how to speak of God in light of human justification by Jesus on the cross. For the preacher, the gospel sermon is not "repent from sin and be saved." Rather, it is "you have been saved from sin, now repent and believe."

This act of giving goes to the heart of what Barth sees as the only possible consideration of *how* Christian preaching is possible: the human word becomes the Word of God through God's own self-revelation in Jesus Christ through the Holy Spirit.[44] In other words, if God is wholly other and if we have no natural capacity to know God because of sin, the only way that a preacher can ever speak of God is if God has first spoken,[45] and *continues* to speak in and through human agency. "The Word," Barth writes, "creates the fact that we hear the Word . . . Up there with Him it is possible for it to be possible down here with us."[46] When this event happens it is always a miracle that is "essentially response and not essentially source."[47] This is Barth's theme, tirelessly proclaimed, which he applies to every homiletic consideration.

From a human standpoint, all that it is possible for The Preacher as Herald to do is to serve the Word faithfully by announcing the *kerygma*—the good news of the revelation of Jesus Christ for the world. The preacher's role is to simply and humbly announce what God himself wills to communicate, which is Jesus Christ, God himself for us. The preacher begins to fill this role by staying within the constraints of the canon.[48] Thus, only sermons inspired by Scripture have any hope of experiencing the eventfulness of revelation.

44. Barth understands the question of revelation in regards to preaching as the question of Christology itself. "The difficulty of preaching," said Barth, "is none other than that of trying to say who and what Jesus Christ is. Theologians must go both ways, the way of descending and the way of ascending thought" (Barth, *Homiletics*, 45). This means that The Preacher as Herald must point to the ascended Christ so that he might in grace descend to us. Only when God descends to speak through the preacher's voice at the moment of proclamation can humanity have any hope of ascending to knowledge of God.

45. Barth, *Homiletics*, 41, "God's holy majesty is something our sinful and darkened minds are incapable and unworthy of contemplation. Revelation occurs, therefore, to reverse the epistemic consequences of the fall."

46. *CD* I/2, §16.2, 48, vol. 4, (247).

47. Hart, "Revelation," 41.

48. In this light, revelation is not a fixed deposit of any human document, it is always the self-revealing presence of the Word itself. To confuse anything other than the resurrected Christ to be the content of God's self-revelation would be idolatrous. See Watson, "Bible," 59–61.

In this sense, the sermon is never mere human words spoken over the congregation, it is a media for the Holy Spirit to reveal who God is, or a lightning bolt of divine discourse that is beyond the preacher's capacity to conjure, control, or calculate.

Barth used the image of the herald to remind modern preachers that they are radically dependent on the "eventfulness" of revelation to say anything about God.[49] In other words, the witness can only speak to what is witnessed. Barth likens our effort to describe revelation to the attempt to draw a bird in flight, or the effort to describe lightning when all we have to go on is what is left after lighting strikes.[50] Therefore, this identity stresses that revelation is not something that we have or hold, but always something that God gives, fresh, new, and each time it happens it is a miracle.[51]

Barth's belief that our salvation is finished and accomplished has pragmatic implications for the preacher's homiletic practice. In the sermon, everything is "downhill": "The real need is not so much to get to the people as to come from Christ. Then one automatically gets to the people. Nothing should be said on any other level than that of the Word made flesh. No position need to be taken vis-à-vis the gospel. The preacher should simply believe the gospel and say all he as to say on the basis of this belief. This means that the thrust of the sermon is always downhill, not uphill to a goal. Everything has already taken place."[52]

The preacher's sermon proceeds "downhill," working from the summit of our already accomplished salvation in Christ. There is no need to persuade a hearer to believe in order to be saved, rather because of what God has accomplished in Christ, the preacher can proclaim that the hearer is saved, and therefore should believe. Even though we preachers can work, plan, and provide, we must not be so misguided as to think that any strategy or rhetoric on our part can give what can be "received only as a free gift."[53]

---

49. Nicholas Wolsterstorff notes Barth's "relentless eventism" as Barth's determination to keep revelation in God's hands rather than ours. Barth is determined to keep revelation miraculous. See Wolsterstorff, *Divine Discourse*, 71–72.

50. Barth, *Word of God*, 283.

51. What Barth says of our confidence of Scripture can be transposed directly to the event of preaching. "Only when and as the Bible grasps at us. . . . If the prophets and apostles tell us what they have to tell us, if their word imposes itself on us . . . all this is God's decision and not ours. . . . The Bible is God's Word to the extent that he speaks through it . . . The Bible, then, becomes God's Word in this event, and in the statement that the Bible is God's Word the little word 'is' refers to its being in this becoming" (*CD* I/1, §4.2, 106-7, vol. 1, (109-110)).

52. Barth, *Homiletics*, 53.

53. Ibid.,

Barth says that preaching can never be justified by us, but only in the work of God's justification.[54]

One of the benefits of this emphasis on an actualized justification gives the preacher a particular freedom from the burden of having to "save" the hearers with skillful rhetoric and winsome messages. As Barth retains the rigorously theological, gracious, miraculous quality of preaching, he frees preaching from its tendency to degenerate into merely moralistic, anthropological exercises of advice-giving, scolding, and helpful hints for making it through the week.[55] For The Preacher as Teacher, the sermon can easily become a "work" designed to garner "effect," "conversion," or "decision,"[56] whereas the identity of The Preacher as Herald liberates the preacher from this burden. According to Barth, it makes little difference if the preacher is a good communicator or not, because only God can persuade us to faith. God produces faith, not us.[57] Thus, within the internal logic of this model, it would be strange, even blasphemous, to think that a preacher could rearrange a few words in a sermon, adjust the style, or adapt the form and thereby make God better known through any rhetoric bent on persuasion.[58]

The Preacher as Herald does not strive to find creative ways to "connect" or make a sermon more aesthetically pleasing for the ear in the hopes that it will persuade the hearer to listen. Thus, originality and creativity are not virtues often associated with this model. As Thomas Long comments, "heralds do not aspire to be artists; they aspire to be servants of the Word."[59]

Preaching for Barth is not intended to be the place for novelty, rather it is, "human talk about God on the basis of the self-objectification of God which is not just there, which cannot be predicted, which does not fit into any plan, which is really only in the freedom of His grace, and in virtue of which He wills at specific times to be the object of this talk, and is so according to His own good pleasure."[60]

In other words, preaching is what we do; revelation is what God does. Barth encourages us, therefore, to think of the task of preaching as a human task, as a response or affirmation to divine grace. By the grace of God, preaching is both an objective and subjective event, as God's initiative and

54. Ibid., 72.

55. For more on this see chapter 4, "Rhetoric, Style, and Barth" in Willimon, *Conversations with Barth*, 83–113.

56. Barth, *Homiletics*, 8.

57. Hart, "Revelation," 40.

58. Andre Resgner Jr. suggests that this why the traditional legacy of Augustine's appeal to the use of rhetoric "suffered a Barth attack." See Resner, *Preacher and Cross*, 58.

59. See Long, *The Witness of Preaching*, 25.

60. *CD* I/1, §4.1, 89, vol. 1, (92).

as human response. Jesus Christ is not only the subject who is proclaimed in preaching, but through the Holy Spirit, also the gracious preacher, whose sermon is always an event that is *particular, personal,* and demands our *active* response.[61] In summary the theological presupposition informing The Preacher as Herald model is that the human words in preaching are appropriated by and assumed into divine action.

This identity is scandalous to some because it exalts the identity of the preacher. It suggests a privileged relationship where the human preacher has been personally commissioned by God himself to announce the good news of his arrival.[62] This announcement that the Word has come points to the center of history by declaring that the Word was made flesh and dwelt as a total person among us (John 1:14). For The Preacher as Herald, the Word to be proclaimed is the proper name of a human person—the Son of God, Immanuel, the Christ—who is himself the self-giving God. Word, or Logos, is his divine name, and Jesus is his human one. The very idea of Christian preaching has its origin in identifying this divine Word as the subject and object of Christian proclamation. Proclaiming this name of the subject and object of history itself is the primary purpose of the preacher. For in proclaiming the name of the Word, Jesus Christ, what *has* happened, *is* happening in time through the Holy Spirit.[63] It is because of God's incarnation in Jesus that Christianity not only is situated in time but is actually participating in an event that transcends time, pulling the past and future into one moment in the eventfulness of revelation.

Nein! to Apologetics and Rhetoric

Barth's theology of revelation broke any confident appeal to the use of rhetoric or apologetics, as it placed primary confidence in God's speech rather than in humans'. Only God can speak for God. Only God can make God known. No human ingenuity of language or argument could improve or aid what only God can do. Therefore, Barth rejected any method or strategy that would suggest otherwise, including rhetoric and apologetics. Apologetics is the branch of theology that is concerned with proving the truth of

61. Hart observes three significant points that arise out of this claim. See Hart, "Revelation," 47–49. The first point is that *the event of God's self-revealing is particular not general* (CD I/1, §5.2, 137-38, vol. 1, (140)). Second, *revelation takes the form of personal address* (CD I/1, §8.2, 34, vol. 2, (329)). And third, *revelation is not just an event but an action* (CD I/1, §6.3, 196-97, vol. 1, (120)).

62. This exalted humility of preaching points precisely to one of the most controversial aspects of the herald's identity. See Hart, *Regarding Karl Barth,* 39, 38.

63. See CD I/1, §4.1, 91-92, vol. 1, (95) and CD I/2, §22.1, 2-4, vol. 6, (745-46).

Christianity, and rhetoric, as we have discussed, is the art of using language to persuade the hearer with eloquence. Barth perceived that both rhetoric and apologetics in and of themselves were fine, but he strongly objected to the idea that they could be tools to aid the event of revelation.

Let us look at both in order to understand how this reaction shapes the identity and practice of The Preacher as Herald. Let us begin with Barth's suspicion towards apologetics. It should be observed that Barth's anti-apologetic stance puts this identity in counterintuitive tension with a significant emphasis for many of today's homileticians. Barth, however, was never shy about swimming against the current. He would argue that the job of the preacher is not to appeal to this world using rational arguments to persuade the hearer into faith; rather the purpose is always to proclaim another world that this world could not make sense of without the miracle of faith. In this sense, the Christian preacher is about a more imperialistic enterprise than a deferential pleading to help make sense of the world. We are to let God at one and the same time destroy and recreate a world through the inbreaking of his Word, as is made possible through human proclamation. That creation of a new world is more than an anthropological matter or a cultural-linguistic construction, it is a gift of the world-creating God through the mouth of his servant when the Word is faithfully preached. In this sense, the preacher privileges conversion over apologetics, transformation over conversation.

Barth would argue that God is not a formula we can prove with reason or any other natural capacity known to us. We know God only by God's speaking, not through arguments for God's existence. Since the unbeliever lacks faith, the one requisite for true knowledge, there is no wonder that apologetics is viewed with suspicion. Where God fails to convince the unbeliever, there is little that we can do to convince. For example, in the middle of his lectures that became *Dogmatics in Outline*, Barth was asked, "Are you not aware that many are sitting in this class who are not Christians?" Barth says that he laughed and responded, "That makes no difference to me."[64] This statement may be taken as evidence of Barth's lack of concern for the non-Christian, or it may be better interpreted as a theological statement that arises out of Barth's peculiar regard for the non-Christian. The working assumption of The Preacher as Herald is that the preacher as apologist has no means of making the Christian faith more accessible than it already is. Barth believed that all the preacher who cares about evangelism should do is redescribe and point to the alternative world of the kingdom of God

64. Barth, *Dogmatics in Outline*, 93–94.

in order to invite the nonbeliever into the linguistic universe of the Scriptures.[65] In other words, the preacher treats people like insiders, using the
church's language, stories, and presuppositions of faith to make sense of the
world, instead of assuming people are outsiders and using the categories of
the world to make the faith seem reasonable or relevant to them. Thus, this
identity fails to make much distinction between "believers" and "nonbelievers," believing that the homiletic task is the same for both. In terms of the
doctrine of the church, this is important because it means that the church
would, in a positive way, always see preaching as primarily evangelistic, no
matter who is listening.

One of the reasons for this belief is Barth's doctrine of election, which
softens the difference between the believers and nonbelievers. Barth taught
a revolutionary doctrine of double predestination. Theologians in the Reformed Church traditionally taught that God elects some for salvation,
some for damnation. In volume II/2 of *Church Dogmatics*, Barth turned this
understanding of election on its head, when he taught that in Jesus Christ,
God has in eternity elected God's self for rejection, damnation, and death,
but sinful humanity for election into salvation, grace, and forgiveness. Jesus
Christ is both God's *yes* and God's *no*. God has, in Jesus Christ, chosen rejection for himself but salvation for humanity.[66]

Barth is often charged with adherence to the doctrine of *apokatastasis*,
universal salvation. Barth does not directly teach this, but he does suggest
that the ultimate fate of everyone must remain an open question in light of
the actual justification accomplished in Christ. He believed that salvation
for all must be our hope, and this is not an impossible hope considering
the triumph of God's grace in the person and work of Christ. The preacher's
responsibility is to testify to God's decisive *yes* in Jesus Christ. This is the
preacher's main service to both believer and unbeliever. The main difference
between the nonbeliever and the believer is a noetic, not an ontic difference.
The Christian knows a fact about the world that the non-Christian does not
yet know. Believers and unbelievers are bound together both by our solidarity in sin and by our solidarity in grace. This is how Barth stated the church's
relationship to the unbeliever: "To the extent that we may be Christians in
spite of our non-Christianity, our real distinction from non-Christians will
consist in the fact that we know that Jesus Christ himself, and he alone, is
our hope as well as theirs, that he died and rose again for those who are
wholly or partially non-Christians, that his overruling work precedes and

65. See Jenson, "Scripture's Authority," 37.

66. For two different but illuminating discussions of Barth's doctrine of election, see
Jenson, *Alpha and Omega* and McCormack, "Grace and Being," 92ff.

follows all being and occurrence in our sphere, that he alone is the perfect Christian, but that he really is this, and is in our place."[67]

The nonbeliever "does not yet participate in the knowledge of Jesus Christ and what has taken place in him."[68] For those who do so participate, however, this participation is everything. All have sinned, says Paul, yet, in Jesus Christ, God was reconciling the world to himself. Period. The affirmation that all are enemies of God and that all have been redeemed by the work of God in Christ is the basis for Barth's connection between believers and nonbelievers. Evil, "the Nihil," is thus likened by Barth to stupidity.[69]

Barth suggested that it is a tragic mistake for preachers to convince unbelievers that Christianity is rational, reasonable, or historically credible through apologetics, because every attempt to defend Christianity inevitably takes its stand at some point outside the Christian faith.[70] The real god of apologetics is the god of reason, or historicity, or some other idol than the living, speaking God of Israel and the church. Apologetic that appeals to any other basis than the Holy Spirit's gifts is an act of unfaith that produces, not faith, but trust in something other than God.

Barth's great concern about apologetics, and intrinsic to his idea of The Preacher as Herald, is that an outside form or method will control Christian proclamation, and in that effort, reduce the message itself. For example, Barth feared that when preachers appeal to even the best of rhetorical devices, it "domesticates" the wild Word of God. He feared any outside influence that could result in the domesticating of revelation. Barth feared the process of making the gospel respectable. As Barth writes:

> When the Gospel is offered to man, and he stretches out his hand to receive it and takes it into his hand, an acute danger arises which is greater than the danger that he may not understand it and angrily reject it. The danger is that he may accept it and peacefully and at once make himself its lord and possessor, thus rendering it innocuous, making that which chooses him something which he himself has chosen, which therefore comes to stand as such alongside all the other things that he can also choose, and therefore control.[71]

67. CD IV/3, §69.4, 327, vol. 27, (342).

68. CD I/1, §72.1, 34, vol. 29, (715).

69. Webster, Barth's Moral Theology, chapter 4. See also Nicholas Wolstorff's article, "Barth on Evil," 584–608.

70 For a detailed examination of epistemic justification in modern theology and the logical incoherence of dependence theories of justification, see Marshall, Trinity and Truth, 50–71.

71. Barth, CD II/1, §26.2, 137–38, vol. 7, 141.

This fear of any outside influence was worked out most publicly in Barth's famous rejoinder to Emil Brunner in 1929, "Nein!" when he objected to Brunner's formulation of natural contact point, or divine-human connection, which the listener already possesses.[72] To assert such a starting point is to dignify unbelief by making it more than it is, and by not giving proper weight to the primacy of faith. Believers who reach out to nonbelievers using apologetics are in danger of assuming the standpoint, the ground that is occupied by the nonbeliever and thus giving away too much territory before the battle begins.[73]

The source for Christian proclamation was a watershed issue for Barth. Where the preacher's starting point originated determined whether revelation was to be understood as the run-off supplying the tributaries of the age of rationality, or whether the trajectory of one's preaching would flow from the ancient witness of historic Christian orthodoxy. This trajectory affirms there is no divine-human continuity, no creaturely *analogy of being* to God, and furthermore, no other starting point for theological method and practice, human or otherwise, apart from the revelation of the Word, as witnessed in Scripture. As Hart writes, "Christian theology, Christian ethics, therefore, could in no sense be held to derive their message from two distinct sources: revelation on the one hand, and nature or reason on the other."[74]

Thus, in Barth's monumental *No*, he was subverting the foundation for a theological rationale for apologetics. He also forestalls any justification of rhetoric as an aid to help persuade the hearer towards belief. To adopt a position that said the preacher could more effectively preach the gospel if she were trained in human rhetoric is akin to saying that preachers can offer a "point of contact" for the revelation of the Word if they will simply obey the human wisdom of rhetoric.[75] In other words, there is something the human preacher can do to assist God in salvation.

The consequence of Barth's theological objection to any "contact point" outside of the revelation for the preacher was that it encouraged the preacher to separate herself from the Augustinian tradition of using rhetoric to help the preacher "teach, delight, and persuade" the listener. As a result, says Long, preaching suffered a "Barth attack" in the twentieth century.[76]

72. This famous written debate between Brunner's *Natur und Gnade: Zum mit Karl Barth* and Barth's response *Nein! Antword an Emil Brunner*, were captured in an English translation by Peter Fraenkel, *Natural Theology*.

73. *CD* II/1, §26.1, 90–94, vol. 7, (93–97).

74. Hart, *Regarding Karl Barth*, 148.

75. See Barth, *Homiletics*, 121–27.

76. Long, "And How?" 174.

For the preacher, to rely on rhetoric in the effort to persuade the hearer is to confuse the issue of who makes revelation effective. Only God, not a rhetorical method that a preacher might master, can speak his Word and make it effective for the listener. In fact, it is not too strong to say that Barth actually recommends that the preacher avoid rhetorical strategies all together. The Word of God should be the only guide for the sermon, not appeals to the itchy desires of the listener in the vain attempt to be relevant.[77] To get this order backwards is to fall down the wrong side of Barth's watershed divide.

Barth's Theology for Preaching

One of the tensions of The Preacher as Herald is that it so stresses and emphasizes God's activity in preaching that it can obscure any gifts or skills or wisdom that the human offers. For preaching, this translates into sermons with little variation of form or style in communication. Barth never ceases to underline that preachers should have no rules or strategies for communication, but must instead simply "reiterate" or "repeat" the Scripture without obscuring it with rhetorical flourish, creative design, or originality of form.[78] For example, Stanley Hauerwas notes that Barth tends to narrate Scripture rather than argue it in his theology, meaning that Barth reasserts, repeats, redescribes rather than arguing or explaining any particular text.[79] Hauerwas astutely notes that Barth's narrative style is, in itself, an argument: "Barth just cannot provide the kind of 'knock down' argument so many desire; but that he cannot is both theologically and philosophically justified."[80] That is, Barth wants to work in such a way that the three forms of revelation are at work through the Holy Spirit, rather than his logical well-formed arguments. Barth speaks the way he speaks for theological reasons. Because the Word of God originates exclusively with God, preaching must always be, in a certain sense, repetition: "The problem of the Word (that is, of course, the Word of God) in theology I understand to be the question of whether and how far theology recognizes its obligation of directing Christian preaching to the repetition in human words of what is said to

---

77. Barth writes, for example, that he found his preaching was most successful when he simply kept to the script of Scripture, rather than trying to figure out what people wanted to hear. See Barth, *Natural Theology*, 79–80.

78. See Barth, *Homiletics*, 104. This emphasis on reiteration of the biblical witness is also picked up by the Barthian homiletician Ritschl in *A Theology of Proclamation*, 127–42.

79. Hauerwas, *With the Grain*, 27.

80. Ibid., 156-57 n. 33.

men through God himself about God, in distinction to which man can say to himself about God."[81]

Therefore, when we use Barth's thought as a guide of this identity, we see that the preacher is called merely to restate what has already been witnessed in Scripture. The preacher's original sin of the pulpit is the effort to be original, for what is expected of the preacher is faithful transmission of the text. One of the first to call attention to the Barthian propensity for restatement as an alternative to rhetorical apologetics was the theologian Hans Frei.[82] Frei argues that Barth, rather than attempting to build bridges to the discourse of the modern world or to constructing arguments with the modern world on the basis of its reigning ideologies, had to "recreate a universe of discourse."[83] This meant that Barth's language, style, and form needed as closely as possible to match the rhetoric of the "strange new world of the Bible." What this means for this identity is that the hearer is welcomed into this alternative reality of God's reign, by showing, not explaining or arguing. Quite unapologetically, The Preacher as Herald invites people to enter a world that has its own rhetorical integrity, its own closed circle of meaning, a world that cannot be accessed by the use of words from other linguistic worlds.[84] Frei reads Barth's narrative style as an exercise in rhetorical transference. Theology, as the exposition of Scripture in its own language and logic, is geared toward transferring the hearer to the world that unfolds before the proclamation of the Word of God. Barth's theology, therefore, is a continual striving towards describing this world breathed to life by the work of the triune God. Consequently, Barth is thoroughly uninterested with the quest of correlating revelation with either an explicit or implicit anthropocentric quest for meaning.

ENGAGING THE PROPHET

Barth's metaphor of The Preacher as Herald has many strengths. First, Barth's theological framework provides a deep and powerful paradigm for understanding the task, language, and performance of preaching. Second, Barth's thought also reinstates God as the subject of preaching, in an era where the turn away from God as the principle subject has been championed. A third strength is that this homiletic identity asks the preacher to depend completely upon the power and initiative of God's grace for a sermon to be truly

81. Karl Barth, *Theology and Church*, 200.
82. See Frei, *Eclipse of Biblical Narrative*, 110.
83. Ibid., 111.
84. Ibid., 115.

effective proclamation. And fourth, by grounding the homiletic identity's emphasis on the revealed Word, congregations are protected from sermons that try to pass off gritty moralisms, tired apologetic strategies, subversive political agendas (from both the right and left), or trendy fads and fashions bought from the ever-burgeoning industry of religious consultants. The uncompromising faith of the transcendent God speaking through the human servant serves as a protection for both congregation and preacher. This is what led Barth to argue that the preacher's only task is to reiterate, or repeat, Scripture in a sermon.

But is it possible to only repeat what is said in Scripture? All reading, at some level, is translation, not simply description. Similarly, we may ask if it is even possible to ignore rhetoric's rule in all communication? Is reiteration really as simple as Barth wants us to believe?

David Buttrick notes that when Barth said no to rhetoric he made some interesting judgments about the work of homiletics.[85] For example, Barth notoriously rejects "in principle" sermon introductions. Introductions suggest "a point of contact," or some point of entry from human experience into the Word of God. He denounces introductions as "a waste of time," except for those introductions that are a brief statement of what the introductory Scripture reading is going to be about. Introductions distract listeners and lull them into thinking that human wit is the means by which they will apprehend the Word of God. Use of quotations from various people and illustrations only cause listeners' minds to wander into areas that have no possibility of becoming revelation.[86] However, Barth violates his own principle in many of his sermons, particularly his later prison sermons. Most of the sermons in *Deliverance to the Captives* have extensive introductions and illustrations.[87] In Barth's actual preaching life, we overhear both rhetorical power and wit that comes not from pure reiteration, but from a mind whose creativity and vision of interpretation found playful freedom within Christian preaching. The dirty little secret about Barth's sweeping strictness against using rhetoric-like introductions and illustrations is that it is something Barth himself did not do.[88] It seems as though Barth was not always faithful to Barth.

---

85. See David Buttrick's introduction to Barth, *Homiletics*, 8.

86. See Barth, *Homiletics*, 122–23.

87. For an example, see Barth, *Deliverance to the Captives*, 54–55.

88. William Willimon writes: "Barth so vividly and successfully utilizes rhetorical strategies of irony, narrative, surprise, hyperbole, and many more in his richly metaphorical theological works like *Romans*. And in *Church Dogmatics* Barth uses a creative, highly complex circular argument. Then he produces sermons that are often so wooden in their presentation. Barth says, of his *Dogmatics*, that he wants to speak to the

While Barth studiously avoids falling into the cul-de-sac of natural theology in his dogmatic theology, it is curious to experience Barth condemning apologetics and rhetoric for preachers, because in many of his sermons he is so heavily polemical, contentious, and rhetorically charged. It may be true that The Preacher as Herald does not aspire to be an artist, but Barth himself was an artist. He was a creative agent, using the full capacity of his human reason, imagination, and wit to absorb, engage, and contribute to his Christian theology. One could say that *The Church Dogmatics* was the canvas where he painted his version of the Sistine Chapel. Instead of a brush and paint, Barth used a pen and words.

It is at exactly this point that Barth's metaphor of the herald attracts criticism. Four concerns are worth reconsidering in light of God's self-revelation in Christ as witnessed to in Scripture: (1) Barth's understanding of rhetoric; (2) his view of human agency or responsibility; (3) his view of orality; and (4) the role of the imagination. Of course, in some ways these concerns are tied together and influenced by each other, but it may be helpful to take each one at a time.

Rhetoric

Barth's theoretical dismissal of rhetoric is problematic for The Preacher as Herald for several reasons. First, and most generally, the dismissal of rhetoric for homiletic reflection limits the options for thinking about *how* preaching is done. Even if a preacher recognizes the nature of revelation and determines to preach the gospel of Jesus as Barth would insist, the preacher still has to make decisions, using the tools of language, form, style, and argument to say it. Barth's dismissal of rhetoric may in fact limit a preacher's ability to use all the resources and options offered. Is it even a fair expectation to assume that any preacher can faithfully proclaim the *kerygma* without giving attention to how it is said?

Indeed, Thomas Long argues that eliminating rhetorical concerns from preaching is really an impossibility. Though it is a silly claim, Long suggests that "there are no Barthians in pulpits today."[89] Richard Lischer echoes this critique and suggests one of the reasons for the unpopularity of this model today is that there is "a scandalous fleshiness to preaching, and

church. That is a rhetorical strategy of the most basic kind. To speak to the church is to self-consciously speak to a distinctive linguistic community, to work within a peculiar realm of discourse where much of the rhetoric is predetermined but also that forces rhetorical decisions at every turn in the road" (*Conversations with Barth,* 189).

89. Lischer, "Before Technique," 178.

while sermons may attempt a 'pure' theology all the way through Saturday night, on Sunday morning they are inescapably . . . rhetorical."[90] Lischer means that preaching is a very human act and requires considerable human emotion, intellect, and bodily presence. Preaching, in this sense, is fleshy. The preacher's task is to put together words, and that work, like it or not, is a rhetorical act that requires levels of discernment. Preachers," says Long, "cannot really avoid rhetorical concerns."[91] Natural capacity, or not, rhetorical decisions are made in the performance of preaching.

Second, it is interesting to note that when Barth eschews the rhetorical tradition, he obfuscates the central role that rhetoric plays in his own preaching. Barth may claim the goal of this identity is to "just preach," or simply to reiterate the words of Scripture, by repeating what has already been recorded in Scripture, but that may mean little more than that the preacher either does not know or is unwilling to admit his own rhetorical goals and strategies. Either way, it is an odd claim. William Willimon goes so far as to suggest a that homiletic model, like Barth's, that is unwilling to acknowledge the human role preachers have in selecting language is not only odd, it is "immoral,"[92] because it is important to acknowledge one's rhetoric as it is an exercise of power by the speaker. In any speaking, preaching included, there are decisions to be made all along the way: stratagems, purposes, conscious and unconscious arrangement of material, assumptions about the listeners, things said one way and not another, all of which is the stock and trade of rhetoric. How an argument is reasoned and how style is used influences how that argument is heard.

Moreover, when reading Barth, one is struck by the highly creative and complex rhetorical arguments involved in his own *Church Dogmatics*.[93] It is one thing to admit to the peculiarly demanding nature of Christian speech about God; but it is another thing to suggest that preachers act as simple transmitters of the words in Scripture, as if merely reciting speech about God.

This leads to a third problem of discouraging the use of rhetoric for preaching. Rhetoric gives serious attention to how language is heard. As suggested above, how we express ourselves does impact how it is heard. Understanding how we are heard requires the preacher to take seriously the life, culture, and experiences of those who listen. Of course, a preacher

90. Ibid.

91. Ibid., 178.

92. Willimon argues that Barth's reluctance to take seriously the significance of the human agency involved in selecting language is immoral. See Willimon, *Conversations with Barth*, 189.

93. Ibid.

can never control or predict how another hears or responds to a sermon. But one does need to pay attention to the context, the mood, the events of the time to perceive or anticipate how a sermon might be interpreted. This requires paying attention to the culture and people one is speaking to. Cultural context influences the messages preached and the message heard. Though Barth does admit preachers need to give attention to the hearer,[94] he offers no serious encouragement about how to do this in practice, nor about how preachers ought to think about the influence culture has in shaping their own reading of Scripture, or the hearers' perception of the gospel.

While the strength of The Preacher as Herald encourages a rich theological reflection on the Word, one of its weaknesses is that when rhetoric is abandoned as a category of priority, the model discourages paying attention to the receiving end of the preacher's equation. The focus is constrained on saying as correctly as one can what has been given to say, so as to be a faithful witness. But even a witness is a translator who is required to find the right words, images, and form to communicate to another. This kind of translation requires a knowledge of those one is called upon to testify to. Barth may concede that it is wise for a preacher to learn about the hearer's culture, but he himself never goes so far as to suggest that any insights learned from this attention should be used to form or frame the sermon's content or style. This lack of emphasis on rhetoric suggests that for Barth, such insights gained are ultimately insignificant to the eventfulness of revelation, since revelation is always a work of God, not a human one. This is nice theory, but is it not a little naive in practice? Are we not all, in some way, guided and formed by our contexts, cultures, and commitments? The consequence of Barth's pure commitment to keep the pulpit focused on the Word of God, not the words of man, results in the preacher ignoring critical insights that could be gained from engaging the culture, stories, language, myths, traditions, and experiences of the hearer. Such an honest engagement is necessary in any missional work.[95] This kind of serious attention is something Barth's understanding of the preacher is formidably suspicious of, as it is believed to misplace the source and norm for revelation.

This suspicion is precisely where Barth himself fails to be true to Barth. Barth contends that preaching must be dependent on and be shaped by the revealed Word written, that is always pointing us to the revealed Word in the form and person of Jesus Christ, the revelation of God in flesh. But preaching within the bounds of the Word, where God speaks to us in the

---

94. Barth, *Homiletics*, 111.

95. For more on how real engagement with human culture is inescapable for the work of mission and preaching, See Walls, *Missionary Movement*.

Bible, and through the incarnation, is itself the exact thing that should lead us to appreciate and replicate the faithful use of rhetoric.

This is one of the more damning critiques of Barth's thought, namely, that in its disdain for rhetoric, the preacher becomes at odds with the witness and example of Scripture itself. As the church fathers, the great exegetes of every age and more recently literary criticism of Scripture have shown us, Scripture employs a rich array of literary forms in order to present the gospel. The Bible was preaching before it was Scripture, and its persuasive, proclamatory intentions led biblical writers to reach for a wide range of literary devices to do their proclamation, as Augustine notes in *On Christian Doctrine*.[96]

The biblical authors show evidence of considerable attention to rhetorical dynamics. In other words, they were concerned not only with *what* they were saying but also with *how* they were saying it.[97] Scripture and her many characters, prophets, apostles, preachers, teachers, heroes and villains all take advantage of metaphors, tropes, analogies, and stories, to communicate. Indeed, John the Baptist, Barth's favorite herald example, was one who used powerful and vivid language to not only point to Jesus, but also to call his culture and its religious leaders to account. John did more than merely reiterate Scripture; he embodied it in such a way that his language became prophetic poetry.

The Preacher as Herald fails to adequately answer the question of why we find the Bible concerned with the very things this model disparages such as techniques of speech borrowed from pagan cultures, poetic forms, mysterious parables, loaded metaphors, story, testimony of personal experience. The rhetorical structures in Scripture were built with the creative tools hanging off the belts of artists embedded in their culture. Is it not these tools that God himself uses to make himself known in the event of revelation? Biblical scholar Amos Wilder has reminded us that the rhetorical strategies of the Bible are not mere ornaments dressing up the gospel to make it more attractive; they are forms and techniques called forth by the creative nature of the gospel itself: "the coming of the Christian Gospel was in one aspect a renewal and liberation of language. It was a 'speech-event,' the occasion for a new utterance and new forms of utterance."[98] Is it possible to read John's apocalyptic vision on Patmos, or read the laments of Isaiah, or the prayers of David, or Paul's letters and diatribes and not come to the conclusion that these preachers were not only creating effects with words in the effort to

---

96. See Augustine, *On Christian Doctrine*, 4.5–8.

97. Ibid., 4.7.16.

98. Wilder, *Early Christian Rhetoric*, quoted in Long, *Witness of Preaching*, 29.

"connect," but they were allowing their creativity to be a means God used as an extension of the Word itself? "Is it not significant," asks Eugene Peterson, "that the prophets and psalmists were also poets?"[99] These forms found in Holy Scripture, suggests something significant about forms appropriate for the Christian preacher.

The most severe critique is that despite Barth's focus on Jesus Christ as the subject and object of preaching, his homiletic advice ignores the way Jesus Christ came and actually preached. Jesus' use of rhetorical devices, like narrative, was not merely to accommodate to the limitations of the hearers, nor was it an exercise of vanity, but rather it was used to include the hearers into a complex, linguistically derived world that is called salvation. There was something about the nature of Jesus Christ that seemed to demand a rich repertoire of linguistic forms in order to do justice to the object of proclamation.[100] Any model that encourages a homiletic identity to be suspicious of rhetorical concerns is ignoring the witness and practice of Jesus, the eternal Word himself.[101] My primary concern with Barth's dismissal of rhetoric is that it dismisses what Jesus himself seemed to take so seriously. Barth is passionate that the Word is to be the only guide for the preacher. Yet, his own homiletic practice fails to reflect the Word's style and tone. For all of Barth's focus on Christ as the central pivot of his robust and rich theological reflection, he refuses to let Jesus' creative methods of speaking shape his homiletic practice or advice to other preachers. Jesus, for example, was a great storyteller, a master of metaphor, parable, misdirection, and poetry.[102] Barth does an excellent job of reminding us that Jesus is God's Word, but he fails to follow Jesus' language down to the streets of cultural experience where the truth is always told slant through the subversive ironies of parable, the prophetic cadences of poetic discourse, or the fictional characters encountered in a story. Unlike Barth, Jesus preached by telling stories that grew out of the experiences, images, and language of his culture. He purposefully used language and narratives that people could relate to and connect with by avoiding abstraction in favor of concrete examples rooted in

99. Peterson, *Contemplative Pastor*, 155.

100. See Alter, *World of Biblical Literature*, 40.

101. Willimon notes that "despite his love for Mozart, there is in the preaching of Barth a kind of tone-deaf quality in his explication of the Biblical text. The style of most of his sermons is direct, upbeat, and declarative. That is often a well-received homiletical style, but it is not the style of the whole of Scripture. Barth's sermons assert and announce but they almost never deduce, entice, cajole, and sneak up upon a hearer. In contrast, the Scriptures do delight in such allurements" (*Conversations with Barth*, 190).

102. This is the argument of Eugene Peterson in *Tell It Slant*. See also Jensen, *Thinking In Story*, 18–22.

human experience. Consequently, people are still relating and connecting with them.

Barth's tireless focus on God as the principal subject of revelation allows the preacher to be free again to focus on the triune God as the primary subject of preaching. But ironically, his model somehow inspires Barth to pass over some of the rich rhetorical possibilities that Scripture and Jesus suggest for preaching. What Barth offers us in this identity is this new way of speaking as an invitation to come to the real life of abundance in God's kingdom. But what this identity misses or ignores is the diversity, creativity, and artistic power witnessed in revelation that comes to us as a sermon in Scripture and the revelation of the incarnation of Jesus. Hans Boersma suggests that this critique is linked to Barth's Christology which, it could be argued, is "Alexandrian'" in that Barth's understanding of the preacher loses the full significance of Jesus' humanity.[103] Even if Barth gives full place to the full humanity of Jesus, his insistence on a doctrine of substitution, and a relative lack of a doctrine of the "priesthood" of Jesus (where what Jesus does "for us" is necessarily linked to what the Spirit does "in us"), would still lead logically to such downplaying of human dynamic in preaching.[104]

Barth fails his own test by ignoring the way Jesus, the revealed and incarnate Word, chose to speak to us. A look at Jesus' own preaching and teaching demonstrates that he cared deeply about not only what was said, but how he was saying it. In other words, Jesus practiced rhetorical and artistic forms of speech that Barth, in the name of Jesus, argues preachers ought to avoid using. For all Barth's talk about reiterating Scripture, he fails to follow the actual practice of Scripture's own rhetorical examples. And for all of Barth's talk about focusing on Jesus, he fails to follow Jesus' own strategies of speaking. Advocates of The Preacher as Herald who deem issues and questions of rhetorical form and method to be nothing more than an issue of natural theology are in fact shying away from the witness and practice of Jesus' own preaching life. And thus, Barth shies away from his own theological call to stay true to the Word written, revealed, and preached by the apostles. In light of these considerations, it must be asked if this identity

103. See Boersma, "Alexandrian or Antiochian?," 263–80. C. T. Waldrop also presses this argument in *Karl Barth's Christology*. It should be noted that George Hunsinger makes a similar point that Barth deliberately alternates between "Alexandrian" and "Antiochian" in his way of describing Jesus' humanity, and offers a strong statement and defense of Barth's views in relation to the Chalcedonian definition. See Hunsinger, "Karl Barth's Christology," 127–39.

104. For more on how Barth develops the doctrine of substitution for the identity of the preacher see Hart, *Regarding Karl Barth*, 31–36.

in fact discourages the church from experiencing the Word of God, in the name of witnessing to the Word of God.

The instinct to be committed to Scripture and to the agency of God in and through human proclamation is one of the reasons The Preacher as Herald is so rich and offers so much for practicing preachers. However, taking this commitment to the level where we trust not only what Scripture and Jesus say but also how it is said, would allow the preacher to expand and explode in ways not encouraged under the current model. We want to take the instinct of rich theological reflection of this identity, where the subject and object of revelation is central, but in a way that honors this centrality by trusting the many creative rhetorical instincts and possibilities a commitment to the Word offers. In this way, we want to push the best of Barth's homiletic identity to embrace the true artistic calling of being a witness to the Word demands.

Orality

A second concern about embracing the model of The Preacher as Herald is connected to the oral dynamics of preaching in our emerging oral/aural communication culture. Barth's encouragement of this identity was linked to the idea that sermons were to be expressed in clear and controlled prose. In other words, God speaks best if the sermon is *written*. When talking about how to preach Barth writes, "The basic prerequisite, in execution is to write the sermon. This condition is so important that a thorough argument in its favor seems to be needed. To be sure, a sermon is a speech. It has to be this. But in this speech we should not leave it up to the Holy Spirit (or some other Spirit!) to inspire the words, no matter whether we have an aptitude for speaking or not."[105]

Barth's homiletic model betrays the literary assumptions of the superiority of the written word for communication. As Walter Ong has argued, those shaped dominantly in a culture of print, as Barth was, often forget the primary oral nature of the gospel. Barth acknowledges that while the sermon is oral, its orality is effective first as literature. The sermon is *written* first. He argues, "Each sermon should be ready for print, as it were, before it is delivered."[106] Barth goes so far as to say that if a sermon is not written word-for-word, it may not even be considered Christian discourse: "Some ministers have acquired such facility in preaching that they feel able to dispense with this discipline (writing sermons), but their sermons are not

---

105. Barth, *Homiletics*, 119.
106. Ibid.

Christian discourses."[107] It could be that Barth means that preachers who do not spend time preparing scripted sermons as a fruit of dense study do more harm than good, because they are unfamiliar with what they are preaching on; or it could be that Barth means exactly what he says, that nothing unwritten can be considered Christian discourse. Barth's advice to preachers is to write down the sermon to ensure careful thought. However, in giving this suggestion, he fails to emphasize the preaching is primarily heard, not read: Just as it was for Jesus, and is still true today, preaching is not fundamentally an act of writing, it is an oral event. In the beginning, God did not *write* the Word, but *spoke* the Word.

It is interesting to note that his focus on writing may also be an argument that Barth is not altogether indifferent to rhetorical prescriptions. This focus on writing suggests that Barth himself was interested in a sermon's human craft. It is a virtue to suggest that a preacher's words be weighed and measured soberly before speaking. But he seems to argue that if our words are not accounted for by writing, than our language may be a hindrance to the event of revelation. But if a sermon not written can actually be a hindrance, are we not more involved in making revelation effective than Barth himself wants to admit? If Barth's objective is to protect the pulpit from unnecessary chatty talk or from sermons that are delivered without preparation, than his concern about rhetoric is understandable. But to suggest that an unwritten sermon is not "Christian discourse" is a dubious claim since Jesus himself, the author of Christian discourse, never wrote anything down.

Moreover, this focus on scripted preaching is inadequate in a multicultural, multiethnic church. Arguably some of the best preachers in the church today are African American preachers, whose homiletic tradition of orality knows no rival. Shaped primarily in an oral tradition and freed from written sermons, their preaching often sharply contrasts with white European models. Eugene Lowry describes African American preaching as "transconscious narrativity."[108] Henry Mitchell says this kind of preaching is a "communally stored wisdom and cultural affinity" that is central to African American homiletic experience.[109] It is a pattern of rhetoric, repetition, rhythm, and rest, a kind of "folk based orality."[110] The African American preacher does not write out the sermon, but rather performs it—sometimes extemporaneously—from a rich oral framework that seeks to pull the con-

---

107. Barth, *Preaching of the Gospel*, 77–78.

108. Lowry, *Sermon*, 25.

109. Mitchell, *Recovery of Preaching*, 29.

110. Ibid., 35.

gregation into the event itself. Would we say that because a traditional African American sermon is not written that it is not real "Christian discourse"? This of course would be a ridiculous claim.

As the "global community" becomes smaller and evolves into a more multiethnic communication culture, preachers must pay closer attention to the wisdom an oral culture offers. As Buttrick observes there is a changing dynamic of orality that preachers in our cultural moment need to take seriously:

> In such moments, we are tempted to withdraw into our Bible-study circles and preserve our souls. But as we shrink, we can either become a somewhat self-righteous cultural anachronism, or we can reach out with the gospel message. The need to speak to the world and thus to human situations in the world may move us toward a different homiletics. Our preaching may well become much more oral and immediate . . . People are thinking, understanding, and speaking in ways that belie the homiletical textbooks we have inherited from the past. So we need to think out the rhetorical ways and means appropriate to contemporary consciousness, a task that ought to keep both homileticians and practicing preachers busy.[111]

This kind of attention is actually attention to the witness of Jesus himself. Jesus' preaching was oral and immediate to his hearers. It is ironic that Jesus, whose words create and form our lives, never wrote a word by his own hand. Jesus was a man of words. He is, after all, the Word made flesh, not the Word made text. Others did write his words down, and there is probably no person whose words have been reproduced in print as often. It is important to keep Jesus' original oral quality in mind. For it was the living voice of Jesus, the words *spoken* that first shaped the disciples. Written words, as important as they are, are a giant step removed from the mind of the original author. A determined effort must be made to hear the speaking voice and listen to it, not just to look at it and study the written word.[112]

This is a significant point. The world is changing, and preaching is beginning to take place in a context that is more "oral and immediate" than it was for Jesus. This emphasis on "thinking out of rhetorical ways" to address our cultural moment will also require preachers to think seriously about the role of the imagination. This is an area where Barth's model is once again limited. Barth's understanding of good communication is controlled by

---

111. Buttrick, *Captive Voice*, 112.

112. Eugene Peterson expands on this "determined effort" in *Eat this Book*.

assumptions ruled by a communication culture of print-literacy that fails to take seriously the role of the imagination in oral communication.

Human Responsibility

A third concern of Barth's version of this identity when working within our cultural moment is the lack of emphasis on the human agency of the preacher. While in many ways Barth is trying to empower the preacher, he ironically downplays the human responsibility of the preacher in evaluating a sermon's faithfulness. Barth correctly names the fundamental and inescapable tension as the relationship between *the Word of God and the Word of man.*[113] It is true that the human can never force God to reveal himself. But on the other hand, one of the unsettling patterns available to The Preacher as Herald in this tension is the ability to sidestep not only the significant human role and selection of words, forms, and even Scripture in the hermeneutic process of preaching the *kerygma*, but also its cultural coloration. Is the *kerygma* as fixed and obvious as this identity implies?

Alvin J. Porteous challenges this notion of a self-evident, ready-to-be-told gospel. Porteous insists that the biblical message is a word of liberation. The church's "social and economic conditioning" as a privileged group of people has resulted in an "ideological skewing of [its] message."[114] Consequently, the church is "faced with the difficult task of disentangling the message of the gospel from these ideological creations and distortions."[115] For centuries the privileged and the powerful have defined the essential *kerygma.*[116] Justo L. Gonzalez and Catherine Gunsalus Gonzalez tell the story of how the interpretation of the Christian gospel by the powerful "became normative and was passed on as authoritative, not only to later generations among the powerful, but also to the powerless, who were left with the

---

113. See John Webster's account of Barth on the relationship between grace and human freedom in *Barth's Ethics of Reconciliation.* This tension between divine grace and human action is the key to understanding Barth's vision of the Christian life and ethics, argues Webster. Here he shows that taking seriously Barth's claim that divine grace is not simply information, but is action eliciting divine activity, is the key to understanding Barth's vision of Christian ethics. Webster writes, "I want to try to show that what commands attention in Barth's ethics of reconciliation is a twofold claim: that the followers of Jesus Christ are invited and entitled to act, and that the invitation and entitlement to action are truly grasped only by those who live in his fellowship and under his good and gracious rule" (19).

114. Porteous, *Preaching to Suburban Captives,* 34.

115. Ibid., 36.

116. Gonzalez and Gonzalez, *Liberation Preaching,* 15.

alternative of either acquiescing to exploitation or rejecting Christianity."[117] These voices raise the critical issue: who gets to define the *kerygma*?

The art of knowing is no longer understood to be a simple activity produced by the apprehension of correct philosophical, scientific, or exegetical method. Affirming this point, Joseph Sittler comments that our "ways of knowing must be as supple and contrapuntal and various as history is—not as clear and clean and simple as philosophy hungers for."[118] Lesslie Newbigin, for example, reminds the church that hermeneutics is a human act that is not done in isolation from one's culture, opinions, private fears, or prejudices.[119] Our social, economic, and educational experiences all shape our selections of what we emphasize, and sometimes more importantly, what we do not emphasize in a gospel presentation. This hermeneutical work is colored by cultural conditions that are not neutral. The image of a herald betrays a belief that the choices of words, form, and style are neutral conditions that God will or will not make his self-revealing Word. A word can say a thousand different things depending on the context, the listener, voice inflection, or even body and facial expression. Do we not need to acknowledge that the preacher could, for example, think he or she was proclaiming the *kerygma* faithfully while still using sexist or racist language? Do we not need a homiletic identity that keeps the responsibility of the preacher at the forefront of our attention?

If Jesus' life, death, and resurrection have any message, is it not, at the very least, that God is never predictable? Barth's legacy, though flawed, does remind us that for human reality to encounter God, it must be infused first with the activity of God himself. Only when the Word encounters us through the open pages of the words in Scripture can the sermon be an instrument and agent of his self-revealing activity. Preachers make conscious choices when selecting what is said—and, perhaps just as significantly, how it is said—so that they are ultimately answerable for the quality and content of a sermon. It is one thing to guard God's activity and freedom and warn preachers away from attempting to commandeer God's work of reconciliation and grace; it is quite another to sever humans so completely from the process that the Word and our human words are perceived to have no significant relationship to each other. Thomas Long notes in his discussion of the homiletics of Barth that "the herald image so stresses that preaching is something which God does, insists so firmly that preaching is divine action

117. Ibid.

118. Sittler, *Anguish of Preaching*, 36.

119. See Newbigin, *Gospel*, 184–97.

rather than human effort, that the role of the preacher is almost driven from sight."[120]

Barth's thought loses the gifts of the human work of the preacher, and in the process diminishes the work of God. Paul Scott Wilson, for example, criticizes Barth's image of the herald by saying that "it is inaccurate, or at least wishful thinking, to define the preacher's role as nothing more than a mere conduit . . . We always speak from the limitations of our own time and culture. God's message changes us, and we also change it for those who receive it from us. Mere instrumentality does not exist in preaching."[121] Sermons are as much conversation as proclamation, and no preacher can claim to be always in monologue.

The demand for the preacher to be an unnoticeable vessel—a pure vehicle of the Word—is potentially delusional. Beware of the preacher who modestly stands before the congregation and says, "Now I am just giving you the pure Word of God, without any adulteration by my own personality, commitments, limits, or sin." More dangerous than hindering the gospel through the defects in my character is that character defect that deludes me into thinking that I can be a pure vessel for the gospel, that my vocation as a preacher has somehow lifted me out of the mire of sin and self-deceit that infects lesser mortals within the congregation. Therefore, as a preacher, I ought not to pray to be a pure, untainted vessel, a herald, but rather that God might make me aware of all the ways that I hinder the proclamation of the gospel through my own sin. Knowing some of the ways that I ought not to be trusted with a biblical text, knowing to some degree the texts that most challenge my own limitations, admitting to some of the ways that I preach myself rather than Christ crucified, can give the preacher a modicum of humility on the way to the pulpit.

Imagination

In the half-light of our late modern world, it is critical that preaching possess an operational root metaphor that takes seriously the powers of the imagination. This is because the intellectual culture of modernity, which believed it had achieved access to certainty for human knowledge and behavior through positivist foundationalism, is giving way to a culture of ideas which acknowledges that in some degree all knowing is dependent on the tacit powers of the imagination.[122] The imagination, suggests Garrett Green,

120. Long, *Witness of Preaching*, 29.

121. Wilson, *Practice of Preaching*, 28.

122. See Grenz and Ranke, *Beyond Foundationalism*. For a discussion on the tacit

is understood "not so much as a particular faculty, but as the integration in human experience of the various human abilities and potentialities."[123] Hart echoes this belief when he writes that the "imagination seems to run through every sphere, layer, dimension, nook, and cranny of our humanity . . . the category of imagination may provide a convenient focus for an accounting of what it means to be human in God's world."[124]

With such a view of the imagination, it is easy to see its importance for the proclamation of Christian faith. The imagination is not so much a specific location, or "organ," of the human body or mind, as it is the mysterious power of humanity to see, interpret, discover, and organize our perceptions, feelings, and experiences in reality. Without the imagination there could be no rationality, belief, art, or the possibility of human communication. The imagination involves every "nook and cranny" of our existence. This must be true for the existence of preaching as well.

If this is true, what is The Preacher as Herald's relationship to and understanding of the imagination for homiletic identity? This identity, as evidenced by Barth, would resist giving the imagination so much significance, or would at the least be suspicious of such a sweeping claim. As with reason and experience, Barth's suspicion of the imagination for homiletic reflection is that preachers cannot try to establish the reality of God through human powers, whether that effort be inspired by rational arguments or through creativity expressed in art forms. [125] Only God can give knowledge of God. Any alleged feeling of absolute dependence (Schleiermacher), yearning for some ground of being (Tillich), or desire for a more fulfilling life (choose any one of a number of contemporary advocates who support this idea) will not provide access to God. The working result of this theological conviction is that the preacher is discouraged from considering the creative capacities of the imagination to be anything other than a temptation towards natural theology, where Christian speech is reduced to talk about ourselves.[126]

In order to engage Barth's assumptions about the nature of the imagination in human experience, we need to remember Barth's relationship with Ludwig Feuerbach as discussed in chapter 1. Feuerbach's critique provided Barth with the insight he needed to assail the liberal theology he absorbed as a student. What Barth appreciated most in Feuerbach was not his notorious idea that Christianity was a mere projection of human religious

power of imagination in epistemology, see Polanyi, *Tacit Dimension*.

123. Green, *Imagining God*, 150.

124. Hart, "Imagining Evangelical Theology," 199.

125. Barth, *Homiletics*, 13.

126. See Green, *Imagining God*, especially chapters 3 and 4.

yearnings, but rather Feuerbach's bald reduction of theology to nothing but anthropology, thus typifying the theology of the age. In modernity, theology had degenerated into anthropology, beginning with various assessments of the "human condition" rather than with, "And God said . . . " Barth saw Feuerbach pushing the process that began with Kant to its logical conclusion. Feuerbach merely exposed theology's great reversal: it had become more interested in humanity than God. From Feuerbach, Barth learned his famous dictum that theology must be more than talking about humanity in a loud voice. Otherwise Feuerbach's charge against "theology" would be simply confirmed by theologians.[127]

In his commentary on Romans, Barth roars against such tame proclamation that either constructs Jacob's ladder or aims to cut God down to our size:

> We suppose that we know what we are saying when we say "God," We assign to Him the highest place in our world: and in so doing we place Him on fundamentally one line with ourselves and with things. We assume that He needs something: and so we assume that we are able to arrange our relation to Him as we arrange our other relationships. We press ourselves into proximity with Him. . . . We make Him night unto ourselves. We allow ourselves an ordinary communication with Him, we permit ourselves to reckon with him. . . . We serve the No-God.[128]

Because of what he saw as preaching more interested in humanity than God, Barth was determined to ground preaching not in tacit human experience, or bodily faculties, but only in God's own self-revelation of the Word, made known to sinful humanity through the Holy Spirit. Understood in this way, Christianity is always a response to the God of grace.

The point we are pressing is that when Barth accepted the modernist dichotomies of Feuerbach between reason and imagination, he quickly dismissed the imagination as a serious category for theology and, consequently, for Christian proclamation. Thus Barth does not see much use for the imagination when it comes to thinking about homiletic practice. Any homiletic interest in imagination was merely a ruse to conjure false images of God, rather than to, "in plain truth without embellishments," portray Christ, "who will utter his own truth."[129] Therefore, the preacher should not aspire to nurture a homiletic imagination—this would lead to the attempt

127. In Feuerbach, Barth found an odd ally whom he used to turn liberal theology back on itself. See Barth, *Protestant Theology*, 520–26.

128. Barth, *Epistle to the Romans*, 44.

129. Barth, *Homiletics*, 13.

to illustrate what cannot be illustrated, or worse, would attempt to create a "No-God" in human likeness.

Barth's suspicion however, warrants a question: If everything depends upon God to speak, on what grounds can Barth argue how not to speak, or of what faculty to trust or distrust? If revelation is contingent on an outside transcendent power of self-revelation, why could not God speak through the imagination, art, or logic? Barth seems, at times, to suggest that if a preacher tries to appeal to reason or imagination, God will not reveal himself. But how else is a preacher to speak? As we have already suggested that we cannot escape rhetorical concerns, we must ask, is it possible to escape the imagination? To suggest that we can seems to be a contradiction. Again, it may be worth noting the imaginative forms of Scripture itself, and the way in which Jesus, the incarnate Word revealed, actually preached.[130]

To argue that there is a wrong way to speak is to argue that there is a right way, and if there is a right way, we have a significant role within the revelation event. For Barth to go so far as to say that a preacher should never try to "capture the imagination of the hearers" is to go beyond his own concern and to prescribe a rule for preaching that ironically, might actually limit the way in which God may choose to reveal himself in a sermon. Why would God use a simple, rationally controlled exegetical sermon any more than a story or a narrative approach to expose the meaning of a text? Is not exegetical preaching any creative or imaginative form or method that exposes the meaning of a text? If God's will is to reveal himself in a revelatory event, Barth's logic demands that no matter what or how we preach, God will make this happen.

Barth suspicion of the imagination is intended to safeguard the preacher from speaking carelessly by discouraging any attempt to risk innovation in a sermon, because innovation might seek to "capture the imagination."[131] Yet too much safeguarding makes preaching safe. Revelation from God inherently poses risk. The Word made flesh bleeds, but this bleeding realizes our salvation. Barth has good reason to be concerned about the abuses of the imagination, and his caution about putting the imagination as the cart before the horse in the event of revelation is to be heeded. Still, Barth seems to undervalue the imagination as a human gift the Holy Spirit can use in the eventfulness of the preacher's proclamation.

There is considerable worth and weight to this identity. It succeeds in maintaining a homiletic identity within the trinitarian framework. In this framework, the Word preached, written, and revealed in Jesus Christ,

130. See Vanhoozer, "Voice and the Actor," 61–106.

131. Barth, *Homiletics*, 13.

shapes the beginning and end of Christian proclamation. Along with Barth and his model, we want to affirm and honor the priority of God's actions in grace, supporting the belief that revelation is a free gift of God, which only God can make possible or access in us. As such, we don't want to fall into the vain effort to try to locate the thing in us, or argue for a natural born "contact point" that when touched by the Spirit actualizes the miracle of faith.[132]

Instead, we want to seek out and develop an identity that trusts in the triune God while following the way of Jesus. In this way, according to Garrett Green, "proclamation can be thought of as singing the scriptural melody so that others may also learn to hear and enjoy it and to join in the singing."[133] The imagination as shaped by Scripture allows the preacher to find an equilibrium that balances the rhetorical side of preaching (concern for form, style, metaphors, etc.), while at the same time maintaining a reliance on revelation. Only when human imagination is given what it could not produce for itself—the true images from Scripture—can it in faith imagine God rightly.[134] The church needs this kind of preacher working out of this kind of homiletic identity, one that takes the power of imagination seriously, because in Jesus, all of humanity's gifts are taken seriously. As Hart suggests, "Imagination, the poetic, can help us bring to expression, for ourselves and for others, reality in its most mysterious and complex dimensions and yet, having brought it to an appropriate level and form of expression, to remain tantalizingly aware of the symbolic shortfall of our utterance. For reality, in all its mysterious depth, is the great iconoclast; and God is the greatest iconoclast of them all."[135]

Preaching holds the possibility of spreading the mysterious reality of God's good news of the Word with imaginative modes of speech—speech that is visionary, dramatic, artistic, capable of inviting persons to join in another conversation. As Walter Brueggemann writes, "reduced speech leads to reduced lives."[136] The sermon may be one of the last best places left in our twilight culture to hear unreduced imaginative speech that permits people to enter into a new life of faith.

---

132. For an example of such an effort that moves the focus to the imagination see Green, *Imagining God*, 40.

133. Ibid., 151.

134. Ibid., 149.

135. Hart, "Imagining Evangelical Theology," 200.

136. Brueggemann, *Finally Comes the Poet*, 3.

CONCLUSION: A FRAMEWORK AND A VOID

What we are suggesting in this exploration of The Preacher as Herald is that Barth's view of the preacher may limit the possibilities of homiletic practice. Preachers think with their mouths open in a complex interplay of hearing, speech, and thought, which involves all of their senses and the imagination, while always being grounded in the Word of God. The major task in our present situation, as was Barth's intent, is to free ourselves from enslavement to the detached modern self. We are after a homiletic identity that holds the possibility of recovering the sermon as the occasion of an encounter with something other than ourselves.

Barth's homiletic identity gives us a significant trinitarian framework, but its lack of emphasis on human agency, specifically in relation to the dynamics of orality and the imagination, is a void that leaves us wanting. How can we maintain this framework, while at the same time making room to honor the actions and responsibilities of the preacher? The proposal that we will consider in the next chapter is that the preacher's craft is analogous to the work of an artist. Artistry is never merely about self-expression. It is focused on the "otherness" of reality, which makes room for the primary event of revelation. Thus, to speak of humans making a work of art is not to suggest the work begins *ex nihilo*, not only in the sense that the artist brings to the task all of the insights, ideas, and inclinations of the humanity of the artist but also in that the artist must confront the stuff of his or her art—a piece of stone, a canvas and some paint, or the limitations and potential of a musical instrument. The artist must not only confront these materials but must master their histories, traditions, and skills to make them come to life in new and different ways for their context. The violinist speaks of wrestling with the violin. The writer tells of the terror of staring at the blank page. Art requires respect for the medium and constant practice with the limitations and possibilities that are inherent in the medium. The artist must be willing to be challenged, confronted, and limited by the otherness and malleable objectivity of the medium. Some of the artist's subjectivity will need to be sacrificed in the task of bringing the art to visible or audible expression. The art is never the unconstrained exercise of the artist's will upon the medium. Most artists have a great respect for, sometimes even a great fear of, and often a deep love and infatuation for the medium of their art. They speak of the clay telling them what sort of pot ought to be made, they complain of the stone that demands to be cut in a certain way, they tell of the characters in a novel taking on a life of their own. They are led in ways that they never intended to go, indeed would not have gone without the encounter with and submission to the medium.

Analogously, the preacher submits to the Word, revealed in Jesus Christ, as well as the Word written in Scripture. It is precisely in relationship to the specifics of the Word that the sheer "otherness" of the world becomes most clear to the preacher. The sermon is not a mere projection of the preacher's feelings, experiences, and thoughts. The Word always stands there in defiant, sometimes loving, otherness. The Word is not infinitely pliable to the preacher's will, but always a reality to which the preacher must submit. The Word may point the sermon in a direction that the preacher may not have intended it to go. This kind of openness requires an intuitive trust of the Word's work upon our imaginations. The Word, the material of the sermon, has secrets that it may or may not reveal to us. Sunday upon Sunday, it is the otherness of the Bible that overwhelms the preacher, challenges him or her, and demands to be spoken in a voice not exclusively the preacher's own. And it is this otherness that enlists the imagination to think in ways that allow this world to respond to its ever-speaking Creator.

This is an otherness rooted outside of us, in another imagination, which takes ours and frees it to speak with the creativity and power of a revelation that saves. This is made possible by the vicarious humanity of Jesus Christ, the one who took advantage of all the creative gifts of imagination, orality, rhetoric, and embodied action to proclaim the good news that the kingdom of God had come near. We will explore the significance of the vicarious humanity of Christ, that is the double ministry of Christ made possible through the incarnation, for a homiletic identity that honors both human creativity and divine agency in the next chapter.

5

The Preacher as Liturgical Artist

My father was very sure about certain matters pertaining to the universe. To him, all good things—trout as well as eternal salvation—come by grace and grace comes by art and art does not come easy.—NORMAN MACLEAN

INTRODUCTION: GRACE, ART, AND PREACHING

A Presbyterian preacher from Montana, the father of Norman Maclean identifies grace as the bedrock of all good things—"trout as well as eternal salvation." I want to argue that this recognition of dependence on God's grace could not be more true of the work of Christian preaching. If we recast the art of catching a trout with a dry fly as the art of using language to catch the imagination of a hearer, we may discover a helpful way of thinking about the identity and practice of the preacher. Like fly-fishing, preaching requires skills guided by tacit judgment, creativity, traditional wisdom, subversive instinct, and attention to environmental conditions, as well as the need to stay alert to the variety of forms hidden in the shadows of living water. Yet both the fly-fisherman and the preacher are always responding to something first set in motion by God. Preaching, we might say, comes to us by grace, and this grace comes by art; but art, Maclean reminds us, does not come easy.

How might this understanding of preaching as an art that is a means of grace shape homiletic practice? In this chapter we will argue that the development of an identity that seeks to bring grace through acts of human art may illustrate a helpful way forward for understanding *who* preachers are and *what* preachers do. In other words, to understand the preacher as an artist who works within a specific context of Christian worship, with and for a specific audience and people, within a working tradition of a people that are *liturgically* formed, may encourage a fresh and creative homiletic practice guided not by rhetorical technique, but by a renewed understanding of artistic identity and activity within the artistry of Word's ongoing ministry of proclamation. In this sense, the acts of Christian preaching have something to do with artistry, the imagination, and creativity within Christ's artistry, imagination, and creativity. Consequently, artistry and creativity are fundamental to the homiletic identity of a preacher whose God is the primary agent that shapes the practice of this art form. Thus, I want to propose a new metaphor for the preacher: The Preacher as Liturgical Artist.

INTRODUCTION OF THE PREACHER AS LITURGICAL ARTIST

In this chapter, the metaphor of The Preacher as Liturgical Artist will demonstrate a way to move forward. Preachers are artists that have a role in God's drama of salvation as they are called to faithfully and creatively reiterate the gospel. They are called to speak the truth beautifully as they witness to the person of Jesus and the work of his Father. Their work is enlivened by the Holy Spirit to invite God's people to participate in the continuing creativity of the Word. As Flannery O'Connor argues, "The basis of art is truth, both in matter and in mode. The person who aims for art in his work aims after truth, in an imaginative sense, no more and no less."[1] In this spirit of truth telling, artistry can be considered fundamental to a preacher's identity, which in turn shapes the practice of preaching "in matter and in mode." The metaphor of identity of The Preacher as Liturgical Artist assumes that the creative powers of imagination are given by God to be used in preaching not primarily so that preachers might persuade others, taking over the role of the Spirit, but so that they might offer back to the Father their human gifts that are redeemed in Christ. Therefore, the initial difference between The Preacher as Teacher and The Preacher as Liturgical Artist is that the former puts the focus squarely on human agency, while the latter embraces responsible human action as a way of offering back to God what God has provided to humanity. This means that the preacher keeps the primary work of conversion in God's hands, while at the same time the preacher participates in that conversion by giving to God the use of his or her human gifts.

1. O'Connor, "Writing Short Stories," 92.

This allows the wisdom of both The Preacher as Teacher and The Preacher as Herald to find convergence in a new identity, namely the liturgical artist.

As noted above, Flannery O'Connor argues that "the basis of art is truth, both in matter and in mode." While O'Connor roots the task of the artist in truth, others base their artistic endeavors on notions of beauty or personal expression. Pablo Picasso, for example, suggests that "art is not the application of a canon of beauty but what the instinct and the brain can conceive beyond any canon. When we love a woman we don't start measuring her limbs."[2] Definitions and descriptions of art vary, but a basic description of the task of the artist at the least includes the following entailments:

1. An artist is one who works with a given material.

2. An artist adds value to what he or she lays hold of, offering back more than is given.

3. An artist works within a tradition of training and skill.

4. An artist has a "gift" which he or she must exercise responsibly.

5. An artist is "creative."

6. An artist works imaginatively.

7. An artist performs for an audience within a given context.

Theologically, describing The Preacher As Liturgical Artist entails a number of theological assumptions about *creativity, imagination, the nature of art,* and the role of *tradition* in human endeavor. This description of the preacher also requires a fresh understanding of *performance, the relationship of the preacher and congregation*, the *context* for preaching and, most importantly, the *character of Jesus' priestly ministry*, which was thoroughly artistic and beautiful. As the argument of this chapter develops, these various issues will be discussed in relation to the person and work of Jesus Christ, who is both the source and the model of our proposed homiletic identity.

What we mean by artist as we describe the metaphor of The Preacher as Liturgical Artist is not the tortured Romantic notion, but rather the classic sense of a skilled artisan who absorbs a tradition and whose skills are grounded in a larger framework of participation in God's ongoing work of creation that might best be expressed within an aesthetic theory along the lines of Nicholas Wolterstorff's art in action.[3] This understanding of the artist takes human imagination and creativity seriously, but not as rivals to

---

2. Quoted in "Statement By Picasso: 1935" in Barr, *Picasso*, 16.
3. Wolterstorff, *Art in Action*.

God. Instead, The Preacher as Liturgical Artist seeks to engage with what has been given in the fallen world by taking things that have been created and redeemed and offering them back to God with added value. In this sense, proposing the term artist is not an attempt to suggest one definitive answer to the question of what an artist does. That would be an impossible reduction. Instead, we are using the term to suggest a way of encouraging the preacher to employ human gifts and capacities that have been redeemed in Christ and to offer these gifts back to the Father in gratitude. This understanding of the artist is captured beautifully by T. S. Eliot:

> Lord, shall we not bring these gifts to your service?
> Shall we not bring to your service all our powers
> For life, for dignity, grace and order,
> And intellectual pleasures of the senses?
> The Lord who created must wish us to create
> And employ our creation in his service
> Which is already His service in creating.[4]

To develop this concept of the artist faithfully, we have to put it in a trinitarian framework and let Jesus Christ lead the way forward. Following the way of Jesus in relationship to the Father and the Holy Spirit also requires a particular understanding of creativity in conversation with the triune God. The contribution of this project is the application of the artist metaphor to the ongoing liturgical task of preaching. Others have considered and are considering the beauty of worship and the call to be faithful artists in this context. The emphasis of this project, however, is on putting the preacher in relationship to this beauty, with the end of showing how the image of The Preacher as Liturgical Artist sends us back to Jesus Christ where we can find a place in his ongoing work with the Father and the Spirit.

Therefore, we need to frame an understanding of artistry and preaching within the doctrines of the Trinity and the incarnation. We will do this by appealing to a theology of communion and the priesthood of Christ developed in the trinitarian thought of T. F. Torrance and J. B. Torrance. In so doing, we will uncover the significance for preaching of the vicarious humanity of Christ, whose double ministry of God to humanity and humanity back to God redeems our humanity and all of our gifts and thereby sets us free to offer our best—our reason as well as our imagination and creativity—back to God with gratitude.

---

4. Eliot, "Choruses from 'The Rock,'" 111.

RECOVERING THE PRIESTLY SYNTHESIS
OF THE INCARNATION AND CREATION

What we are pursuing is a theology of preaching that will help us to find an identity for the preacher that is both framed by the doctrine of the Trinity and encourages the full use of a range of human gifts, such as creativity and imagination. What we need is a homiletic identity that can hold the holy tension between divine and human agency in the work of Christian preaching. For such a synthesis we turn to T. F. Torrance's theology of communion and his emphasis on the incarnation. Of particular interest is the way that Torrance understands the ministry of Jesus and the notion of the vicarious humanity of Christ.

Trinity and the Vicarious Humanity

Throughout his work, Torrance wants to ground an understanding of worship, including acts of preaching, in the double ministry of Christ. He emphasizes the twofold ministry of Jesus Christ, where "he ministered the things of God to man and the things of man to God. That man-ward and God-ward ministry are to be thought of as an inseparable whole in the oneness of our Lord's Person as God and Man, of his life to its culmination in his vicarious death and resurrection, but also as extending after his ascension into his heavenly intercession as our High Priest and Advocate before the Face of the Father."[5] It is by reclaiming this stress upon the double ministry of Christ that the church and its preachers are set free to rest in the gospel of grace and not of works.

> As the incarnate Son of the Father Jesus Christ had been sent to fulfill all righteousness both as priest and as victim, who through his one self-offering in atonement for sin has mediated a new covenant of universal range in which he presents us to his Father as those whom he has redeemed, sanctified and perfected for ever in himself. In other words, Jesus Christ constitutes in his own self-consecrated humanity the fulfillment of the vicarious way of human response to God promised under the old covenant, but now on the ground of his atoning self-sacrifice once for all offered this is a vicarious way of response, which is available for all mankind.[6]

5. Torrance, *Incarnation*, 73.
6. Ibid., 76.

It is in the light of the incarnation, the true light of God, that we understand the nature of divine and human action and their proper interaction.
This begins with the recognition that Christ fulfills the covenant from both
sides.[7] From this starting point it is possible to think clearly about God,
humanity, and the reconciliation of the two through the life, death, and resurrection of Christ Jesus.

In this perspective, we must think of preaching as taking place within
the relations of covenant partnership and reciprocity between God and
humanity. Christian preaching is grounded in and governed by the belief
that through the incarnation, Jesus Christ has proclaimed the message of
the Word of God as the Word of God. It is also grounded in the belief that
through the incarnation, Jesus Christ has responded to this Word as a human on behalf of other humans. He not only brings God to humanity but
humanity to God in himself.

Of particular interest is the way that Jesus stands in our place before
God, making himself our sermon, in the sense that Jesus is *the* Word and
revelation of God. From this perspective, Jesus is a sermon not in word or
even only in an act, but in his personal being. This insight is based on the
vicarious humanity of Jesus, meaning that everything that the Son did when
he took up our humanity, he did with and for us. What he did in the flesh
he did for us, whether this was living, dying, and rising again or preaching
the word of God to the people of God. It is as the truly human one that Jesus
Christ stands in our place in the pulpit, even as we stand there, so that from
deep within our humanity, where he has united himself to us, he continues
to stand in for us before the Father and before the world. That is to say, Jesus
Christ is both the preacher and the message preached. As Torrance writes,
"Jesus Christ acts in our place and on our behalf in both a representative
and a substitutionary way so that what he does in our stead is nevertheless
effected as our very own, issuing freely and spontaneously out of ourselves."[8]

Thus in all our preaching, we come before God in such a way as to let
Jesus Christ take our place, replacing our words with his own self-offering as
the Word made flesh, for he *is* the sermon through or in which we respond
to the love of the Father. This notion of vicarious redemption and vicarious
participation calls us to preach with a faith that makes Jesus our mediator,
for in him the message and the messenger are the same, and in him we are
gathered up, so that with him we preach as we could not otherwise preach.[9]

7. This is the central thesis of J. B. Torrance in *Worship, Community, and the Triune
God of Grace*.

8. Torrance, *Incarnation*, 88.

9. Ibid.

This work between God and God's people and between God's people and God is fulfilled through the vicarious humanity of Jesus.

In other words, truly human preaching is proclamation in the name of Jesus Christ that rests in his ongoing ministry before his Father and God. It is thus with utter peace and joy that we are free to preach with creativity and freedom as the Holy Spirit hides our words in the words of Christ. The work of Christ assures us that as we preach and listen to preaching, we are caught up within the dynamic life of the triune God, within the sighs of inarticulate intercessions of the eternal Spirit from whose love nothing in heaven or on earth can ever separate us.[10] This centrality of the double work of Christ means that if Christ's vicarious humanity is lost for preaching, preachers themselves are lost.[11]

Torrance makes this critical and clarifying point with greater specificity in an essay entitled "The Mind of Christ in Worship: The Problem of Apollinarianism in the Liturgy." Here Torrance argues for recovering the essential place of the human mind of Jesus Christ in the mediation of our worship of God. Torrance claims that once we lose sight of the vicarious role of the mind of Jesus in its oneness with the mind of the Father, the whole meaning of worship changes and with it the basic structure and truth of the liturgy.[12] He argues that over time the church's liturgy, in reaction to Arianism, elevated the divinity over the humanity of Jesus. The eternal Word superseded and then obscured the humanity of Christ. Thus, the church, in both the East and the West, failed to hold in tension the christological foundation of Chalcedon that teaches that in his life and death Jesus Christ is one with God and one with humanity, truly God and truly human. As Torrance writes:

> In allowing no room for the mental and moral life of Jesus as a human and in denying to him authentic human agency in his saving work, it left no place for the vicarious role of the human soul and mind and will of Jesus in the reconciling "exchange" of like for like in the redemption of man. And by destroying his representative capacity, it had no place for his priesthood or human mediation in our worship of the Father, and by the same

10. This is why J. B. Torrance argues that if a trinitarian framework for preaching is lost, so is the church, which is why recovering this doctrine needs to be one of the essential ministries of the church. Torrance writes, "There is no more urgent need in our churches today than to recover the Trinitarian nature of grace—that it is by grace alone, through the gift of Jesus Christ in the Spirit that we can enter into a life of communion with God our Father" (*Worship*, 59).

11. Torrance, *Incarnation*, 95.

12. See Torrance, "Mind of Christ," 140.

token it took away the ground for any worship of God with our human minds. A mutilated humanity in Christ could not but result in a mutilated Christian worship of God.[13]

The effect of this failure throughout the centuries, according to Torrance, was to thrust Christ up into the majesty and grandeur of the Godhead in such a way that the ancient biblical and patristic stress upon the High Priesthood of Christ and his human mediation of prayer to the Father was diminished if not lost. Thus the continuing work of Christ and his ongoing mediation of our work was lost and humans were left with either the sense that they have to do everything on their own or that they can do nothing but wait for God to do God's thing. The notion of participation in Christ and the role of the Spirit were also obscured as the basis of both was forgotten. This neglect led to an overemphasis on the human priest who was seen as substituting for Jesus, which led to a sense that the preacher rather than Christ was responsible for administering grace.

Torrance's claim is that without the human mind of Christ mediating on our behalf to God, the divinity of Christ subsumes the ongoing human work of God and, consequently, we are "thrown back on ourselves."[14] In this perspective, our human gifts, such as reason, creativity, imagination, and performance, become vain attempts to do what only Christ, a human/divine mediator, could offer for us. Hence, Torrance draws out the implication that when the church loses this vision of Jesus the true High Priest, grace is seen to be mediated through three physical means: *institutional physicalism, social physicalism, and spiritualistic phenomenalism*.[15] Each of these emphases, according to Torrance, misplaces the unique role that the human mind of Christ plays in our acts of Christian worship. Consequently, the true nature of Christian worship as mediated through the human mind of Christ is lost, and with it our true communion with God.

The true nature of divine worship, however, in spirit and in truth through the Son, is such that we are given access to the Father beyond the limits of the visible and the tangible and our

13. Ibid., 150.

14. Ibid., 204.

15. Ibid., 206–7. *Institutional physicalism*, according to Torrance, is when salvation is sought to be mediated through ecclesiastical institutions, including liturgical institutions, regarded as spatio-temporal forms of behavior before God. *Social physicalism* is what Torrance describes as an effort to ground salvation in human works. And in *spiritualistic phenomenalism*, Christ himself tends to be thrust into a subsidiary place, for what is primary is what the worshipper himself does in the Spirit, which leads spiritual phenomena, acts of healing or speaking in tongues to become the criteria of genuine worship in the Spirit.

minds are lifted up into a region that transcends what we know but which we are assured through the mediation of Christ is in complete harmony with what the Father has revealed of himself through the Son . . . Christian worship stands or falls with the ascension of the crucified and risen Christ into the holy of holies, and with access through the veil of his flesh into the uncreated Light of God.[16]

Torrance argues that what is needed for true worship to be realized is the restoration of the Christological foundation of the church's faith by maintaining the integrity of the human will and mind of the Incarnate Son mediating to the Father, through the Spirit, on our behalf. It is through this priestly mediation that we learn to worship the Father through the name of Christ, in the Spirit. This relationship is the heart of the Christian gospel. When we realize that this intercession is happening every day, it transforms our acts of worship—our praying, preaching, singing, and sacraments—to be knit together in Christ, and thus our lives begin to take shape within the context of Christ's holiness in worship. Torrance suggests that this is deeply significant to our understanding of the implications of the vicarious humanity of Christ. When grasped and indwelled, this points us to the true nature of reconciliation that allows for communion with God that sets us free to respond to God with all of our selves. In *Incarnation*, Torrance describes this theology of communion in relation to Christ:

> We are to think of the whole life and activity of Jesus from the cradle to the grave as constituting the vicarious human response to himself which God has freely and unconditionally provided for us. That is not an answer to God that he has given to us through some kind of transaction external to us or over our heads, as it were, but rather one that he has made to issue out of the depths of our human being and life as our own. Nor is it an answer in word only but in deed, not by way of an exemplary event which we may follow but which has no more than symbolical significance, but by way of a final answer to God actualized in the flesh and blood of our human existence and behaviors and which remains eternally valid. Jesus Christ is our human response to God. Thus we appear before God and are accepted by him as those who are inseparably united to Jesus Christ our great High Priest in his eternal self-presentation to the Father.[17]

16. Torrance, *Incarnation*, 207.
17. Ibid., 80.

What the vicarious humanity of Christ means for our purposes is that since we are redeemed in Christ and united to Christ, we can bring all our best human efforts to God, not as a way to make God's revelation happen, nor to justify our salvation, but as a free response to God's grace in Christ through the Spirit. As J. B. Torrance emphasizes, "our repentance is thus a response to grace, not a condition of grace."[18] Likewise, our preaching is a response to grace positioned in the ongoing work of Christ and the Spirit and so not a condition of grace. In other words, because of Christ's priestly work—because of the vicarious humanity of Jesus—our reason, our creativity, even our imagination are set free to be used as ways to give glory to God through Christ.

To reclaim this human freedom in and with Christ, Torrance suggests that the church must ground worship in the life and work of the triune God. The central points of reference for this reconstruction begin, first, with a proper emphasis on the incarnation. When the "Word became flesh," Jesus, the Son of God, took our human nature and healed and sanctified it in himself, so that he might offer it up to God in and through his own self-consecration and self-presentation to the Father on our behalf: "At the heart of that lies the fact that Christ identified himself with us in our alienation and disobedience, made our distorted sonship and worship his own and thereby transformed them in union with his own. It is on that ground that he continues to take up our prayers into himself, moulds and shapes them in and through his own self-offering, in which his life and prayer are one and indivisible, and so offers them continually to the Father mediated through his own."[19]

The second dynamic that must be reclaimed within a theology of communion is the work of the Holy Spirit. The work of the Holy Spirit is critical for our understanding of human freedom in Christ before God the Father. In other words, through Christ we have access in one Spirit to the Father because he has sent his own Holy Spirit to dwell in us. This is the same Spirit by whom he lived and prayed and through whom he offered himself without spot to the Father. "Thus the presence of his Spirit in us," argues Torrance, "means that Christ's prayer and worship of the Father are made to echo in us and issue out of our life to the Father as our own prayer and worship."[20] When applied to preaching, this means it is possible that through a sermon the presence of Jesus Christ is actualized by the presence of the Holy Spirit.

18. Torrance, *Worship*, 59.
19. Torrance, "Mind of Christ," 208.
20. Ibid., 209.

Finally, we must come to understand that it is Jesus Christ himself who grounds our human prayers and preaching in worship. It is only with Christ as humanity's High Priest, our one and only mediator to the God the Father, that any human being can worship or preach faithfully. As Torrance explains:

> We worship God and pray to him as Father only through the mediation of Christ our High Priest, but since he is both Priest and Sacrifice, Offerer and Offering, made on our behalf, we worship and pray to the Father in such a way that it is Christ himself who is the real content of our worship and prayer: we offer Christ to the Father through our prayers, for in the Spirit the prayer that ascends from us to the Father is a form of the self-offering of Christ himself. Really to pray to God, therefore, is to pray with Christ who prays with us and for us, and to pray with him is to pray his prayer, the prayer of his life which he offered in our place and on our behalf, and in which through union with Christ in the one Spirit we are made continually participant.[21]

The crucial point in all this is the vicarious humanity of Christ in which his truly human mind, will, and soul are given their undiminished place in his saving work. That means that it is in the complete integrity of Christ's humanity that he acts, as a human for us humans, in all that we are called to do by way of response to the creative and redemptive love of God. In obeying and believing, in repenting and surrendering, in asking and receiving, in serving and praising, in loving and adoring God the Father Almighty—all of which Christ does for our sake—Jesus redeems, converts, and re-creates our humanity in himself. By saving us from the inside out Christ restores our human nature, mends our relationship to the Father, and enables our ongoing lives of communion with God. In other words, it is because, "the unimpaired human nature of Christ is inseparably united in him to the Creator Son and Word of God, making his humanity quickening and creative, indeed humanizing humanity, that as through union with him in the Spirit we share in his humanity we on our part are so profoundly humanized that our obedience and faith, our repentance and surrender, our service and praise, our love and adoration may be the spontaneously free and glad self-offering of the sons of God to their heavenly Father."[22]

In this light, we could say that all human efforts to preach take place within the life of Jesus Christ, whose life is one of continual worship, prayer,

21. Ibid.
22. Ibid., 210.

and praise to the Father on our behalf. Our preaching, then, happens through the mind of Christ, which is to say it happens through Jesus' own worship of the Father. In Christ, the human work of preaching is grounded in such a way that we may come before God the Father without thinking that we are playing the primary role, without having to look anxiously over our shoulder lest our preaching be wrong, unworthy, or done simply out of a desire to be (or appear to be) pious.[23] In so far as preaching is through, with, and in Christ, it is not primarily a form of our personal self-expression, autonomy, or artistic freedom. All of these human instincts take place in Christ's artistic freedom, which is always obedient to the will and desire of the Father.

What we mean by Christ's artistic freedom is the insistence that *in Christ* we are free to be creative precisely because our exercise of freedom, here as elsewhere (e.g., in moral action) is always held together with and "clothed" by Christ's perfect exercise of freedom on our behalf. In effect our creative freedom is an extension of the doctrine of justification by faith, which sets us free from the fear associated with failure, free to make mistakes in the confidence that God's purposes and promises do not hinge on the quality of our performance.

By grounding preaching in the grammar of the Trinity and, more specifically, within the vicarious work of Christ, preachers are freed to be creative agents, working with rhetorical dexterity amidst a shifting culture. It is precisely because preaching is shaped and structured by the vicarious humanity of Christ that preachers are consequently freed up to proclaim the gospel in a variety of ways and in a variety of contexts. Because Christ assumed and redeemed all of our human nature, we are free to use all our human gifts as we work with and in him. This is critical because preachers who face an increasingly multicultural and globalized world need a theology that encourages preaching the gospel with all their creative gifts. Today's preacher must be able to adapt with fluidity to a variety of human situations, societies, cultures, languages, ethnicities, and ages, not to mention differing aesthetic tastes and popular appeals, without falling victim to the temptation to reduce ministry to pragmatic strategies and techniques. Torrance argues that by objectively grounding our worship in Christ, by way of his priestly office of mediation between God and humanity, we are free to use and adapt creative forms of language and culture in our preaching of God, "without being imprisoned in time-conditioned patterns, or swept along by constantly changing fashions, and without letting preaching and

23. Ibid., 211.

our worship dissolve away into merely cultural and secular forms of man's self-expression and self-fulfillment."[24]

To connect this discussion with the larger goals of this book, I am attempting to synthesize two fundamental dynamics of preaching. The first is the importance of taking seriously the human agency of the preacher. The second is the need to place this work of human agency within the larger framework of God's grace and ongoing work in Christ on our behalf. In other words, I want to reconcile the responsible and "creative" nature of the preacher without falling into Pelagian quicksand. Torrance's theology of communion and his description of Christ's vicarious humanity offer a way forward.

If Jesus' vicarious humanity can itself be construed as a "work of artistry" (that is a work of human and divine artistry), then the "artistry" of preaching (and, indeed, artistry proper) can be made sense of as an active participation in Christ's human response to the Father in a direct and unambiguous sense. From this perspective, human artistry is a sharing in Christ's own artistic response to the creative goodness and beauty of the Father. This response, as well as the reality that all of humanity and humanity's gifts have been redeemed in Christ's vicarious humanity, makes possible the homiletic identity of the preacher as a liturgical artist.

What Torrance offers us is a rich theological framework in which to understand Jesus as an artist, which consequently frees preachers to see themselves in a similar light. Rowan Williams gives us an account of "art" as a creative and redemptive engagement with what is given in the created and fallen world, as it requires us to take the things of creation and life and offer them back to God with "added value."[25] The theology of communion, as offered by Torrance, allows us to develop a Christology in which Jesus' priestly assumption of our humanity, and redemptive transformation of it, is an act of creative artistry: taking the "raw materials" of our created and fallen nature, like reason or the imagination, "adding value" to them through his acts of obedience, and then offering our humanity back to the Father in the redeeming power of the Holy Spirit.

Within this theological framework, it is clear that the preacher is not an original creator or "counter-creator" in any sense that would rival God's sovereignty,[26] but can more properly be understood as a "sub-creator" or

24. Ibid., 213.

25. See Williams, *Grace and Necessity*.

26. See Steiner, *Real Presences*. Steiner argues that artistic creation is a theological consideration. He suggests that "there is aesthetic creation because there is *creation*. There is formal construction because we have been made form" (201). Despite this, Steiner suggests that art, and artists, are constantly reaching beyond these bounds as a

"re-creator."[27] This means that the artist is freed in Christ, through the Spirit, to use all the imaginative and creative gifts of humanity in the work of Christian proclamation. By rooting preaching in the vicarious humanity of Christ, we keep Christian proclamation in the soil of the Trinity as we grow up into Christ and so enjoy the full fruits of human agency. Through a more clear appreciation of the salvation and ongoing priesthood of Jesus and the role of the Spirit, preachers are free to avoid a Pelagian quagmire as they perform the act of preaching. The "constraint" of the triune God is the necessity we need to allow our human agency to find its fullest expression.[28] In other words, our true freedom is a response to the work God has achieved through the Holy Spirit in and through the double ministry of the incarnation of the Son.[29] Thus, all offerings to God in preaching are nothing but acts of response to the triune God of grace, offered through the ongoing ministry of Christ.[30] This allows the preacher to embrace the wisdom of The Preacher as Teacher's emphasis on human gifts, while at the same time keeping fellowship with The Preacher as Herald's emphasis on always and ever beginning with God.

This notion of participating in the human work of Christ raises the question of human responsibility and human action. Is it the case, as Tom Smail argues, that if Jesus does everything in our place, then that leaves

---

kind of protest to empirical exactitude or reproductive fidelity. Why? Because artistic creation is at root a grab for freedom: "I believe that the making into being by the poet, artist and . . . composer, is *counter*-creation . . . it is radically agnostic. It is rival. In all substantive art-acts there beats an angry gaiety. The source is that of loving rage. The human maker rages at his coming *after*, at being, forever, second to the original and originating mystery of the forming of form" (203).

27. See Hart, "Tolkien," 39–53. Hart identifies "sub-creation" as a theme introduced by J. R. R. Tolkien in his essay "On Fairy Story," delivered in 1938–39 for the Andrew Lang Lecture at the University of St. Andrews. See below for more on this idea. For now, it will suffice to say that the idea of "sub-creation" is rooted in the idea of a creativity that functions within the limits of our given necessities as human creatures. In this way, it does not aspire to rival or challenge God's sovereignty over creation, but rather find its full expression and possibility within the given limits in creation.

28. See Begbie, *Theology, Music, and Time*, 235–42. Here Begbie argues, "The freedom of the artist requires God's as well as our own agency, the agency of the Spirit who brings about that particularity-in-relation which constitutes our freedom and which has already been actualized in the Son" (240).

29. Ibid., 240. Begbie makes this emphasis in his discussion on the meaning of human freedom: "In short, the freedom of the artist requires God's as well as our own agency, the agency of the Spirit who brings about that particularity-in-relation which constitutes our freedom and which has already been actualized in the Son."

30. Again, this emphasis on our response to grace, rather than our acts providing a condition for grace, is at the heart of Torrance's *Worship, Community, and the Triune God of Grace*. See 57–58.

nothing for us to do?[31] Smail's concern is that the emphasis on the vicarious humanity of Christ means that Christ "repents" on our behalf, and thus neglects the reality of injustice, or personal and structural sin. This is a potential vulnerability in Torrance's argument. However, I am suggesting that the vicarious humanity of Christ calls us to a life of freedom and gratitude. In Christ, we are freed to use all our human gifts redeemed in Christ to actually live into the will and obedience of God. Without Christ's work, it would be impossible for us to do any of it. In other words, my argument is precisely that Jesus' vicarious humanity does *not* leave us with nothing to do; rather, it is what makes our *doing* a possibility.

An essential aspect of Torrance's theological vision is that the Holy Spirit empowers or perfects Jesus' human work and our participation in Jesus' recapitulation of all things to God. It is through the Holy Spirit that we are united to Christ and that our re-creative works are offered as redemptive gifts back to God.[32] Indeed, this claim makes a significant call upon the preacher, because the vicarious humanity of Christ does not leave us with nothing to do, but calls us to offer all our work as a re-creative response back to the triune God.

In the next section of this chapter, we will deal with this pragmatically rather than conceptually, asking how Jesus took the raw material of creation and gave it back to God as a means of grace. We will do this by looking more closely at the ways in which Jesus' preaching represents a re-creative artistry in human action.

Jesus the Artistic Preacher

The preacher's identity is grounded in the life of Christ, and we participate in this life through the Spirit. This means that "our ministry" finds its true place in the ministry of Jesus before the Father and before the world. The ministry of Jesus Christ, the Word made flesh, continues as the risen and ascended Jesus gives his Spirit to all those he calls to follow him and continue his work of proclaiming good news. This is what the vicarious humanity of Christ is all about, as Jesus takes up our humanity to redeem it and indwells it in such a way that we can live with and for him through the Spirit. In this way, Christ ministers as a mediator between God and humanity, and we are given the freedom through him to live as truly human persons with him for others. Thus, the vicarious humanity of Christ understood within a wider Trinitarian theology serves as our outer framework for understanding and

31. See Smail, "Can One Man Die?" 73–92.
32. Trevor Hart makes this argument in "Givenness, Grace, and Gratitude."

taking seriously human agency; Jesus' life for us and before the Father in the Spirit grounds our understanding of what preachers do and who they are in Christ. Working within this theological framework, we need to consider who Jesus is and what he did. More specifically, we need look directly at the work and preaching of Jesus to understand what it means to be an artist caught up in the action of the triune God.

To begin to appreciate the life work of Jesus the artist we will take our lead from Kenneth Bailey. In *Poet and Peasant*, Bailey argues that we too often miss the aesthetic power of Jesus' own ministry of proclamation as an artistic drama of encounter.[33] This, according to Bailey, is because we in the West are often prejudiced against viewing the forms of story and metaphor as serious intellectual work. He argues that in the Western tradition, serious theology has almost always been constructed from ideas held together by abstract reasoning and logic. In such an intellectual milieu, the more intelligent the preacher, or theologian, the more abstract he or she usually becomes, and, consequently, the more difficult it is for the average person to follow what is being said. He suggests that we all too often miss the important ways Jesus communicates his ideas *through* imaginative forms that were typical of this time, place, and people, namely story, simile, parables, and irony, as well as creative faithfulness within his own Jewish tradition. Jesus used these forms, which may be considered more in the realm of the art of poetry, to announce the good news of God.[34] Bailey argues that because we have tended to emphasize Jesus' concepts and sidelined his imaginative and artistic forms of preaching, we have made Jesus fit into our world of conceptual and abstract thinking, rather than letting our conceptual and abstract thinking fit into his cultural ways of communicating that focused on story and parable.[35] Just as Jesus is understood in abstraction from the Father, his teachings are "understood" through a process of abstraction that attempts to remove the message from the medium. Again, we need to let the actual person and work of Jesus reframe the thought, perception, and performance of preachers.

The popular perception of Jesus is that of a village troubadour spinning folktales for fishermen, merchants, soldiers, and farmers. He preached using stories that children, the illiterate, as well as the Pharisees and the Sadducees could understand. But when we examine with care his sermons that so often come to us as parables, says Bailey, we encounter not just powerful stories,

---

33. See the introduction to Kenneth Bailey, *Poet and Peasant*, 15–26.

34. This focus on retrieving the teachings of Jesus by locating them as close to the social and historical context of Jesus as possible is the theme of Bailey, *Jesus Through Middle Eastern Eyes*.

35. See an expanded argument along these lines in Jensen, *Thinking in Story*, 45–66.

we are confronted with the serious theology that presents an alternative reality to adjust ourselves too. Jesus' preaching reflects an astute preacher/theologian, but primarily, "a *metaphorical* rather than a *conceptual*" one.[36] The difference between the two may have to do with how one understands how metaphors function in communicating complex and significant ideas. Bailey writes, "Consider the following. We know that God is Spirit and is neither male nor female. Yet in the Scriptures we are told that the believer is 'born of God' (1 John 3:9). Here John uses female language to describe the relationship between God and believers. Similarly, when Jesus addressed God as 'Father,' he used a male metaphor/title to help us understand the nature of God. Scripture uses male and female images to enrich our understanding of God, who is Spirit and thereby beyond male and female."[37]

As we have seen in chapter 2, a metaphor communicates in ways that rational arguments cannot. Metaphors can offer us pictures instead of detached arguments. This has profound implications and possibilities for our ethical lives.[38] A "metaphorical" preacher like Jesus understands that a powerful picture or image communicates meaning that a thousand words cannot express. We encounter Jesus as a "metaphorical," or artistic, preacher in his use of parables such as "The Camel and the Needle" (Luke 18:18–30), "The Great Banquet" (Luke 14:15–24), "The Two Debtors" (Luke 7:36–50), "The Good Samaritan" (Luke 10:25–37), "The Rich Fool" (Luke 12:13–21), "The Pharisee and the Tax Collector" (Luke 18:18–30), "The Obedient Servant" (Luke 17:7–10), "The Lost Sheep and the Lost Coin" (Luke 15:4–10), or "The Unjust Steward" (Luke 16:1–8). We can see Jesus' use of metaphor as preaching in his seven "I am" statements in the Gospel of John (6:35; 8:12; 10:7; 10:11–14; 11:25; 14:6; 15:1). Also his dramatic use of symbol and gesture in the last supper (Matt 26:17–19; Mark 14:12–25; Luke 22:7–13), or the foot-washing to begin the upper room discourse in John (13:1–38); this, of course, is not intended to be an exhaustive list, but it supports the idea that Jesus preaches through stories, pictures, symbols, and parables.

These examples "illustrated" nothing at all, but are invitations into the history of the kingdom of God. In the West we think the story, parable, or dramatic metaphor is mere bench support for the starting proposition. Illustrations, says T. W. Manson, are too often seen as "the sugar coating on the theological pill."[39] Manson argues that to understand Jesus' creative

36. Bailey, *Jesus Through Middle Eastern Eyes*, 280.

37. Ibid.

38. See Hauerwas, *Vision and Virtue*, 2. Hauerwas agues that if we want to change our way of life, acquiring the right image is far more important than diligently making an argument.

39. See Manson, *Teaching of Jesus*, 73.

speech, vivid imagery, metaphors, stories, and parables as mere illustrations, is to miss the profound theological meaning Jesus is proclaiming within his context. It misses Jesus as an artistically astute preacher in his own right. Manson has stated this most profoundly where he observes that "minds trained in Western modes of thought" are accustomed to theological arguments set forth in abstractions. Then to help "popularize these conclusions" they may be illustrated from ordinary life. But, says Manson, "the true parable . . . is not an illustration to help one through a theological discussion; it is rather a mode of religious experience."[40]

Understanding what Manson is saying can perhaps best be seen by offering an imaginative comparison. In Luke 9:57–58 the text reads, "As they were going along the road a man said to him, 'I will follow you wherever you go.'" If Jesus had been a Western PhD student writing a dissertation, he might have responded something like this: "Bold statements are easy to make but you have to consider seriously what it will cost you to follow me. It seems evident that so far you have yet to do so. I must say to you plainly that I can offer you no salary or any benefits. If my point is not yet clear, perhaps an illustration will help. For example, I do not even have a bed of my own to sleep on."

But Jesus simply and imaginatively replies: "Foxes have holes, and the birds of the air have nests; but the Son of man has nowhere to lay his head" (Luke 9:58).

Rather than the abstract statement followed by a clarifying illustration Jesus has a dramatic confrontation, briefly stated in metaphorical, if not poetic terms. A lofty affirmation about the person of Jesus permeates his metaphorical answer. Theological implications oblige the mind to move out from this compact center in a number of directions. All this takes place at once in an intense imaginative encounter. To assume that we can capture all that happens in a parable in an abstract definition is to misunderstand the nature of Jesus' own preaching.

As a preacher, Jesus trusts creative and artistic speech, the use of story, parable, and metaphor to do more than just color and clothe the meaning of abstract reasoning; rather, he uses his imaginative forms to create meaning.[41] This is how we should properly understand Jesus' preaching through parables. As Kenneth Bailey argues, Jesus' stories and parables serve as extended metaphors "and as such it is not a delivery system for an idea but a house in which the reader/listener is invited to take up residence."[42]

---

40. Ibid.

41. For more on Jesus' parables as art, and Jesus as an artist, see Jones, *The Art and Truth of the Parables.*

42. Bailey, *Jesus,* 281.

What all of these examples suggests about Jesus' own preaching, is that he trusted his artistic creativity as he used all the resources available within God's creation to create meaning for others. His own selected images, metaphors, forms, and pictures appealed to the hearer's own imaginative powers in ways that propositional and abstract statements of truth cannot rival.[43] In this sense, we see Jesus' own human agency at work in preaching as an artist in action bringing us into communion with the Father, through the work of the Spirit. In other words, Jesus the man used his human creativity and imagination in ways that invited ours, so that we might participate in the love of the Father and Son. Meaning, this Jesus used his human creativity to invite all our cognitive capacities to live into his Father's kingdom and will. In this way, all the work we do with our minds changes as we try to love God with all our life in response to Jesus. This suggests to us that Jesus had a much fuller sense of what poetic preaching could accomplish, and opens up the door to take seriously his own creative and artistic witness. It is this artistic witness of Jesus in action that is significant as we think of proposing a new "as" for a homiletic identity.[44]

This relationship between art and preaching is echoed by Edward Farley, who argues preaching is a performance of aesthetic art.[45] Just as Bailey gives us categories to see how Jesus worked artistically within his given cultural context, so Farley gives us some framework to thinking about how the preacher's work is fundamentally artistic. Farley sees preaching as an art form because it embodies, and at the same time, transforms three primary features of artistic activity: engagement with the world, creativity, and imagination.[46] First, he suggests that art is accomplished only in and through the distinctive way the artist engages the world: the way the world evokes a distinctive, personal response. Another way of saying this is that art is a way of *seeing* the world. In artistic disciplines, like painting, sculpture, or composing music, individual experience of the world is part of the artistic expression of the artist.[47] In this sense, preachers have something in common with traditional artists, because each sermon is an artistic expression that speaks to human experience in the world.

43. It is important to note that the two are linked, and both are critical for the task of theology and the preaching life. Pictures easily trump, but do not necessarily replace, abstract arguments.

44. See for example, Brueggemann, *Bible*, 15–16.

45. Farley, "Can Preaching Be Taught?" 171–80.

46. Ibid, 173.

47. See Williams, *Grace and Necessity*, 137–74. Here Williams suggests that this opening to the world is what allows our knowing of the world to be always unfolding by how we see and experience reality.

Second, Farley understands preaching to be an art because it reflects the skill of creativity. "No poet," says Farley, "is content to clone someone else's poem—someone else's experience bodied forth and woven into words."[48] The personal experience of being drawn out creatively in one's encounter with the world never simply repeats the ordinary, everyday activities of another. It adds something to what was before. Likewise, the preacher's work is communicating deeper realities that resist copycat expressions. It must be said that though human creation is not a copycat, nor is it a rival to God's creating *ex nihilo*, it is a response to a "wager on transcendence."[49] The sermon, like the sculpture, the poem, the painting, the dance, is always in some way pointing towards the possibility of faith—of something outside of ourselves that we are trying to see clearly or arrive at.

Third, Farley suggests that because both art and preaching are a creative expression of an individual discovery and response, both require the human powers of imagination.[50] The imagination is a human gift that would take a lifetime to clarify and examine. But for our purpose we are using the term imagination in its most basic sense, which is "having an image or concept of something *not* presently perceived," which is the pervasive human capacity to feel or portray the nonexistent—the mere possibility of an unrealized future.[51] This gift of the imagination is the key to all possibility of experiencing hope. The power to imagine an alternative reality or future is the power to transcend our present circumstances. Preaching, if nothing else, involves the imagination because the sermon is the place to envision the possibilities of a "glory yet to be revealed" (Rom 8:18). In other words, preaching is an act that allows one to envision an alternative *telos* in and beyond the actualities in which we are immersed.[52]

If we apply these insights to Jesus' own preaching ministry, we see in some sense that his preaching was artistic because his preaching embodied all three of these formal features of aesthetic art. First, Christ's preaching was accomplished in and through the distinctive way he experienced the world, or the way the world evoked a distinctive way of *seeing* reality in light of his unique relationship with the Father and the Spirit. For example, Jesus own message was shaped by his vision of reality that "the Kingdom of God is at hand" (Luke 17:21). This kingdom had a distinct trinitarian

48. Farley, "Can Preaching be Taught?" 174.

49. See Richard Bauckham and Trevor Hart's excellent book, *Hope Against Hope*, 48–49.

50. Farley, "Can Preaching Be Taught?" 174–75.

51. For an excellent philosophical overview to provide conceptual clarification of the imagination, see Stevenson, "Twelve Conceptions of Imagination," 238–59.

52. See Bauckham and Hart, *Hope Against Hope*, 51.

relationship. Christ preached out of a unique experience of unity with the Father and the Spirit (John 14:15–24). Second, Farley suggests that the skill of preaching, like aesthetic art, involves creation or innovation more than repetition or application. Jesus did more than just repeat the tradition. He absorbed it and reframed it creatively in light of his vision of reality. We see this in his reading of the Isaiah text in the synagogue at Nazareth, where Jesus says, "today this has been fulfilled in your hearing" (Luke 4:21). Jesus is creatively suggesting an innovative new way of reading a traditional text in light of his own presence. He did not merely repeat the words, he embodied an innovative new meaning. Likewise, Jesus preached with daring extension of the tradition through his "you have heard it said, but I say to you" pattern of speech in the Sermon on the Mount. In this way, Jesus absorbed and reframed the tradition through his relationship to God as the blessed Son of God. And third we can see Jesus own preaching as art, when Farley suggests that preaching is an expression of imaginative faithfulness to God. He suggests that the call to give language to God's grace always involves imagination, that strange human capacity to feel or portray what is not visible, or give language to the hope of an unrealized future. Jesus' own preaching ministry was marked by such an imaginative hopefulness (John 14:25–31; 16:25–33; 17:20–26); we witness Jesus' imaginative skill in the parables about the kingdom of God (Mark 26:29); we witness Jesus' imaginative hope of an unrealized future, when he prays to God for the forgiveness of those who killed him (Luke 23:34). Jesus' ministry had the marks of aesthetic art—where imaginative interpretation of Scripture and tradition, of his preaching and healing, and his dying and rising were marked by a profound imagination shaped by the hope in the work of God.

By rooting the identity of The Preacher as Liturgical Artist in the soil of Christ's vicarious humanity, it reorients us to see that the sermon is an event that participates in Christ's work of creation. It also suggests that the preacher can preach with the same freedom and creativity that Christ practiced, because the preacher is called to follow the logic and path of God's revelation. By seeing Christ's own preaching through poetic and artistic lenses, we see that Jesus utilizes the full force of his humanity to embody and proclaim the message of the kingdom of God, a message that has the power to shatter our perceived realties. In this light, preaching is an artistic action that participates in the mystery of the Spirit's creative work of Christian formation, and it takes seriously the full discipline, creativity, and craft of Jesus' own human skill and wisdom.[53]

53. Rowan Williams makes a similar point in *Grace and Necessity*, 150. Williams suggests that understanding the work of art as participating in an alternative presence is what holds so much possibility for deepening and forming our understanding of

Jesus, Creation, and Creativity

Developing the identity of The Preacher as Liturgical Artist in light of the vicarious humanity of Christ and the artistically sophisticated preaching ministry of Jesus leads to a nuanced notion of creativity. Essentially, this new metaphor points us in the direction of grounding human creativity in the incarnation. This requires seeing the connection between oneself and Jesus, Jesus and creation, and Jesus in the Trinity.

The incarnation of Jesus relocates divine and human creativity among us. Eugene Peterson suggests that "the birth of Jesus provides the kerygmatic focus for receiving, entering into, and participating in creation, for *living* the creation and not just using it or taking it for granted."[54] In other words, the Christian life is the practice of living in what the Word has done and is doing. In this section it is critical to make the way of living the creation clear. Specifically, it is necessary to describe and define the nature of human creativity under Jesus with the Father in the Spirit.

To understand the nature of creativity in relation to the triune God it is necessary to briefly describe the trinitarian character of creation. In this section we will use the thought of Robert Jenson to help us in this task. Jenson suggests that a proper understanding of creation begins with the affirmation that "God speaks the world into being."[55] This is closely related to his unrelenting assertion that the Word God the Father speaks to be himself and create all things is the person of Jesus.[56] The creation of heaven and earth, according to Jenson, takes place as the Father speaks in and through Jesus, who as a human speaks on our behalf.[57] In other words, it is the incarnate Word of God, who endured every human weakness in his own flesh, who pours out the heart of all humanity before the Father, and who is now standing in our place to speak for us that creates the world with the Father and the Spirit.[58] This understanding of the Trinity and the triune character of creation leads back to the vicarious humanity of Christ and leads on to a unique notion of human creativity.

This first connection to make clear is that Jesus is the key to understanding creation. Barth goes into immense detail (four volumes' worth) to press this point: "We have established that from every angle Jesus Christ

ourselves in relationship to another.

54. Eugene Peterson, *Christ Plays*, 53; emphasis original.

55. Jenson, *Systematic Theology*, 6.

56. Ibid., 7–8.

57. Ibid., 9.

58. Ibid., 270.

is the key to the secret of creation."[59] Starting with this secret, Jenson argues that Jesus is the eternal Word who speaks into existence all things in heaven and on earth, visible and invisible, whether thrones or dominions (Col 1:16). This same Word is spoken into humanity as Jesus in order to take our humanity and recreate it in himself. This is the fundamental insight the Gospel of John presses in the prologue, when the poet remixes Genesis 1 to show that Jesus is the Word made flesh and also the God of creation: "In the beginning was the Word, and the Word was with God, and the Word was God. He was in the beginning with God. All things came into being through him, and without him not one thing came into being" (John 1:1–3).[60] In other words, Jesus is God with the God of Genesis 1 that continues to speak and sustain creation's existence.

If we understand Jesus as the source "of all things in heaven and earth," and we put this work within the context of the Trinity where Jesus acts through and in the Spirit according to the will of the Father, then it follows that human creativity is by necessity a participation in the creative work of the Father, Son, and Holy Spirit. Preachers and theologians are those who understand that they are invited into God's creative work as God's image bearers redeemed in the "first born of creation" (Col 1:15). This self-understanding gives a new direction for our creativity through Jesus as we live in his Spirit. This also grounds the idea of creativity in the vicarious humanity of Jesus, and at the same time opens up a place to focus on the Spirit. Likewise, it is the Spirit that frees us to participate in that work and enlivens our work to be both faithful and beautiful.

In this context, it becomes clear that the key to understanding creativity is to understand who Jesus is and what Jesus does in conversation with the Spirit and the Father. A proper understanding of Jesus' indwelling the human condition, in order to recreate it, relocates creativity in the Trinity's living discourse. Jenson presses this point when he writes:

> The triune God's very life is mutual investment: in the classical
> formulation, a triune identity simply *is* a subsisting relation to
> the other triune identities. And whether you are willing to speak
> of the divine identities' *perichoresis* as divine "history" or not is,
> I think, mostly a matter of conceptual taste. *This* God's salvation,
> the "deification" to which *he* draws us, is not a vanishing into the
> sea of abstract perfection but our total inclusion in the life of the

59. *CD* III/1, §40, 27, vol. 13, (28).

60. The New Testament witness to the christological qualification of creation is neatly assembled by Gunton, *Christ and Creation*, 22–30.

three identities, and that is to say, given John's teaching, in their living discourse.[61]

This clarifies our context for understanding the dynamic relationship between creation and preaching. The sermon's creativity is generative in the Word spoken through the Spirit. The Word spoken cannot help but be creative, because it is the same Word from whom "all things came into being." This means that human creativity is tied to the creativity of the Word. When we speak of the Word, it is also really the Word speaking. When we preach it is really our sermon, but since Christ knows us better than we know ourselves and since he himself was true human for our sakes, it is also really his sermon, and it can become our sermon only because it was his sermon. Meaning, it is the sermon of the human nature assumed by Christ that comes before the Father that allows our preaching to be drawn into God's own proclamation. In this light, we see that encouraging homiletic creativity is not a "rival like unto God," where we are encouraging the preacher to be the "center of consciousness" who must "bring forth an expression of himself in the form of a new creation," or who must "struggle to create in freedom," to "pursue novelty, originality, innovation."[62] Rather, by locating creativity in the Word's eternal dialogue, the preacher is freed to participate in the gift of the Spirit's true creative Word, which when spoken is at one and the same time a command and invitation to participate in the triune God's creative discourse.

The consequence of locating creativity in the eternal dialogue allows us to see that human creativity starts with God. We speak only because the Word speaks, and because this Word speaks for us. Each sermon is an echo of Christ's proclamation of the covenant to the Father for us. Faithful preaching accepts and rejoices in this reality of grace. Jenson makes this point when he argues that it is through the Word that we join Trinity's eternal conversation: "God addresses us, and we respond to what he has said; then we turn to others also, to involve them in the conversation."[63]

The basic point to underline in relationship to human creativity is that we never start from scratch. Rather, human creativity is a consequence of God addressing us, which allows us to respond through our speaking, and participate in the larger conversation of God's ongoing discourse. This discourse not only happened, but also continues to happen because God is loquacious. The triune God is a speaking God. All creation and human

61. Jenson, "Joining the Eternal Conversation," 33; emphases original.

62. Wolterstorff, *Art in Action*, 51–52. For further reflection on the act of creating, see also Beardsley, "On the Creation of Art," 291–304.

63. Jenson, "Joining the Eternal Conversation," 34.

creativity has its source in the simple sermon: "Then God said, let there be
. . ." (Gen 1:3). This God who speaks is the same God who speaks as Jesus
and continues to be speaking in and through the Spirit. In other words,
creativity has its location within a divine dialogue between the Father, Son,
and Holy Spirit. More pointedly, preaching is faithful insofar as the preacher
participates through the Spirit in Christ's creative and beautiful work of responding to the Father. The preacher does this by tracing the connections
between the Word's life and ours in a way that continues his work of reconciling all things to the Father in the Spirit. In this sense, preaching is an act
of continuing re-creation where Jesus is using us to gather up his people in
anticipation of their final entrance into the triune life. This entrance is what
allows Paul to proclaim that anyone in Christ is a new creation, where everything old has passed away, and everything has become new (2 Cor 5:17).

To resist being recreated in and through the Word is to resist what God
is doing to give us total inclusion in God's living conversation. Likewise, to
resist being creative in and through the Word is either to resist the character
of Jesus' works or to insist on a flaccid notion of independence and creativity. We too often think of creativity as an entailment of a freedom from
creation and relationship, and ultimately God, rather than being experienced in a freedom that comes from the specificity of being *for* creation and
relationship. This is one of the central arguments of Barth's understanding
of providence in *Church Dogmatics* III/3, where God's lordship over and in
creaturely occurrence is presented not as restrictive, but by what might be
called an act of purposive integration, through which the definiteness of
the creature is upheld.[64] This means that human creativity can exist only
on the basis of the divine preservation of the creature. Therefore, creaturely
creativity is constantly formed and directed by the permission given to it by
the God of creation. Significantly, this ordering and forming of creativity is
not the degradation, but the glorification of the creature on the basis of the
principle that human agency is defined exclusively out of the event of God's
creative Word, in which God commands and humanity is called to faithful
action. As John Webster points out, "Limitation is not about deficiency, still
less about some divine force inhibiting legitimate human flourishing; it is
rather the creature's quite specific path to glory assigned and maintained
by the ordering acts of God."[65] If human creativity is grounded in this condition of God's activity, then the notion of the tortured artist who suffers
to pursue a creative life through autonomous independence is absurd. It is

---

64. For example, see *CD* III/3, §49.1, 85-86, vol. 17, (86); §49.3, 167-68, vol. 17,
(164); §49.3, 170, vol. 17, (166); §49.3, 195-96, vol. 17, (192).

65. Webster, *Barth's Ethics of Reconciliation*, 72.

within the limits of the Word, and in relationship to the Word through the Spirit, that humans experience true creative possibility and expression. This is due to the fact that the limitation of life on our own has no creative future, whereas participation in the divine dialogue of the Trinity is an opportunity to explore God's infinite character. One of these ways of being creative has a future, and the other does not. The end of resistance to a future in the Word is lifelessness, which is ultimately the elimination of creativity.

Preaching by necessity needs to participate in the work of the Word's new creation that happens anytime the Word is spoken. This is what gives preaching a unique sense of anticipation. Any time the Word is spoken something new is happening. This is why preachers need a homiletic identity that encourages the Word's relationship between creation and preaching. Preachers proclaim a Word that is at the same time the source of creation. If preachers are faithful to this Word, it is impossible for them not to participate in God's continuing creation. This is due to the connection between the Word and the law of God. Following Luther's footsteps, Jenson tries to make this clear by suggesting that the Word that is in the divine being is an uttered word by which something is enjoined. This is what Jenson means when he argues, "The Word that eternally is with God so is God, is discourse, utterance."[66] This discourse is fundamentally creative and commands us to be creative, to have our being and way of preaching and living in and with and under the creative Word, Jesus.

The converse of this is also true. If the preacher's words are not faithful to the Word who creates "all things," then the sermon will fail to participate in the basic dynamic of the incarnation's new creation. The Word is always taking something old and from it making something new. In the incarnation, the Son takes the raw materials of our humanity, transforms them into something beautiful through the power of the Spirit, and offers them back to God as a new creation.[67] In this sense, the act of Christian preaching allows the hearer to be caught up in the creative act of God's new creation that begins with speaking. Failure to see Jesus' work as primarily creative speech is to fail to see the role of the Spirit in the incarnation and the gift of the Spirit that frees us to do what Jesus did. If one is in full participation in the Spirit, it cannot help but lead to a participation in a life of God's creative discourse. Thus, the question is not how can the preacher be creative; rather the question is how can the preacher *not* be creative? Creativity is entailed by a relationship with the Word through the Spirit. What Jesus does in the incarnation to re-create humanity through his Word spoken and embodied,

66. Jenson, "Joining the Eternal Conversation," 32.
67. Jenson, *Systematic Theology*, 160.

is connected to what Jesus is doing through the Spirit to re-create humanity in his image today. The Word spoken is always the command to create, sustain, and fulfill creation.

By putting the identity of The Preacher as Liturgical Artist in the context of the Trinity and the witness of Jesus as an artist, we see there is a connection between the way God creates, sustains, and will ultimately remake the world through his Word *and* the call and act of preaching. Consequently, preachers are creative, not because they are extraordinary visionaries, but because they participate in the creative dialogue of the Trinity that is responsible for the creation we live our life in. Because of the Spirit working with the priestly ministry of Christ, we are invited to live into our identity as God's image bearers and so are given a new source and context for our artistic creativity. This is significant because it grounds the idea of creativity in the incarnation. If God does indeed leave us with things to finish, then creativity may be held to be essential rather than just optional, because it highlights the place of our contribution vis-à-vis the Father's own creative action and purposes in the Son, through the Holy Spirit. This homiletic identity intends to make this connection clear by describing preachers as artists who find their creative role and inspiration in the life of the triune God.

A NEW "AS"

The identity of "The Preacher" includes the best characteristics of the other identities we have considered, while avoiding some of the weaknesses. Emphasizing art in relationship to preaching is wise because art *teaches* and has the power to proclaim like a *herald*. This means that the preacher can embrace the wisdom of the larger homiletic tradition and at the same time push preaching in creative directions by encouraging a new way of thinking about the relationship between the artist and the preacher.

These new directions or possibilities open up when we ground the ministry of proclamation in the double ministry of Christ. By grounding The Preacher as Liturgical Artist in the vicarious humanity of Christ, preachers are challenged to attend to the person of Jesus and the gift of participating in his ongoing work. If the person of Jesus also reframes our notion of human creativity, then his work must also shape our creative work. This is true in the two senses discussed above: Jesus was a creative preacher and is the Word that created all things and continues to recreate all things. If we understand the Word's work of creation to be continuing, not finished, then every act of preaching can be a participation in Christ's creative ministry to "reconcile to himself all things" (Col 1:20). It also means that the act of preaching is formed by his creative ministry recorded in the Gospels. Preaching participates in the ongoing ministry of Christ that seeks to fulfill creation's proper end to glorify God. This possibility of participating with Christ, in the Spirit, to reconcile all things provides an energy and rationale for an identity that encourages the metaphoric relationship between the artist and the preacher.

Working in this framework allows us to propose a new "as," or metaphor, as a way to understand the preacher. Preachers are artists who have a role in God's drama of salvation as they are called to faithfully and creatively reiterate the gospel. Preachers are artists who are called to give witness to the person and work of Jesus and the Father with confidence that the Spirit enlivens their words. Through the Spirit the preacher is an artist in action who invites God's people to participate in the continuing creativity of the eternal discourse of the Trinity within the context of the church's liturgical work. As one of the church's liturgical artists, preachers help God's people imagine a new way to see reality and live a life as a new creation in the context of the revealed light that the darkness cannot overcome. By this revelation, the preacher is freed to use all of humanity's artistic gifts in preaching, because our humanity is fully reconciled in the person of Jesus' ongoing artistic action of creation. By this, the preacher is never thrown back on himself or herself, but is always rooted in the grace of God. This is what we mean by associating the preacher with the identity of an artist.

The idea of art in reference to preaching, even to Christ's preaching, may strike some as a somewhat optimistic, if not an idealistic, description of what goes on in a pulpit. For many, this proposal will be received with suspicion. For some, the very idea of the artist in relationship to the preacher may give the impression that preaching has no frame of accountability or point of reference, or encourages preachers to imagine a new gospel, rather than preaching the witness that has been passed to them within the tradition of the church. Some may also think that offering preachers an artistic identity would encourage a witness concerned more with entertainment and amusement than the faithful proclamation of the Word of God. On the other hand, there are those who would object to the homiletic identity of The Preacher As Liturgical Artist because preachers would defile the idea of the pure artist. For them preachers may conjure an image of a peddler of religious goods and services using the pulpit to fleece the weak-minded or promote an institutional propaganda. Indeed, in the popular imagination, the word "preacher" does not often inspire the thought of the gracious deployment of language in service of *all good things*. The objection is that if preachers are to be perceived through an artistic lens, then the association might in reverse taint artists as those seeking to manipulate fears, control behavior, and inspire guilt.

Richard Lischer addresses these concerns when he argues that if one's notion of art is limited to what is new or restricted to inspired poetic self-expression, and if "art" means inspirational stories and pretty metaphors, then preaching will not be experienced as artistic. However, Lischer comments, "If the idea of art is something the creature, who knows she is a creature, sings back to the Creator with something of the creator's own *pizzazz* (as Annie Dillard put it), then preaching has the potential, at least, to be more like art and less like an endowed lecture series . . . If you think of art as part discipline, part craft, and part mystery, we may be on to something."[68]

This points us in the right direction. What we have been arguing for is something significantly different than our popular notion of the artist. We are suggesting that what is needed is a homiletic identity that encourages a particular way of artistic thinking conceived within the vicarious ministry of Christ. To be sure, this way of thinking may lead to certain habits and assumptions that shape the way one preaches and the way others hear preaching. But what is key is to maintain an identity that refuses to reduce the mystery and power of the Christian gospel to an idea, lesson, technique, or a value we can control. As Barth suggests:

> We must realize that the Christian message does not at its heart express a concept or an idea, nor does it recount an anonymous history to be taken as truth and reality only in concepts and ideas. Certainly the history is inclusive, i.e., it is one which includes in itself the whole event of the "God with us" and to that extent the history of all those to whom the "God with us" applies. But it recounts this history and speaks of its inclusive power and significance in such a way that it declares a name, binding the history strictly and indissolubly to this name and presents it as the story of the bearer of this name. This means that all the concepts and ideas used in this report (God, man, world, eternity, time, even salvation, grace, transgression, atonement and any others) can derive their significance only from the bearer of this name and from His history, and not the reverse.[69]

If we are going to think of the preacher and the artist together, then we must begin with the name Jesus and the confession that we live in Jesus and work in his name as those who embody the redemption of a new creation. The good news of the gospel is that Jesus has not stopped preaching on our

68. Lischer, *End of Words*, 107.

69. *CD* IV/1, §57.1, 14, vol. 21, (16).

behalf. The gospel is not an idea, but is grounded in the continual work of the risen Christ who through the Spirit has now laid out a new creation and put this new action of creation in us. As Eugene Peterson writes, "There is no living worth its salt that is not the consequence of the action of God in Jesus through the Holy Spirit."[70] All gospel preaching is rooted in this confession. The name of Jesus and the story of his life, death, and resurrection launch us into an entire new paradigm of good news to rethink the notion of creativity and artistry in our human experience. The Christian preacher is always working in and with the reality of Jesus' work. In this light, we are invited to rethink the concept of an artist in relation to the artist Jesus Christ. As related to preaching, it requires a renewed reflection on orality, language, imagination, judgment, and performance within Jesus' continuing acts of creation.

It may be helpful to ask again: Where do we see Jesus doing the work of new creation through the Spirit? We see Jesus doing this work in his *words* that when *spoken* have the power to create new dynamics for life. When the Word became flesh and lived among us, the power of God's speech began to bring healing and reconciliation into existence. "Be made clean," Jesus said to the leper, and "immediately his leprosy was cleansed" (Matt 8:3). To the centurion he said, "Let it be done for you according to your faith" (8:13); with those words, the man's servant was healed. "Talitha cumm" (Mark 5:41–42), Jesus said and instantly the little girl rose from her deathly sleep. To people throughout the Gospels he said, "Your sins are forgiven," and with his utterance came the moment of grace. When the stone was rolled away, Jesus stepped into the light to inaugurate a new day, proclaiming the words, "Peace be with you!" to his disciples (John 20:19). These words were not mere words, but the declaration of victory after a long, cold war.

In each of these examples, Jesus is creating something new through his spoken words. The one who created all things with his Father in the Spirit is now alive beyond death and creating a new world as he speaks as the resurrected Lord. In Jesus' proclamation of the kingdom of God, his words create a world for others to step into and be healed, and consequently is understood to move us towards fulfillment, or *telos*, of creation. When the Word speaks to people something creative happens: what is old is transformed into something new, what is broken is healed, what is blind is given sight. In short, the Word creates reality.

Jesus is the key to creation, as he is the perfection of the sermon that begins with the words, "Then God said . . . " (Gen 1:2).[71] This is the case

---

70. Peterson, *Christ Plays*, 230.

71. For example, in the creation story of Genesis only God is attributed the powers

because Jesus is the eternal Word who continues to speak new reality into existence through the Spirit. The Word continues to separate the light from the darkness and orders the chaos into a reality that is best described as intrinsically "good."

It is significant to note that in Hebrew the word for "word" is *dabar*. *Dabar* implies more than a "spoken word," it also entails an "affair," "event," and "action," meaning the act of speaking a word (*dabar*) in the creation narrative has a certain dynamic energy and power of its own.[72] In this context, creation is clearly connected to the act of God's own speech. This relationship between God speaking and creation has clear implications for thinking about preaching. The sermon is a place where God's acts of creation are in motion through the Word spoken in the Spirit. Because the Word spoken is also an event of creation, it holds the possibility that in the acts of preaching something new is embodied through the performance of the preacher's words. This is artistic work that involves making decisions about the language and form of a sermon, as well as the bodily performance of the preacher in space and time. In light of Jesus' work of creation and the way it completes God's way of creating/speaking, how is it possible for the preacher not to embrace an artistic identity?

The preacher participates in the act of creation through preaching the Word, who through the Spirit continues to speak creation into being. Consequently, preaching is an activity that is intimately involved in God's active Word that is unpredictable and uncontrollable, and yet full of possible beauty. For example, out of the mess of Genesis 1:2 came the architectonic glories of vv. 3–31; out of the mess of Mary's out-of-wedlock pregnancy came the glories of the incarnation and the means of the world's salvation; and out of the mess of the pulpit comes the glorious news that a crucified and resurrected King is even now making all things new. Relocating creativity through the Spirit in Christ's vicarious humanity allows the preacher to see that Jesus is still working, still interceding, still speaking on our behalf. Whenever the Word speaks something new is birthed, or something old is

---

of creation or creativity (*Bara*). Human creativity takes place in the context of creation. Our creativity is always preceded by God's creative action. Only God creates (*Bara*) without limit and from nothing. When considering human creativity in relation to the doctrine of creation, there is something that we ignore at our own peril. It is the staggeringly creative power of the Word of God. Everything happens in the creation account because God speaks it into existence. Nine times we are told, "And God said . . ." And correspondingly nine times we are told ". . . and it was so." This haunting Genesis refrain becomes a kind of metronome marking the cadence of creation's first sermon. Out of that sermon reality was created. In the opening of Scripture, we see the Word that creates reality.

72. See Brueggemann, *Genesis*, 24.

redeemed through the Spirit. Christ's speaking has the power to take what is and make surprising new circumstances, new possibilities of what is taking shape through the Spirit. In this context, we can see that the preacher is an artist only as he or she relates to who Jesus is, what Jesus did, and what Jesus continues to do through the Spirit.

The call to see that Christ, in the Spirit, is speaking through us and for us, frees the preacher to trust that the process that seems messy is sometimes the place where there is the potential for the Spirit's most creative work. The sermon often leads to surprises that the preacher may never have intended, resulting in an experience never imagined. The words that were crafted for the sermon take on a life of their own in the sermon. Thus, the preacher is freed from a writ formula for preaching, but leans into the text, listening to its forms, its language, its wisdom, and from this crafts a fresh and unique reflection that is new to the church. In the Spirit, each sermon and its process is a call to participate in the work of the Word's ongoing creation. This means that the sermon is a craft that trusts that something like ordinary language is charged with extraordinary meaning. In other words, Jesus' oral creativity opens the possibility that the preacher's own speech participates in the triune God's eternal discourse.

We see Jesus using words carefully and creatively. We are reminded that God's Word never returns empty (Isa 55:11). If preachers take seriously the call to speak the Word into the messiness of the real world, then they will experience the gift of new creation through the Spirit that hovers over it all. This vision of preachers as artists forming goodness out of the messiness of the broken creation invites and challenges the preacher to use words wisely. Those who preach the Word are called to be stewards of words, by crafting new worlds with a language that is "able to accomplish abundantly for more than all we can ask or imagine" (Eph 3:20). Words are both the preacher's tools and materials used by Christ. In other words, the preacher's words spoken or listened to, written or read—are intended to do something *in* us, giving us a wholeness, pointing to holiness, wisdom, and hope in God, because they echo the divine discourse of the Word. The use of words is always an active performance that forms us. Eugene Peterson writes, "It is the very nature of language to form rather than inform. When language is personal, which it is at its best, it reveals; and revelation is always formative—we don't know more, we become more. Our best users of language, poets and lovers and children and saints use words to *make*—make intimacies, make character, make beauty, make goodness, make truth."[73]

---

73. Peterson, *Eat This Book*, 24; emphasis original.

Richard Lischer suggests precisely this when he argues that the goal of preaching is not to inform, it is rather to "*form* those who hear and share them for a life of faithfulness."[74] This formation, argues Lischer, is the consequence of artistic forms of preaching.

Words shaped by Jesus and offered in the Spirit are always forming something new in us. In this sense, crafting words is a primary ally in God's work of revelation. Like a brush in the hand of a skilled painter, so is the right word from the mouth of a preacher; it can reveal or open us up to a new world to ponder. Therefore, the call to creative preaching entails crafting words as a responsibility. As an artist for Christ, the preacher is the protector and steward of the church's language, keeping it from misuse, exploitation, and harm.[75] By attending to words with the discipline and skill of a master artist, preaching has the power to draw those who hear a sermon into a deeper communion with Jesus the Word, his Father, and their Spirit.

Preachers are called to preach with and like Jesus as they depict a world in which the radical claims of the gospel may be spoken with faithful clarity. This clarity requires us to reconsider the nature of words and reconsider the significance of a disciplined imagination.

Imagination is what makes human life meaningful and engagement with the world possible. No human being can really thrive without it. Imagination is the foundation of human perception, of understanding and interpretation, and of whatever deep probings we may make into the significance, meaning, and mystery of human life and reality. It is not just a cognitive phenomenon, although it is the foundation of all cognition. "Its impetus comes," according to the philosopher Mary Warnock, "from the emotions as much as from the reason, from the heart as much as from the head."[76]

The Preacher As Liturgical Artist understands the powers of imagination as one of the chief glories of Jesus; through his vicarious ministry on our behalf, our imagination finds redemption in him. This is why Eugene Peterson argues that the imagination is essential for Christian ministry, "Right now, one of the essential Christian ministries in and to our ruined world is the recovery and exercise of the imagination. Ages of faith have always been ages rich in imagination . . . Is it time to get aggressive, time for the Christian community to recognize, honor, and commission its pastors

74. Lischer, *The End of Words*, 107.

75. The idea of the preacher as the steward of the church's language was inspired by Lindbeck, *Nature of Doctrine*.

76. Warnock, *Imagination*, 196.

as Masters of the Imagination, joining our poets, singers, and storytellers as partners in evangelical witness."[77]

It is the call to commission preachers as "masters of the imagination" that this identity seeks to fulfill. The imagination is essential for the Christian life, argues Samuel Wells, because "it is the task of the imagination to change or challenge the presumed necessities of the world, to resist the implication that what the Christian community receives are givens rather than gifts."[78] It is in precisely the *redeemed* imagination in Jesus that The Preacher As Liturgical Artist experiences God pushing us out of the presumed world where most of us are trapped.[79]

Jesus' own preaching life was shaped with the possibility of a disciplined imagination. Jesus could do this because he himself was the imaginative embodiment he was pointing others to see. The mustard seed could represent the kingdom of God. The bread could be Christ's body. The wind could be the Spirit. Two loaves and five fish could be a feast. Jesus' imagination saw the ordinary pregnant with extraordinary meaning in light of his own presence. Jesus not only embodies the meaning, he is the meaning of the message. Jesus is the meaning because he is the person, fully human and fully divine, the active agent of our salvation who lives in perfect union with the Father through the Spirit, and who is beyond reproach. This extends even to his imagination. Jesus' homiletic imagination is an extension of his communion with the Father through the Spirit. Jesus is free to imaginatively experience covenantal promise, Scripture and sacrament, prayer and preaching, fellowship and hospitality in a way that assumes this eternal communion of the Trinity. This life of communion does not reduce Jesus' imagination, rather it expands it so that it sees and invites all creation to find new life and meaning in him, and in him, through the Spirit, in a new life of obedience to the Father. Consequently, it also expands our imagination. For in Christ is the possibility of a communion with the source of all creation. Jesus is so powerful, so unsettling, and so buoyant because as a preacher he has a tongue salted by an eternal conversation with the Father that both exhibits and establishes the mutual "indwelling" or "perichoretic unity" of the triune God of grace.[80] In short, Jesus is the master example of a preacher

77. Peterson, *Under the Unpredictable Plant*, 171–72.

78. Wells, *Improvisation*, 125.

79. See Brueggemann, *Finally Comes the Poet*.

80. See Torrance, *Worship*, 31–32. "A *two-fold relationship*" is thus established between the triune God and ourselves, through the Spirit. It is a relationship between God and humanity realized vicariously for us in Christ and at the same time a relationship between Christ and the church, that we might participate by the Spirit of Jesus' communion with the Father in a life of intimate communion. In both, there is a bond of mutual love and mutual self-giving—of mutual "indwelling" or "perichoretic unity."

who embodies the disciplined imagination entailed by the identity of The Preacher As Liturgical Artist.

In this sense, there may be such a thing as a "homiletic imagination." Preachers in every tradition have an imagination and an intelligence that enables them to pull together what they perceive in the world and what they contemplate in their souls in the process of creating new works of artistic performance, what we call a sermon, which in turn helps the rest of us apprehend reality in entirely new ways. The imagination relies on individual gifts but is also shaped by community, education, artistic tradition, and above all, the relations of the perichoretic unity.

The Preacher As Liturgical Artist is a homiletic identity that seeks to speak out of this unity, in that it desires to reflect and unleash the human powers of Jesus' imagination. The imagination of Jesus is the bridge the Holy Spirit uses to close the gap between the strange new world of the Scripture and our world. When this bridge is crossed, the Holy Spirit baptizes our imagination so that we might be transformed, or "sanctified" into a new life, a life where human desire is transformed and relocated in the life of the Son, the eternal Word made flesh for us and for our salvation.

This is significant to note because the imagination is a primary concern of both artist and preacher, though with one respective differences. Imagination is a necessary condition for any artist's work because it requires imagining possibilities of "*seeing as.*" But not all artists require a sense of hopeful possibility in God. Many artists are content to use their imagination to portray what is, with little regard to what could be in light of God's revelation in Jesus. This means that not all artists are required to *see* hope, but the imagination of the Christian preacher is. The homiletic imagination deals in the economy of hope—that is of God's gracious promise to "wipe away every tear" (Rev 21:19). Indeed, Richard Bauckham and Trevor Hart argue that this quality of hope is essential for our making of any meaning of life: "The quest for meaning, truth, goodness and beauty is closely bound up with hope as an activity of imagination in which we seek to transcend the boundaries of the present, to go beyond the given, outwards and forwards in search of something more, something better, than the given affords us."[81]

Locating preaching in Christ allows every preacher, despite the circumstances, to hope in a "glory yet to be revealed" (Rom 8:18), because Christ, right now, is raised and "is at the right hand of God, interceding on our behalf" (Rom 8:34). Preachers seek to see the world wholly, but unlike other artists, the Christian preacher is compelled to see from this hopeful

---

81. Bauckham and Hart, *Hope Against Hope*, 53.

lens that "nothing can ever separate us from the love of God in Christ Jesus our Lord" (Rom 8:39).

Hence, if we are to take seriously the ability of preachers to imagine beyond assumed reality and into another possibility where God is making all things new, then preachers cannot flinch from using or appealing to the powers of the imagination. The preacher's daring imagination of the possible is a passport to travel deeper into the truth of an eschatological vision that is breaking upon us even now. The imagination becomes the medication used by God to awaken us from our spiritual coma.[82] It is the act of speaking to this daring vision of the gospel where the imagination finds expression in the artistic work of preaching, as preaching is nothing less than effort to imagine the Word, or *Logos*, in its most exalted mood.

The imaginative power of the preacher is an evocative vision of seeing possibilities of Christ's vicarious humanity break apart fixed conclusions and press the hearer always toward new, dangerous, and imaginative possibilities of hope.[83] Announcing the gospel requires the preacher to draw on the metaphoric power of identity in Christ. Might not another way to aid preachers be to offer a homiletic identity that takes seriously Christ's preaching as a work of artistic action? If Christian preaching means preaching Christ, it cannot but reflect Christ's own creative, imaginative, and hopeful vision of reality. Arguably, preaching then cannot but be a work of aesthetic art—and preachers cannot but be artists.

Every human being lives by the power of the imagination. As Leslie Stevenson highlights, the human imagination is a complex integrating process that provides linkages between our bodies, minds, and emotions, indeed our very souls that make sense or meaning out of the world.[84] It is by means of the imagination that we are able to come really to "see" and

---

82. See Williams, *Grace and Necessity*, 147. Williams comments that the imagination is central for waking up to life: "Imagination produces not a self-contained mental construct but a vision that escapes control, that brings with it its shadow and its margins, its absences and ellipses, a *dimensional* existence as we might call it. The degree to which art is 'obedient'—not dependent on an artist's decisions or tastes—is manifest in the degree to which the product has dimensions outside of its relation to the producer, the sense of alternative space around the image, of real time and contingency in narrative, of hinterland."

83. See Bauckham and Hart, *Hope Against Hope*, 53: "The quest for meaning, truth, goodness and beauty is closely bound up with hope as an activity if imagination in which we seek to transcend the boundaries of the present, to go beyond the given, outwards and forwards in search of something more, something better, than the given affords us."

84. See Stevenson, "Twelve Conceptions of Imagination," 238. See also Johnson, *Meaning of the Body*.

understand anything at all—even, in a sense to "see" God.[85] The point we are making is that this is as true for Jesus as it is for us. Jesus lives by the power of the triune imagination, and through the Spirit, so do we.

Grounding the identity of The Preacher As Liturgical Artist in the vicarious ministry of Christ calls the preacher to not only take language and the imagination, but also the importance of human judgment, seriously. It requires the preacher to judge like an artist, by considering all things with aesthetic discernment. Preaching is not a matter of merely telling, it is a matter of showing. Flannery O'Connor, an artist from whom preachers would be wise to learn, writes this about writing fiction: "For the writer of fiction, everything has its testing point in the eye, and the eye is an organ that eventually involves the whole personality, and as much of the world as can be got into it. It involves judgment. Judgment is something that begins in the act of vision, and when it does not, or when it becomes separated from vision, then a confusion exists in the mind which transfers itself to the story."[86]

This judgment is as true for preaching as it is for the writer of fiction. Sunday after Sunday, preachers craft a world in which the radical narrative of the gospel is told with a kind of creative clarity that invites all to be full participants. But to make this invitation appealing requires a wise eye for discernment. The preacher, like the artist, needs to luxuriate in the freedoms of choice. The preacher chooses words, approximately fifteen hundred of them on a Sunday morning and three million in a vocational career.[87] These choices speak into existence an alternative reality, a projected narrative, where God's grace is understood to sustain and permeate reality. In this porous context, preachers serve as liturgical artists within the church, offering to the gathered the creative Word that invites all to respond to the triune God without coercion or manipulation. This invitation requires honoring how people experience reality.

The point being pressed is that the kind of preaching that uses the senses begins first with a particular vision of reality. This kind of vision, or *seeing*, is not something that can be bought or sold, downloaded or digitalized. When sermons suffer, preachers often look for a strategy, something practical, like a technique that promises "seven steps" to better preaching. But technique by itself is deadly. What is needed is the vision to go with it,

85. For further discussion of the nature of the imagination and its relation to the life of faith, see Dykstra, *Vision and Character*, chapter 3. There you will find an extended discussion of the sources and uses of the imagination and of the relation between imagination and revelation.

86. See O'Connor, "Writing Short Stories," 92.

87. Snow, *Impossible Vocation*, 53.

and this does not come from a formula. The kind of vision we have been discussing has its source in the revelation of the vicarious humanity of Christ. This revelation is not a commodity that can be consumed; it can only be given as a gift. When we receive this gift, we are never the same again, because our humanity is transformed in Christ's ministry of reconciliation that recreates us into new creatures who hunger with an appetite for God's presence.

This kind of seeing shapes a "habit of being" performed in Christ.[88] If we understand preaching to share in Christ's ongoing work of redemption, then preachers are performers who participate in the ongoing ministry of Christ on our behalf.[89] Kevin Vanhoozer's recent work *The Drama of Doctrine* makes this point when he suggests that the theologian and the preacher might best be understood if the metaphor of dramaturge is used, the one who advises on how best to interpret and perform the script.[90] In this sense, preaching embodies the promise to be a "faithful performance" that involves a script of the Scriptures, rehearsal of embodied movement and voice, and entails interaction with the congregation and other dramatic qualities.[91] Trevor Hart suggests the notion of artistic performance is a natural metaphor to apply in a broader way towards the Christian life, "At the very least, perhaps, the metaphor of artistic performance is suggestive in theological terms because of the fundamental religious conviction that human life is indeed lived (a work 'played out') not just in the sight or hearing of other people, but before a God who (however he may be held to be involved in things) looks on and listens with great interest, and makes judgments about what he sees and hears. This conviction grants all life lived in terms of it a 'performative' aspect from beginning to end."[92]

In this light, preaching is a performance that involves active participation by all present.[93] Preaching is a part of that dialogical liturgical move-

88. A phrase borrowed from a collection of letters by Flannery O'Connor, *The Habit of Being*.

89. For a discussion on the nature of preaching as performance, see Childers, *Performing the Word*, 15–35.

90. See Vanhoozer, *Drama of Doctrine*.

91. For more on the how the notion of performance furnishes a potentially helpful model for thinking theologically about the Christian life and Christian ministry, see Hart and Guthrie, *Faithful Performances*.

92. Ibid., 3.

93. For an example of those who have appealed to the notion of artistic performance in relation to the reading of Scripture in the church, see Lash, "Performing the Scriptures," and Young, *Art of Performance*. Neither goes beyond exposition to consider the actual phenomenology of preaching, but both are excellent resources for exploring the idea of performance that can be applied to preaching.

ment of performance that involves not only those who perform, but also those who attend the performance. Clayton Schmidt suggests that to ignore the performative quality of preaching is an error of judgment, "to shy away from matters of performance is to misunderstand the nature of the current arts that make up worship. In any public form of expression there is a time of preparation, often known as rehearsal, and a time of presentation, usually known as performance. To perform in worship is simply to do what preachers and worship leaders train and prepare to do: to give public expression to musical, dramatic, dance, or discursive forms that make up the patterns of worship."[94]

In a sense, there is no audience in worship—only performers—who all begin in the initial performance of Christ doing the will of the Father through the Spirit. Even though worshippers, like theatergoers, sit in rows and listen to the reading of the Word or the sermon, the "audience" is invited to respond in Jesus' vicarious performance on our behalf. Christ performs our needed intercession to the Father through the Spirit in our preaching and praying, in our singing, serving, and receiving the real performance of Christ in the sacraments. Thus, Christ not only performs with those who worship in his double ministry, but he also performs as the lead role that all other roles respond to. As Wells says of the ethical shaping power of performing worship, "Thus in worship Christians seek in the power of the Spirit to be conformed to the image of Christ—to act like him, think like him, be like him."[95] The preacher performs best by watching the performance of Christ—in the hope to become like him. What preachers do, as do all who worship, is respond to God's "self-performance" in Christ.[96] Consequently, as Hart highlights, God is not just the director of the performance, but an active character in his own drama:

> In the incarnation, of course, he takes flesh and becomes an actor on the stage together with us; but while his involvement in the action is certainly concentrated here it is not limited to this particular part. More widely, the perception of Christian faith is, as one recent study has it, that "If Christian faith is from start to finish a performance" it is so precisely because "our God is a performing God who has invited us to join in the performance that is God's life."[97]

94. Schmidt, *Too Deep for Words*, 30.

95. Wells, *Improvisation*, 84.

96. Bartow, *God's Human Speech*, 3.

97. Stanley Hauerwas (with James Fodor) in Hauerwas, *Performing the Faith*, 77.

The point to emphasize is that in the Spirit, the resurrected Jesus is still performing on our behalf. This performance takes place within the vicarious ministry of Christ as our words are taken by Christ, in the Spirit, and offered back to God as Christ's own. What we cannot do, God has done for us in Jesus Christ. Jesus Christ performs for us, in our name, to offer that perfect performance of submission to the Father. In this way, Jesus calls the preacher to be identified in a "wonderful exchange" as Christ's priestly performance of intercession through the Spirit, frees our performance through the vicarious "exchange" that happens when God comes to us in Jesus to fulfill his purposes of a new creation.[98]

We see then, that the triune God is still active in the preacher's performance of the Scriptures. God is not a spectator watching us perform them; rather our performance in worship is always a response to the performance God has already begun. [99] Jesus is God's self-performance, and we are able to join that performance through the Spirit because our humanity is vicariously performed in Christ, through the Holy Spirit, to the Father. Thus, The Preacher As Liturgical Artist's emphasis on mastering performance is not focused primarily on mastering our performance. Instead, this identity encourages preachers to participate in the ongoing performance of the vicarious humanity of Christ, who is performing with us, in the Spirit, for the Father, who wills and commissions this performance on our behalf.

This may seem obvious, but many preachers lose sight of this trinitarian dynamic of our human performance. It is easy to do. In any kind of creative work (especially work that takes place in public and often under considerable pressure), it is our natural tendency to attend primarily to our own performance, to our own action, to what we ourselves are doing, to how well we are performing—and, perhaps, especially, to how other people think we are doing. But the performance and imagination, the language and judgment of the preacher are not something to be achieved or attained. It comes as a gift. At the very heart of the preaching model we are discussing lies the good news of a power that is not our own, a performance that ultimately is not our work, a voice that transcends our mouths, a grace that is not of our own doing. The notion of The Preacher As Liturgical Artist is not so much one of earnest striving as it is of an active participation that is experienced when we allow ourselves to be embraced, or let ourselves be fed by the Word that can energize us for the artistic action of proclaiming the reality that "Jesus Christ is Lord."

98. Torrance, *Worship*, 15.
99. Hart and Guthrie, *Faithful Performances*, 6.

The confidence that arises when preachers themselves know, in a deeply personal way, that they too can rest confidently in God's upholding arms enables them to let go of the anxieties that can plague and defeat the art of preaching when it is driven by compulsive striving. In Christ, preachers are freed from such conditions. They are freed to attend to how Jesus' art in action is living out its intentions in a people within a place. The preacher's own preaching is always in service to their ways of proclaiming the gospel. Similarly, we can also see that what matters is not our own liturgical performance but rather the performance of Christ on behalf of the people Christ claims as his own.

Preaching like this has a kind of beauty and allure that is almost irresistible. And so it replicates itself by drawing more and more people into it, forming and shaping their lives and imaginations, and launching them into new ministry in turn. Such ministry has about it a freshness, an improvisatory character, a liveliness that is itself infectious. And thus an imagination that is at the heart of "seeing" with hope turns out to be an imagination full of creativity with Jesus—an imagination that sees what is "not yet" and begins to embody it.

In this vicarious dynamic, the preacher's human performance is reconceived by the work of the Spirit as preachers come to see themselves in relation to Jesus, the master of creation, who is nothing less than the incarnate and resurrected artist in action.

PUTTING THE ARTIST IN CONTEXT

An awareness of the context of the liturgy is essential for the homiletic identity of The Preacher As Liturgical Artist. Preaching does not exist in a vacuum. In most places and at most times, preaching takes place within the context of the work of God's people, the communal liturgy of worship. It is difficult to underestimate the power that Christian liturgy offers preachers. It is also difficult to overestimate the way this can and should shape the call to preach as artist in and with Christ.

Liturgical scholars have long been attuned to the aesthetic dimensions of liturgical experience. The twentieth century in particular has witnessed comprehensive scholarly reflection on the aesthetic dimension of liturgy.[100] The primary contribution of liturgical scholars like Gordon Lathrop,

---

100. The first wave of that reflection was part of the Liturgical Movement that led up to and immediately followed Vatican II and is exemplified by books such as H. A. Reinhold, *Art and Liturgy*.

Geradus van der Leeuw, Don Saliers, and Janet Walton has been their evocative writing on the aesthetic dimension of corporate liturgy in worship.[101]

These scholars are passionate connoisseurs of liturgical arts and are eager to promote the awareness of its value for the church. This reflection and passion develop out of the conviction that liturgical arts are so intrinsic to liturgy because liturgy itself *is* art. For example, van der Leeuw states, "whether it is rich or impoverished, developed or truncated, the liturgy of the Church is in any case drama, and it is in any case art."[102] Similarly, Saliers suggests that, "Liturgical action does not simply use art, it is art—dialogue with God in symbolic form." In other words, the liturgy itself "requires all that art requires: form, material, discipline, imagination, and pain."[103] Liturgy is experienced through perception; it evokes immediate response; it inevitably involves interpretation and evaluation.[104] Liturgy is multivalent, allusive, metaphoric, and symbolic. In all these ways, liturgy *is* art.

But at this point, we must take caution. Liturgy is not the child of a single artisan, nor does it reveal a single person's subjectivity, but it belongs to the actions and beliefs of a community that shares an identity as "the body of Christ."[105] Moreover, it is with Christ as its head and Christ as its high priest that the liturgy finds its highest artistic expression. In other words, liturgy is the work of the people, as it is the work of Christ in and among the people, through the Spirit. This means that the liturgy is an art in action that finds its meaning within the intentions of the worshipping body. Liturgical scholar Cyprian Vagaggini writes, "The end of art is at the service of a higher end, the liturgy's own end: the Church's sanctification and worship in Christ."[106] In Christ's work on our behalf to God, through the Spirit, we find not only our end in worship, but also our true freedom to be artists in action, artists in community, artists with the mission of preaching and embodying and enacting the gospel.

---

101. See Lathrop, *Holy Things*; Leeuw, *Sacred and Profane Beauty*; Saliers, *Worship as Theology*; and Walton, *Art in Worship*.

102. Leeuw, *Sacred and Profane Beauty*, 110.

103. Saliers, *Worship As Theology*, 206.

104. Witvliet, "Liturgical Aesthetics," 36–39.

105. See Foley, *Creativity*, 244. Here Foley points to an important dissimilarity, one that concerns the difference between Christian liturgy and other kinds of artwork that we most often encounter. Artists, as we have seen, have been valued in the modern Western culture for being creative geniuses who are perceived to agonize or suffer to find the inspiration to produce an innovative, daring, and emotion-laden work. However, art that serves liturgy, as Foley points out, does not strive for such emotional singularity, innovation, or identification with individual human subjectivity.

106. Vaggagini, *Theological Dimensions*, 51.

This work of Christ on our behalf reframes our expectations in worship. By keeping the focus of our worship grounded in Christ, the subjective aesthetic experience as such is not the primary aim of the liturgist or the preacher, nor is it the ultimate end for worship. The praise and glorification of God and the transformation toward the holy through the vicarious humanity of Christ is the highest aspiration of Christian preaching in liturgical worship.[107] Hence, The Preacher As Liturgical Artist is at the service of a higher end, the liturgy's own end: the church's sanctification and worship in Christ.

All parts of the liturgy are to serve this proper end and find their fullest expression within the limits of our Christ. Wolterstorff writes, "Liturgy without art is something the church has almost always avoided . . . But unless distortion creeps in, art in the liturgy is at the service of the liturgy . . . Good liturgical art is art that serves effectively the actions of the liturgy . . . that the actions . . . be performed with clarity . . . without tending to distract persons from the performance of the action . . . without undue awkwardness and difficulty."[108]

It is critical to understand that the sermon is an artistic action within the liturgy. This gives preaching its context of relationship to the congregation. Because preaching is act within the larger actions of the liturgy it gives the church's proclamation a framework of accountability and protection. Charles Rice argues, "Placing preaching firmly in the liturgy is more likely to keep us close to the gospel and away from chauvinism, moralism, parochialism, and the unworthy agendas that crowd upon us."[109] Indeed, keeping preaching close to the context of the liturgy is the best way to prevent its temptation to perversion, as William Skudlarek tells us:

> Worship, or liturgy, or sacrament, then is far more than the setting of the sermon. It is even more than the kairos of preaching . . . it is, to use that old but at times still helpful philosophy, the "final cause" of preaching: its end, purpose and goal. To say this is not to deny that preaching is to bring people to faith, or that it is to have an influence on their behavior. Rather, it is to affirm that faith and obedience are to go one step further and be transformed into praise and thanksgiving. Unless this step is taken faith can all too easily degenerate into doctrinal rigidity, and obedience into legalistic conformity. Authentic praise and thanksgiving—that is, praise and thanksgiving flowing out of a

---

107. Saliers, *Worship As Theology*, 205.

108. Wolterstorff, *Art in Action*, 184–85.

109. For reflections on the relationship between preaching and liturgical art, see Rice, *The Embodied Word*, 56.

recognition of the graciousness of God (faith) and propelling us to actions of love and justice (obedience) is ultimately the mark of effective proclamation of the word of God.[110]

Thus, The Preacher As Liturgical Artist calls preachers to work within the symbiotic relationship between preaching and the whole liturgy for the ultimate end of protecting the art of preaching so it can always be freed to glorify the triune God.[111] This means working with other liturgical artist like readers, musicians, visual artists, architects, and the artistic mob that is the congregation. Working in this school of art, the preacher must integrate the sermon into a kaleidoscopic range of forms and events that together honor God and lead the people into his presence.

It is because preaching takes place within the liturgy of the baptized community that the preacher is called to be a responsible servant to the community. In other words, the sermon's faithfulness is judged to the degree it serves the work of God's people in worship. This work, as we have been arguing, is not primarily rooted in merely our work—our prayers, our singing, our preaching, our intercessions—but rather the liturgy is always and ever focused on the one minister of grace, Jesus Christ. In this very real sense, the church's liturgy is where Christians learn the grammar of grace, as Jesus continues to be the priest leading the church's liturgy. As J. B. Torrance suggests:

> Jesus Christ is, on the one hand, God's Word of grace to a faithless world, the one in whom God makes a new covenant, bringing forgiveness (Jer 31:31ff.). But on the other hand, he is the one whose whole vicarious life in our humanity is a faithful obedient response to the Father's purpose in electing him—in being the Lamb of God to take away the sin of the world—that through him Israel's destiny to be a light to the Gentiles might be fulfilled. Here is the one true priest, the one true worshiper, the leader of our worship (the *leitourgus*) in whom alone "the ordinances of worship" (*dikaiomata latreias*) are perfectly fulfilled and through whom alone we can draw near to God. So worship is God's gift of grace to us in Christ.[112]

This double role of Jesus reveals why the liturgy, and preaching within the liturgy, is seen as an ordinance of grace. On the one hand, in the liturgy the prayers of the people are offered to Jesus Christ as God. In worship, we pray to the Father and to the Son and to the Holy Spirit. But on the

110. Skudlarek, *Word in Worship*, 69.

111. See Foley, *Creativity*, 4, 268.

112. Torrance, *Worship*, 63.

other hand, Jesus Christ is seen as our great high priest, as a human being praying to the Father, the one who intercedes for us and leads our worship of adoration and praise. He is the one who gives us access to the Father in the Spirit as he prays with us and among us as our brother. This double role and ministry is the center that gives the grace of the liturgy its center. In other words, Jesus receives and leads the worship of his people and in this dynamic double movement the artistic movements of preachers and others can be faithful expressions of God's truth, beauty, and goodness.

The God we pray to in the liturgy is the same God who is praying for us in Christ through the liturgy. God comes to us in Jesus Christ to be our high priest who leads our life of continual acts of worship. The liturgy and those who perform it are never called to take over the priestly role of Christ in our worship. That leads to the error of making the human church the high priest for humanity, who assumes the role of being the mediator of grace. However, a proper understanding of the church's liturgy within the double role of Jesus always calls the church back to the sole priesthood of Christ as both the object of our worship and the leader of our worship. The liturgy within this context allows the church to be the royal priesthood that shares by grace in the priesthood of Christ. Only in this way can we understand the liturgy of Christian worship to be an instrument of grace, where Christ alone is the high priest who mediates on our behalf. We come to God our Father both in Christ and through Christ, and only through Jesus Christ.

This means that the preacher as an artist finds the fullest expression of freedom within the constraints of the liturgy of Christ's body, the church. The significance of this confession is that it challenges the notion of artistic freedom rooted in the subjectivity of the individual. Not only does it challenge this notion, it invites the preacher to discover the freedom experienced in the confession of a community. The best artists are not tortured geniuses working without rules or constraints. On the contrary, the most significant artists have been those who first mastered an aesthetic tradition, and then made a contribution within their respective discipline as a service to the wider community.

In Western Antiquity and up through the Middle Ages the term for art (*techne* in Greek or *ars* in Latin) could apply to any activity or product of skillful, knowledgeable, and admirable making—everything from ordinary leather-work and masonry to painting and architecture.[113] Alternatively, "art" referred to intellectual accomplishment and teachable knowledge, as in the seven "liberal arts." In this sense, any artist is one who works out of a defined tradition, craft, or guild of discipline. It is only by endeavoring to learn

113. Brown, *Good Taste*, 27.

the activities necessary within the tradition that one can make meaningful variations on it.[114] It is thus not through escaping the tradition but through mastering the tradition that something new takes on form and shape.[115] Artists—like all human makers, thinkers, and doers—do not ever create in total isolation, without reference to what has gone before. Historically in the arts, one was typically an apprentice before one could be considered a master. The apprentice who submits to the master becomes the artist who is uniquely educated and skilled to know what an original contribution would be, as he learns the skills necessary to make something without it being considered a copycat cliché.

It is through absorbing the porous liturgical tradition of the church that the preacher serves the body of Christ as an artist. It is the liturgy where the preacher learns to locate one's individual expression within the larger expression of Christ's high-priestly intercession on our behalf. This is the cornerstone of human freedom. True freedom is when our individuality is set free to live within the constraints of God's work and the work of God's people. However, many preachers are mesmerized by the misconception that freedom opposes all limits, when in fact true freedom is experienced within the constraints of Christ. Working within this constraint in Christ is what gives "Christian freedom a restful restlessness," according to Jeremy Begbie.[116] In any creative activity, whether art or scholarship, there is a restlessness to risk pushing beyond the boundaries, to try something new, or make a new discovery. In this sense, there is a tension between being faithful to a tradition and extending that through new work that is within and beyond the bounds of what has been. But before an artist can push beyond, he or she first must learn what has already been done or discovered. The most significant artists are those who work within this tension; they rest within a tradition, learning from others, and then allow their restlessness to begin pushing toward new options that expand the scope of the tradition's wisdom. Tradition serves as a master to the apprentice, not to stifle or restrict artistic freedom, but to give it context for freer explorations and discoveries.[117] Likewise, a preacher with no boundaries, or a preacher without the desire to be a student of the liturgical tradition where Christ is kept at the center, will fail to cultivate his or her gifts and serve the body as Christ calls him or her to do.

114. Begbie notes that T. S. Elliot makes a similar argument in an essay "Tradition and the Individual Talent" (*Theology, Music, and Time*, 220n35).

115. See Crowther, *Critical Aesthetics and Postmodernism.*

116. Begbie, *Theology, Music and Time*, 244.

117. For another essay that engages the relationship between artistic freedom and tradition, see Wolterstoff, "Work of Making," 101–30.

We need not look any further than Jesus to see a preacher who masters his tradition in such a way that he can push it in new and exciting directions. For Jesus, as the eternal Son of God, embodied in his person the fulfillment and climax of Israel's tradition. In this way Jesus could say truthfully, "do not think that I have come to abolish the law or the prophets, I have not come to abolish but to fulfill" (Matt 5:17).[118] Often we fail to see Jesus as a "Jewish theologian," who was always and ever working in and through the faithful tradition of God's chosen people.[119] In this light, Jesus' teachings, like those of his followers, reflect a distinct ethnicity and culture. Thus to properly understand or appreciate Jesus as a preacher, we need to understand how he operated within his Jewish tradition.[120]

The Christian church was birthed not by Jesus fleeing the traditions of Israel to satisfy his own individual conscience or agenda, but by Jesus living fully into the faithful traditions of Israel. As Geza Vermes highlights, "the general picture of Jesus emerging from the Synoptic Gospels is that of Jew who conforms to the principle religious practices of his nation."[121] Jesus lived within the traditions of his people, in style of dress, in eating habits, in manner of worship and prayer, in observance of traditional festivals and holidays, and liturgy and prayers. In fact, Jesus is regularly associated with synagogues, the centers of Jewish liturgical worship and teaching. There are general references to his frequenting them in Galilee, sometimes specifically on the Sabbath. Two of these synagogues, one at Capernaum (Mark 1:21; Luke 4:31) and the other at Nazareth (Luke 4:15), are explicitly named. He was, it seems, a familiar figure in those circles, a much sought-after teacher and preacher of great originality within his tradition.

Jesus was one who was immersed and saturated within Israel's living tradition of worship and teaching and personal prayer. In other words, Jesus never set himself against his tradition, he was always trying to let people know that he was there as its perfect embodiment.[122] For example, when asked what is the fulfillment of the law, he offers the two greatest commandments from the tradition of the law, combines them, and then tells the

118. For an excellent account of how Jesus fits into the tradition of the Jewish law and custom, see Vermes, *Religion of Jesus*, 11–45.

119. See Young, *Jesus the Jewish Theologian*, on how Jesus served primarily within his religious and cultural tradition.

120. Wilson, *Our Father Abraham*. "The Bible reflects a view of reality which is essentially Hebraic . . . The evidence found in the New Testament is abundantly clear: as a mother gives birth to and nourishes a child, so Hebrew culture and language gave birth to and nourished Christianity" (12).

121. Vermes, *Religion of Jesus*, 13.

122. Peterson, *Tell It Slant*, 13.

story of the good Samaritan to turn the whole tradition on its head (Luke 10:25–37). As a preacher, Jesus did not just echo the tradition. Instead, he turned it upside down, with the suggestion that the tradition of the law and prophets was witness to his work and person.

Faithfulness to Jesus requires of the preacher the patient development of this same instinct to master tradition and use it in a way that can help us see the work of God in a fresh way. For example, we see this in the Revelation of St. John. The 404 verses of the book of St. John's Revelation contain no less than 418 quotes or allusions from the Old Testament. If we consider the Apocalypse of St. John to be a sermon, then the sermon is in fact the most derived and borrowing book of the Bible. St. John mastered the Scriptures not to say something new, but to say something old in a new way. In other words, because the preacher is an artist in Christ, he refuses to throw out the wisdom of the past. One of the key ways to learn and understand and communicate this past is through a disciplined participation in the tradition of the liturgy of the church. Specifically, preachers need to learn the psalms, traditional prayers, songs, hymns, habits of performance, the rich liturgies of the eucharist and the ways of preaching that have been developed and passed on through the liturgical tradition.

If the preacher is to be an artist, it will require the patient obedience of a student who is willing to submit to the constraints of the church's liturgical tradition. Just as arts like painting, sculpture, dance, and singing have a tradition to be trained in, so does Christian preaching as an action of Christian liturgy. This tradition demands of the preacher to learn classic skills and form habits of thinking that are a result of centuries of the church's best reflection and practice. It is through learning the classic skills within the aesthetic tradition of the liturgy that preachers learn how to free themselves from their own subjectivity, in order to harmonize one particular voice within the "chorus of witnesses" singing from the Christian pulpit.[123] Preaching as an art is not a call to private performance, but to master a public symphony to be played for all. To learn how to sing the score of the gospel, the preacher is first required to "guard the deposit" that has been committed to the church (1 Tim 6:20). Thus, to encourage a homiletic identity where preaching is associated with the artist in the context of the liturgy is an encouragement to master, not deviate from, the tradition of Christ working among the people.[124]

123. For examples of sermons that take advantage of the homiletic tradition and in so doing offer the church fresh and creative preaching, see Long and Plantinga, *Chorus of Witnesses*.

124. See Oden, *Rebirth of Orthodoxy*.

The Preacher As Liturgical Artist is a homiletic identity that—at its best—embodies the purposes of the liturgy itself. It seeks to be a means by which Christ's ongoing work for and in the church through the Spirit draws people into a deeper relational communion in the Trinity. At its best, the event of preaching is one aesthetic part of a larger liturgical action where we are encountered by Jesus the high priest, who is leading the people to its proper voice. The sermon needs to fit a liturgical context because the liturgy is the art in action of the community of faith in Christ and not merely one person. As Wolterstorff suggests: "Liturgical art is not the artist 'doing his own thing,' the artist 'doing her own thing,' with the rest of us standing by as appreciators and critics. Liturgical art is the offering of the artist to the liturgical community for its praise and confession and intercession. In liturgical art, the liturgical community finds its artful priestly hands and voice."[125]

This is how The Preacher As Liturgical Artist understands the work of the sermon within the body of Christ. It is an offering to the body to respond in the freedom of grace and experience together the union with Christ through the Spirit. Worship involves the human acts of speaking, reading, and singing among others; these actions generate an aesthetic experience into which others can enter and respond. Even bodily movement, posture, and space create aesthetic impressions others perceive. Thus, we conclude that the aesthetic dimension of worship itself is inevitable. In other words, there is no such thing as a non-aesthetic worship experience or sermon, whether the service is high or low church, in regards to liturgical expression. For these reasons it is wise to consider the preacher not just an artist, but also a liturgical artist. In this sense, the preacher takes the role of a public servant, joining worshipers within an ongoing aesthetic experience that points us to God in and through the vicarious ministry of Christ and just so to the community that frees all who gather to offer praise and prayer, songs and sermons.[126]

For The Preacher As Liturgical Artist, the liturgy of the church is the context where the preacher learns the tradition and enters into the larger work of Christ among the people. In the acts of liturgy, Christ calls us into his body through the work of the Spirit. This body, the church, is the context of the preacher's liturgical art in action. Moreover, it is in this context that the preacher's individuality is freed from himself or herself in order to serve God's people faithfully. And it is in the work of this community, the liturgy, that the individual preacher learns the resources necessary to be faithful, or

125. Wolterstorff, "What is This Thing," 7.
126. See also Lathrop, Holy Things, 223.

to be a responsible servant, to the community of Christ in the artistic action of preaching.

CONCLUSION

In chapter 1 we asked the question what might be a fitting homiletic identity for our cultural moment. In light of the twilight of modernity, the significance of the imagination for epistemology, and the emerging dynamics of orality, what is an identity that will recognize these changes not simply as challenges to overcome, but as opportunities that could enhance the work of Christian proclamation? What image can guide our experiences of God's creation and shape our performances as preachers without letting the cultural moment dictate working assumptions?

What we have suggested in this chapter is that the doctrine of the incarnation, specifically the priestly office of Christ's mediation between God and humanity, gives us a model or framework to describe preaching as an artistic action. Working within this theological framework it becomes clear that the ministry, especially the preaching ministry, of Jesus was connected to the life of an artist in action who spoke with vivid language, taking advantage of transforming images, metaphors, and stories that announced the kingdom of God as present. Finding our place with Jesus and our method in his ministry, we find ourselves confronted with the call to be attuned as artists working with and for God the Father in the power of the Spirit in Jesus' name. The Preacher As Liturgical Artist is a homiletic identity that encourages the preacher to work artistically for and with Jesus. This artistic freedom enables the preacher to change, adapt, and (sub-)create sermons to respond to the variety of forms in Scripture as well as to fit the aesthetic taste of diverse and divergent human situations and societies, cultures and languages, ages and races, and even popular appeal. This freedom for creative and imaginative diversity in preaching is made possible by the particularity of Christ's ministry, whose vicarious sacrifice on the cross "ransomed for God saints from every tribe and language and people and nation, and made them to be a Kingdom and priests serving our God" (Rev 5:10–11).

This project puts the preacher's identity squarely in relationship to Jesus, his creative work and life, and the ongoing work of his people. By grounding The Preacher As Liturgical Artist in the context of Christ's vicarious humanity, and not in individual self-expression, rhetorical skill, or any particular human performance or cultural context, the preacher is freed to use all the gifts of humanity as gifts redeemed for artistic preaching within the context of the church. This creative freedom to preach as an artist is primarily experienced in Christ's vicarious ministry offered to all humanity for all times and in all places. This experience of ministering with and for Jesus as an artist in action is nothing other than the call to live in the Spirit who is the power of God to create and redeem all things that are true, good, and beautiful.

It is precisely because this proposed identity of The Preacher As Liturgical Artist is objectively grounded in Christ that preaching is freed to use and adapt diverse forms of language and culture for proclamation, while at the same time is prevented from being imprisoned or reduced by static patterns conditioned by our culture or swept along by constantly changing aesthetic currents blowing through the church. Indeed, it is the invocatory character of Christ's own proclamation which fulfils the preacher's identity as he or she calls upon Christ to come among us, for it is Christ's Spirit which shapes and adapts sermons to be a message to and from the Father, through the Son, no matter what the cultural conditions in which the preacher finds himself or herself. This is a homiletic identity that allows the life and ministry of Christ to inform the Spirit's creative movement from text to sermon. In this way, the preacher is freed from preoccupations and obsessions with technique, as each sermon shares in the proclamation of Christ, in whom the Father is well pleased. While we do not know how to preach as we ought, the good news for the preacher is that the ascended High Priest sends us his own Spirit who helps us in our weakness by enabling our preaching to become a participation in Christ before "the one who is seated on the throne" of grace (Rev 4:1).

The Preacher As Liturgical Artist is an identity that takes our cultural moment seriously as an act of loving one's neighbor. From Augustine we learned that discussions concerning aesthetic judgment that are near to the hearts of people, both personally and religiously, must demonstrate the rule of love. When tastes are mutually shared, a certain bonding between people can occur. But equally, when tastes are not shared, they can be divisive, especially if considered in the liturgical realm of worship.[127] In other words, aesthetic judgment is never neutral. Furthermore, aesthetic discernment is always connected to one's culture, education, experiences, and ethnicity.[128] There is no biblically enfranchised cultural mode of preaching. Preaching is always a culturally constructed phenomenon.

127. Brown, *Good Taste*, 9. Brown argues that aesthetic *taste* matters to Christian faith *at a basic and critical level*. Aesthetics are important, he suggests, because it is one of the areas, wittingly or unwittingly, that most forms, defines, and thus divides people's spiritual life.

128. Ibid., 23.

The Preacher As Liturgical Artist invites preachers to discern the most fitting language, forms, and presence for a sermon as an act of obedience to the rule of love. This requires taking other people's tastes seriously. As Frank Burch Brown writes, "Such a form of Christian taste learns to appreciate the value of 'alien' tastes it can never hope to enjoy personally, due to human limitations. To enjoy another's enjoyment is already an act of love."[129] This sensitivity is part of the responsible service the preacher owes the congregation. The enjoyment of another's enjoyment is an extension of Jesus' commandment to love one's neighbor. Being aware of the ears through which others hear is an act of loving and honoring the other. In this sense, the preacher reflects the wisdom of Paul who preached as a Jew to the Jews, as a Greek to the Greeks, or in his words, as a "slave to all, so that I might win more of them" (1 Cor 9:20).

This practice of love urges the preacher to learn the skills that are necessary to preach using different aesthetic forms, genres, and styles. The choice of language, content, and form are aesthetic decisions that are fashioned into a public performance for others as an act to honor them. In other words, preachers practice aesthetic judgment every time they step into the pulpit. This kind of attention to aesthetics brings together the sensitivity and subtlety of an artist that is working at the height of his or her powers. In the moment of performance, the mastery of words, orality, tradition, the imagination, creativity, art, and other skills are required for the preacher to be present in a way that is appropriate, or fitting, to the cultural and liturgical conditions of those who may be listening to the sermon. Yet even more critical to this identity is the awareness that in this moment of performance, there is another who is performing in our place, and whose performance actually frees us to offer our best performance in response to the Word who transcends our words.

The Preacher As Liturgical Artist is proposed as a homiletic identity that encourages an awareness of this vicarious performance. It is a metaphor that places the preacher within the ongoing mystery of Jesus' double ministry, and that allows our humanity to participate in, but never to dominate, the work of Jesus' creation in and through a sermon. It preserves human agency while at the same time locating it within the agency of the Trinity. In this sense, the preacher is an artist who acts in response to the creative work that Jesus Christ has already done and continues to do for us and in us through the Holy Spirit for the glory of God the Father.

129. Ibid., 24.

Bibliography

Allen, Ronald J. "The Preacher as Teacher." In *Preaching and Practical Ministry*, 29–46. St. Louis: Chalice, 2001.

———. *The Teaching Sermon*. Nashville: Abingdon, 1995.

Alter, Robert. *The World of Biblical Literature*. New York: Basic Books, 1992.

Amos, Thomas. "Augustine and the Education of the Early Medieval Preacher." In *Reading and Wisdom: The De Doctrina Christiana of Augustine in the Middle Ages*, edited by Edward D. English, 23–40. South Bend, IN: University of Notre Dame Press, 1995.

Aristotle. *Nicomachean Ethics*. Translated by J. A. K. Thomson. New York: Penguin, 2003.

———. *Poetics*. Edited by Stephen Halliwell and W. Hamilton Fyfe. New York: Putnam, 1927.

Arnold, Duane W. H., and Pamela Bright. *De Doctrina Christiana: A Classic of Western Culture*. South Bend, IN: University of Notre Dame Press, 1995.

Augustine. *On Christian Doctrine*. Translated by D. W. Robertson Jr. Upper Saddle River, NJ: Prentice Hall, 1997.

———. *Teaching Christianity: De Doctrina Christiana*. Introduction, translation, and notes by Edmund Hill. Vol. I/11 of *The Works of St. Augustine: A Translation for the 21st Century*, edited by John E. Rotelle. Brooklyn, NY: New City, 1996.

Babin, Pierre. *The New Era in Religious Communication*. Minneapolis: Fortress, 1991.

Bailey, Kenneth. *Jesus Through Middle Eastern Eyes: Cultural Studies in the Gospels*. Downers Grove, IL: InterVarsity, 2008.

———. *Poet and Peasant*. Grand Rapids: Eerdmans, 1976.

Barbour, Ian G. *Myth, Models, and Paradigms*. New York: Harper & Row, 1976.

Barr, Alfred H., Jr. *Picasso: Fifty Years of His Art*. New York: Museum of Modern Art, 1946.

Barth, Karl. *Church Dogmatics*. Study edition. Edited by T. F. Torrance and G. W. Bromiley. Translated by G. W. Bromiley et al. 31 vols. London: T. & T. Clark, 2010.

———. *Deliverance to the Captives*. New York: Harper & Row, 1961.

———. *Dogmatics in Outline*. Translated by G. T. Thomason. New York: Harper & Row, 1959.

———. *The Epistle to the Romans*. London: Oxford University Press, 1933.

———. *Homiletics*. Louisville: Westminster John Knox, 1991.

------. *A Karl Barth Reader.* Edited by Rolf Joachim Erler and Reiner Marquard. Grand Rapids: Eerdmans, 1986.

------. *Karl Barth's Table Talk.* Edited by J. D. Godsey. Edinburgh: Oliver and Boyd, 1963.

------. *Natural Theology.* Translated by Peter Fraenkel. London: Century, 1946.

------. *The Preaching of the Gospel.* Translated by B. E. Hooke. Philadelphia: Westminster, 1963.

------. *Protestant Theology in the Nineteenth Century: Its Background and History.* Translated by Brian Cozens and John Bowden. Grand Rapids: Eerdmans, 2002.

------. *Theology and Church.* Translated by Louise P. Smith. London: SCM, 1962.

------. *The Word of God and the Word of Man.* New York: Harper, 1957.

Bartow, Charles L. *God's Human Speech: A Practical Theology of Proclamation.* Grand Rapids, Eerdmans, 1997.

Bauckham, Richard, and Trevor Hart. *Hope Against Hope: Christian Eschatology at the Turn of the Millennium.* Grand Rapids: Eerdmans, 1999.

Beardsley, Monroe C. "On the Creation of Art." *Journal of Aesthetics and Art Criticism* 23 (1965) 291–304.

Begbie, Jeremy. *Theology, Music, and Time.* Cambridge: Cambridge University Press, 2000.

Berger, Peter L. *The Sacred Canopy: Elements of a Sociological Theory of Religion.* New York: Anchor, 1967.

Binkley, Timothy. "On the Truth and Probity of Metaphor." *Journal of Aesthetics Art Criticism* 33 (1974) 136–53.

Bizzell, Patricia, and Bruce Herzberg, eds. "General Introduction." In *The Rhetorical Tradition: Readings from Classical Times to the Present.* 2nd ed. New York: Bedford/St. Martins, 2001.

Black, Max. "Metaphor." *Proceedings of the Aristotelian Society,* n.s. 55 (1954–1955) 273–94.

------. *Models and Metaphors: Studies in Language and Philosophy.* Ithaca, NY: Cornell University Press, 1962.

------. "More about Metaphor." In *Metaphor and Thought,* edited by Andrew Ortony, 19–43. Cambridge: Cambridge University Press, 1979.

Boersma, Hans. "Alexandrian or Antiochian? A Dilemma in Barth's Christology." *Westminster Theological Journal* 52/2 (1990) 263–80.

Bonner, Gerald. *St. Augustine of Hippo: Life and Controversies.* Philadelphia: Westminster, 1963.

Broadus, John A. *Sermons and Addresses.* New York: George H. Doran, 1886.

Broadus, John A., and Vernon L. Stanfield. *On the Preparation and Delivery of Sermons.* 4th ed. San Francisco: HarperSanFranisco, 1979.

Brown, Frank Burch. *Good Taste, Bad Taste, and Christian Taste: Aesthetics in Religions Life.* Oxford: Oxford University Press, 2003.

Brown, Peter. *Augustine of Hippo: A Biography.* Berkeley: University of California Press, 1967.

Brown, Richard Harvey. *Society as Text: Essays on Rhetoric, Reason, and Reality.* Chicago: University of Chicago Press, 1992.

Brueggemann, Walter. *The Bible and the Postmodern Imagination.* London: SCM, 1993.

------. *Finally Comes The Poet: Daring Speech for Proclamation.* Minneapolis: Augsburg Fortress, 1989.

————. *Genesis*. Interpretation. Atlanta: John Knox, 1982.

Brummer, Vincent. *Speaking of a Personal God: An Essay in Philosophical Theology*, Cambridge: Cambridge University Press, 1992.

Burke, Kenneth. *Permanence and Change: An Anatomy of Purpose*. New York: New Republic, 1935.

Bush, Eberhard. *Karl Barth: His Life from Letters and Autobiographical Texts*. Grand Rapids: Eerdmans, 1975.

Buttrick, David. *A Captive Voice: The Liberation of Preaching*. Louisville: Westminster John Knox, 1994.

————. *Homiletic: Moves and Structures*. Philadelphia: Fortress, 1987.

————. "Interpretation and Preaching." *Interpretation* 35 (January 1981) 46–58.

Cameron, Averil. *Christianity and the Rhetoric of Empire: The Development of Christian Discourse*. Sather Classical Lectures 55. Berkeley: University of California Press, 1991.

Caplan, Harry. "Classical Rhetoric and the Medieval Theory of Preaching." *Classical Philology* 28/2 (April 1933) 73–96.

Casenave, Gerald W. "Taking Metaphor Seriously: The Implications of the Cognitive Significance of Metaphor for Theories of Language." *Southern Journal of Philosophy* 17 (1979) 19–25.

Cavanaugh, William T. *Theopolitical Imagination: Discovering the Liturgy as a Political Act in an Age of Global Consumerism*. New York: T. & T. Clark, 2002.

Childers, Jana. *Performing the Word: Preaching as Theater*. Nashville: Abingdon, 1998.

Chopp, Rebecca. *The Power to Speak: Feminism, Language, God*. New York: Crossroad, 1991.

Clapp, Rodney. *A Peculiar People: The Church as Culture in a Post-Christian Society*. Downers Grove, IL: InterVarsity, 1996.

Clark, Tony. *Divine Revelation and Human Practice: Responsive and Imaginative Participation*. Eugene, OR: Cascade, 2008.

Cohen, Ted. "Metaphor and the Cultivation of Intimacy." *Critical Inquiry* 5/1 (1978) 3–12.

Cox, James W. *Preaching: A Comprehensive Approach to the Design and Delivery of Sermons*. San Franscisco: Harper & Row, 1985.

Craddock, Fred B. *As One Without Authority*. Nashville: Abingdon: 1987.

Crowther, Paul. *Critical Aesthetics and Postmodernism*. Oxford: Clarendon, 1993.

Davidson, Donald. "What Metaphors Mean." In *The Philosophy of Language*, edited by A. P. Martinich, 416–37. New York: Oxford University Press, 1985.

DeMan, Paul. "The Epistemology of Metaphor." *Critical Inquiry* 5/1 (1978) 13–30.

Derrida, Jacques. *Margins of Philosophy*. Translated by Alan Bass. Chicago: University of Chicago Press, 1982.

————. *Writing and Difference*. Translated by Alan Bass. Chicago: University of Chicago Press, 1978.

Descartes, Rene. *Discourse on Method*. Translated by F. E. Sutcliffe. New York: Penguin, 1968.

Dodd, C. H. *The Apostolic Preaching and Its Developments*. London: Hodder & Stoughton, 1936.

Dorrien, Gary. *The Barthian Revolt in Modern Theology*. Louisville: Westminster John Knox, 2000.

Dunne, John S. *A Search for God in Time and Memory: An Exploration Traced in the Lives of Individuals from Augustine to Sartre and Camus*. London: Macmillan, 1969.

Dunne, Joseph. *Back to the Rough Ground: Practical Judgment and the Lure of Technique*. Notre Dame, IN: University of Notre Dame Press, 1997.

Dunn-Wilson, David. *A Mirror for the Church: Preaching in the First Five Centuries*. Grand Rapids: Eerdmans, 2005.

Dykstra, Craig. *Vision and Character: A Christian Educator's Alternative to Kohlberg*. Mahwah, NJ: Paulist, 1981.

Edwards, O. C., Jr. "History of Preaching." In *Concise Encyclopedia of Preaching*, edited by William H. Willimon and Richard Lischer, 184–227. Louisville: Westminster John Knox, 1995.

———. *A History of Preaching*. Nashville: Abingdon, 2004.

Egan, Kieran. *Imagination in Teaching and Learning*. London: Routledge, 1992.

Eliot, T. S. "Choruses from 'The Rock.'" In *The Complete Poems and Plays: 1909–1950*. New York: Harcourt Brace, 1967.

Eskridge, James Burnette. *The Influence of Cicero upon Augustine in the Development of His Oratorical Training for the Training of the Ecclesiastical Orator*. Mensha, WI: George Banta, 1912.

Eslinger, Richard. *A New Hearing: Living Options in Homiletic Methods*. Nashville: Abingdon, 1987.

———. *The Web of Preaching*. Nashville: Abingdon, 2002.

Farley, W. Edward. "Can Preaching Be Taught?" *Theology Today* 62 (2005) 171–80.

Feuerbach, Ludwig. *The Essence of Christianity*. Edited by George Elliot. New York: Harper & Row, 1957.

Foley, John. *Creativity and the Roots of Liturgy*. Washington DC: Pastoral, 1994.

Fosdick, Harry Emerson. "What Is the Matter with Preaching?" *Harper's* (July 1928) 133–41.

Freeman, Harold. *Variety in Biblical Preaching: Innovative Techniques and Fresh Forms*. Waco, TX: Word, 1987.

Frei, Hans. *The Eclipse of Biblical Narrative: A Study in Eighteenth and Nineteenth Century Hermeneutics*. New Haven, CT: Yale University Press, 1980.

Gatch, Milton McCormick. "Basic Christian Education from the Decline of Catechesis to the Rise of the Catechism." In *A Faithful Church: Issues in History of Catechesis*, edited by John H. Westerhoff and O. C. Edwards Jr., 79–108. Wilton, CT: Morehouse Barlow, 1981.

Gay, Craig M. *The Way of the (Modern) World: Or Why It's Tempting to Live As If God Doesn't Exist*. Grand Rapids: Eerdmans, 1998.

Gerhart, Mary, and Allan Melvin Russell. "The Cognitive Effect of Metaphor." *Listening* 25 (1990) 114–26.

Goldingay, John. *Models for Scripture*. Grand Rapids: Eerdmans, 1994.

Gonzalez, Justo L., and Catherine Gunsalus Gonzalez. *Liberation Preaching: The Pulpit and the Oppressed*. Edited by William D. Thompson. Nashville: Abingdon, 1980.

Goodman, Nelson. *Languages of Art*. Indianapolis: Bobbs-Merrill, 1968.

Green, Garrett. *Imagining God: Theology and the Religious Imagination*. Grand Rapids: Eerdmans, 1998.

———. *Theology, Hermeneutics and Imagination*. Cambridge: Cambridge University Press, 2000.

Greenhaw, David M. "As One *With* Authority: Rehabilitating Concepts for Preaching." In *Intersections: Post-Critical Studies in Preaching*, edited by Richard L. Eslinger, 105–22. Grand Rapids: Eerdmans, 1994.

Grenz, Stanley, and John Ranke. *Beyond Foundationalism: Shaping Theology in a Postmodern Context*. Louisville: Westminster John Knox, 2001.

Gunton, Colin. *Christ and Creation*. Grand Rapids: Eerdmans, 1992.

Gutting, Gary, ed., *Paradigms and Revolutions: Appraisals and Applications of Thomas Kuhn's Philosophy of Science*. Notre Dame, IN: University of Notre Dame Press, 1980.

Halling, Steen. "The Imaginative Constituent in Interpersonal Living: Empathy, Illusion, and Will." In *Imagination and Phenomenological Psychology*, edited by Edward L. Murray, 140–74. Pittsburgh: Duquesne University Press, 1987.

Harrison, Carol. "The Rhetoric of Scripture and Preaching: Classical Decadence or Christian Aesthetic." In *Augustine and His Critics*, edited by Robert Dodaro and George Lawless, 214–30. London: Routledge, 2000.

Hart, Trevor. "Creative Imagination and Moral Identity." *Studies in Christian Ethics* 16/1 (2003) 1–13.

———. *Faith Thinking: The Dynamics of Christian Theology*. London: SPCK, 1995.

———. "Givenness, Grace, and Gratitude: Creation, Artistry and Eucharist." New College, University of New South Wales, New Zealand. September 4, 2008. http://www.ncv.unsw.edu.au/audios/audio-archives.

———. "Imagining Evangelical Theology." In *Evangelical Futures: A Conversation on Theological Method*, edited by John Stackhouse, 191–200. Grand Rapids: Eerdmans, 2000.

———. *Regarding Karl Barth: Essays Toward a Reading of His Theology*. Carlisle, UK: Paternoster, 1999.

———. "Revelation." In *The Cambridge Companion to Karl Barth*, edited by John Webster, 37–50. Cambridge: Cambridge University Press, 2000.

———. "Tolkien, Creation, and Creativity." In *Tree of Tales: Tolkien, Literature, and Theology*, edited by Trevor Hart and Ivan Khovacs, 39–54. Waco, TX: Baylor University Press, 2007.

Hart, Trevor, and Steven Guthrie, eds. *Faithful Performances: Enacting Christian Tradition*. Hampshire, UK: Ashgate, 2007.

Harvey, David. *The Condition of Postmodernity: An Enquiry into the Origins of Cultural Change*. Oxford: Blackwell, 1990.

Hauerwas, Stanley. *Performing the Faith: Bonhoeffer and the Practice of Nonviolence*. London, SPCK, 2004.

———. *Vision and Virtue*. Notre Dame, IN: University of Notre Dame Press, 1981.

———. *Wilderness Wanderings: Probing Twentieth-Century Theology and Philosophy*. Boulder, CO: Westview, 1997.

———. *With the Grain of the Universe: The Church's Witness and Natural Theology*. Grand Rapids: Brazos, 2001.

Hayakawa, S. I. *Language and Thought in Action*. New York: Harcourt, Brace, and Jovanovich, 1978.

Hayes, Richard. *Echoes of Scripture in the Letters of Paul*. New Haven, CT: Yale University Press, 1989.

Hegel, George Wilhelm Friedrich. *Vorlesungen uber Rechtsphtsphilosophie 1818–1831*. Vol. 2. Edited by Karl-Heinze Ilting. Stuttgart: Friedrich Frommann, 1974.

Hesse, Mary, "The Cognitive Claims of Metaphor." *The Journal of Speculative Philosophy* 2 (1988) 1–16.

Hopkins, Gerard Manley. *The Letters of Gerard Manley Hopkins to Robert Bridges.* Edited by C. C. Abbott. Oxford: Oxford University Press, 1955.

Hunsinger, George. "Karl Barth's Christology." In *The Cambridge Companion to Karl Barth,* edited by John Webster, 127–42. Cambridge: Cambridge University Press, 2000.

Hunter, James Davison. *American Evangelicalism: Conservative Religion and the Quandary of Modernity.* New Brunswick, NJ: Rutgers University Press, 1983.

Jenkins, Phillip. *The New Christendom: The Coming of Global Christianity.* Oxford: Oxford University Press, 2002.

Jensen, Richard A. *Thinking in Story: Preaching in a Post-Literate Age.* Lima, OH: CSS, 1993.

Jenson, Robert W. *Alpha and Omega.* Nashville: Thomas Nelson, 1963.

———. "Joining the Eternal Conversation." *Touchstone* 14/9 (November 2001) 32–37.

———. "Scripture's Authority in the Church." In *The Art of Reading Scripture,* edited by Ellen Davis and Richard Hays, 27–37. Grand Rapids: Eerdmans, 2003.

———. *Systematic Theology: The Works of God, Vol. II.* Oxford: Oxford University Press, 1999.

———. "What Is Post-Christian?" In *The Strange New World of the Gospel,* edited by Carl E. Braaten and Robert W. Jensen, 21–31. Grand Rapids: Eerdmans, 2002.

Johnson, Mark. *The Body in the Mind: The Bodily Basis of Meaning, Imagination, and Reason.* Chicago: University of Chicago Press, 1987.

———. *The Meaning of the Body: Aesthetics of Human Understanding.* Chicago: University of Chicago Press, 1999.

———. *Philosophical Perspectives on Metaphor.* Minneapolis: University of Minnesota Press, 1981.

Johnson, Mark L., and Glenn W. Erickson. "Toward a New Theory of Metaphor." *The Southern Journal of Philosophy* 18 (1980) 292.

Jones, G. V. *The Art and Truth of the Parables.* London: SPCK, 1964.

Kant, Immanuel. *Foundations of the Metaphysics of Morals and What Is Enlightenment?* Introduction and translation by Lewis White Beck. Indianapolis: Bobbs-Merill, 1959.

Kearney, Richard. *The Wake of Imagination: Toward a Postmodern Culture.* London: Routledge, 1988.

Kennedy, G. A. *Classical Rhetoric and Its Christian and Secular Tradition from Ancient to Modern Times.* Chapel Hill: University of North Carolina Press, 1980.

Kennedy, Rodney. *The Creative Power of Metaphor: A Rhetorical Homiletics.* Lanham, MD: University Press of America, 1993.

Kenneson, Philip D. "Selling [Out] the Church in the Marketplace of Desire." *Modern Theology* 9 (1993) 325–26.

Killinger, John. *Fundamentals of Preaching.* London: SCM, 1985.

Koestler, Arthur. *The Act of Creation.* London: Pan, 1964.

Kuhn, Thomas S. *The Structure of Scientific Revolutions.* 2nd ed. Chicago: University of Chicago Press, 1970.

Lakatos, Imre, and Alan Musgrave, eds. *Criticism and Growth of Knowledge.* New York: Cambridge University Press, 1970.

Lakoff, George, and Mark Johnson. *Metaphors We Live By*. Chicago: University of Chicago Press, 1980.

Lash, Nicholas. *Holiness, Speech, and Silence: Reflections on the Question of God*. Aldershot, UK: Ashgate, 2004.

———. *Theology on the Way to Emmaus*. London: SCM, 1986.

Lathrop, Gordon. *Holy Things: A Liturgical Theology*. Minneapolis: Fortress, 1993.

Lawless, George. "Augustine of Hippo as Preacher." In *Saint Augustine the Bishop: A Book of Essays*, edited by Fannie LeMoine and Christopher Kleinhenze, 13–38. New York: Garland, 1994.

Leeuw, Gerardus van der. *Sacred and Profane Beauty: The Holy in Art*. Translated by David Green. New York: Holt, Rinehart & Winston, 1963.

Levin, Samuel R. "Metaphor." In *A Companion to Aesthetics*, edited by Stephen Davies et al., 423–25. 2nd ed. Oxford: Blackwell, 2009.

Lewis, Alan. "Kenosis and Kerygma: The Realism and the Risk of Preaching." In *Christ In Our Place*, edited by Trevor Hart and Daniel P. Thimell, 70–91. Exeter: Paternoster, 1989.

Lewis, Ralph Loren, and Gregg A. Lewis. *Inductive Preaching: Helping People Listen*. Westchester, IL: Crossway, 1983.

Lindbeck, George. *The Nature of Doctrine: Religion and Theology in a Postliberal Age*. Louisville: Westminster John Knox, 1984.

Lischer, Richard. "Before Technique: Preaching and Personal Formation." *Dialog* 29 (1990) 178–82.

———. *The End of Words: The Language of Reconciliation in a Culture of Violence*. Grand Rapids: Eerdmans, 2005.

Locke, John. *Essay Concerning Human Understanding*. Oxford: Clarendon, 1894.

Long, D. Stephen. *John Wesley's Moral Theology: The Quest for God and Goodness*. Nashville: Abingdon, 2005.

Long, Thomas G. "And How Shall They Hear? The Listener in Contemporary Preaching." In *Listening to the Word: Studies in Honor of Fred B. Craddock*, edited by Gail O'Day and Thomas G. Long, 167–88. Nashville: Abingdon, 1993.

———. *Preaching and the Literary Forms of the Bible*. Philadelphia: Fortress, 1989.

———. *The Witness of Preaching*. Philadelphia: Westminster, 1989.

Long, Thomas G., and Cornelius Plantinga Jr., eds. *A Chorus of Witnesses: Model Sermons for Today's Preacher*. Grand Rapids: Eerdmans, 1994.

Loscalozo, Craig. "Rhetoric." In *Concise Encyclopedia of Preaching*, edited by William H. Willimon and Richard Lischer, 409-16. Louisville: Westminster John Knox, 1995.

Lowry, Eugene L. *Doing Time in the Pulpit: The Relationship Between Narrative and Preaching*. Nashville: Abingdon, 1985.

———. *The Homiletical Plot: The Sermon as Narrative Art Form*. Louisville: Westminster John Knox, 2000.

———. *The Sermon: Dancing on the Edge of Mystery*. Nashville: Abingdon, 1997.

Lyotard, Jean-François. *The Postmodern Condition: A Report on Knowledge*. Vol. 10 of *Theory and History of Literature*. Translated by Geoff Bennington and Brian Massumi. Manchester, UK: Manchester University Press, 1984.

MacCormac, Earl R. *Metaphor and Myth in Science and Religion*. Durham, NC: Duke University Press, 1976.

MacKenzie, Norman. *A Reader's Guide to Gerard Manley Hopkins*. London: Thames and Hudson, 1981.

Manson, T. W. *The Teaching of Jesus: Studies in Its Form and Content*. London: SCM, 1964.

Marshall, Bruce. *Trinity and Truth*. Cambridge: Cambridge University Press, 2000.

McCormack, Bruce. "Grace and Being: The Role of God's Gracious Election in Karl Barth's Theological Ontology." In *The Cambridge Companion to Karl Barth*, edited by John Webster, 92–110. Cambridge: Cambridge University Press, 2000.

McFague, Sallie. *Metaphorical Theology: Models of God in Religious Language*. Philadelphia: Fortress, 1982.

McLuhan, Marshall. "The Medium is the Message." In *The Anthropology of Media: A Reader*, edited by Kelly Askew and Richard Wilk, 18–26. Oxford: Blackwell, 2002.

Miller, George A. "Images and Models, Similes and Metaphors." In *Metaphor and Thought*, edited by Andrew Ortony, 357–400. Cambridge: Cambridge University Press, 1993.

Milosz, Czeslaw. *The Collected Poems, 1931–1987*. Hopewell, NJ: Ecco, 1988.

Mitchell, Henry. *The Recovery of Preaching*. San Francisco: Harper & Row, 1977.

Mitchell, Jolyon P. *Visually Speaking: Radio and the Renaissance of Preaching*. Edinburgh: T. & T. Clark, 1999.

Newbigin, Lesslie. *Foolishness to the Greeks: The Gospel and Western Culture*. Grand Rapids: Eerdmans, 1986.

———. *The Gospel in a Pluralist Society*. Grand Rapids: Eerdmans, 1989.

Noll, Mark A. *America's God: From Jonathan Edwards to Abraham Lincoln*. Oxford: Oxford University Press, 2002.

———. *The Scandal of the Evangelical Mind*. Grand Rapids: Eerdmans, 1994.

O'Connor, Flannery. *The Habit of Being*. New York: Farrar, Straus & Giroux, 1979.

———. "Writing Short Stories." In *Mystery and Manners: Occasional Prose*, edited by Sally Fitzgerald and Robert Fitzgerald, 87–106. New York: Farrar, Straus & Giroux, 1969.

Oberhelman, Steven M. *Rhetoric and Homiletics in Fourth-Century Christian Literature: Prose Rhythm, Oratorical Style, and Preaching in the Words of Ambrose, Jerome, and Augustine*. Atlanta: Scholars, 1991.

Oden, Thomas. *The Rebirth of Orthodoxy*. San Francisco: Harper, 2003.

Old, Hughes Oliphant. *The Reading and Preaching of the Scriptures in the Worship of the Christian Church*. Vol. 2. Grand Rapids: Eerdmans, 1998.

———. *The Reading and Preaching of the Scriptures in the Worship of the Christian Church*. Vol. 6. Grand Rapids: Eerdmans, 1998.

Ong, Walter. *Orality and Literacy: The Technologizing of the Word*. London: Methuen, 1982.

———. *The Presence of the Word: Some Prolegomena for Cultural and Religious History*. New Haven, CT: Yale University Press, 1967.

Ortony, "Metaphor: A Multidimensial Problem." In *Metaphor and Thought*, 1–16. New York: Cambridge University Press, 1979.

Osborn, Ronald E. *Folly of God: The Rise of Christian Preaching*. Vol. 1 of *Preaching and Preachers in Christian History*. St. Louis: Chalice, 1998.

Pasquarello, Michael, III. *Christian Preaching: A Trinitarian Theology of Proclamation*. Grand Rapids: Baker Academic, 2007.

Pearson, Roy Messer. *The Preacher: His Purpose and Practice*. Philadelphia: Westminster, 1962.

Pelikan, Jaroslav. *Jesus Through the Centuries: His Place in the History of Culture*. New York: Harper & Row, 1985.

Pepper, Stephen C. *World Hypothesis: A Study in Evidence*. Berkley: University of California Press, 1942.

Peterson, Eugene. *Christ Plays in Ten Thousand Places: A Conversation in Spiritual Theology*. Grand Rapids: Eerdmans, 2005.

———. *The Contemplative Pastor: Returning to the Art of Spiritual Direction*. Grand Rapids: Eerdmans, 1989.

———. *Eat This Book: A Conversation in the Art of Spiritual Reading*. Grand Rapids: Eerdmans, 2006.

———. *Tell It Slant: A Conversation on the Language of Jesus in His Stories and Prayers*. Grand Rapids: Eerdmans, 2008.

———. *Under the Unpredictable Plant: An Exploration in Vocational Holiness*. Grand Rapids: Eerdmans, 1992.

Polanyi, Michael. *The Tacit Dimension*. New York: Anchor, 1967.

Porteous, Alvin J. *Preaching to Suburban Captives*. Valley Forge, PA: Judson, 1979.

Postman, Neil. *Amusing Ourselves to Death: Public Discourse in the Age of Show Business*. New York: Penguin, 1985.

Quicke, Michael. *360-Degree Preaching: Hearing, Speaking, and Living the Word*. Grand Rapids: Baker, 2003.

Reinhold, H. A. *Art and Liturgy*. New York: Harper & Row, 1966.

Reno, R. R. *In the Ruins of the Church: Sustaining Faith In An Age of Diminished Christianity*. Grand Rapids: Brazos, 2002.

Resner, Andre, Jr. *Preacher and Cross: Person and Message in Theology and Rhetoric*. Grand Rapids: Eerdmans, 1999.

Rice, Charles L. *The Embodied Word: Preaching as Art and Liturgy*. Minneapolis: Fortress, 1991.

Ricoeur, Paul. "The Critique of Religion." *Union Seminary Quarterly Review* 28 (1973) 205.

———. *Dialogues with Contemporary Continental Thinkers*. Manchester, UK: Manchester University Press, 1984.

———. *History and Truth*. Evanston, IL: Northwestern University Press, 1965.

———. *Interpretation Theory*. Fort Worth: Texas Christian University Press, 1976.

———. "The Metaphorical Process, as Cognition, Imagination, and Feeling." *Critical Inquiry* 5/1 (1978) 143.

———. "The Problem of the Will and Philosophical Discourse." In *Patterns of the Life-World*, edited by James M. Edie, Francis H. Parker, and Calvin O. Schrag, 273–89. Evanston, IL: Northwestern University Press, 1970.

———. *The Rule of Metaphor*. London: Routledge & Kegan Paul, 1978.

Ritschl, Dietrich. *Theology of Proclamation*. Louisville: John Knox, 1963.

Roberts, M. *The Jeweled Style: Poetry and Poetics in Late Antiquity*. Ithaca, NY: Cornell University Press, 1989.

Robertson, A. T. *Life and Letters of John Albert Broadus*. Philadelphia: American Baptist Publication Society, 1901.

Robinson, Haddon W. *Biblical Preaching: The Development and Delivery of Expository Messages*. 2nd ed. Grand Rapids: Baker, 2001.

Rogness, Michael. *Preaching to a TV Generation: The Sermon in the Electronic Age.* Lima, OH: CSS, 1994.

Rorty, Richard. *Objectivity, Relativism and Truth?* Cambridge: Cambridge University Press, 1991.

Rose, Lucy Atkinson. *Sharing the Word: Preaching in the Roundtable Church.* Louisville: Westminster John Knox, 1997.

Saliers, Don. *Worship as Theology: Foretaste of Glory Divine.* Nashville: Abingdon, 1994.

Schaublin, Christoph. "De Doctrina Christiana: A Classic of Western Culture?" In *De Doctrina Christiana: A Classic of Western Culture*, edited by Duane W. H. Arnold and Pamela Bright, 47-67. South Bend, IN: Notre Dame University Press, 1995.

Schmit, Clayton. *Too Deep for Words: A Theology of Liturgical Expression.* Louisville: Westminster John Knox, 2002.

Sittler, Joseph. *The Anguish of Preaching.* Philadelphia: Fortress, 1966.

Skudlarek, William. *The Word in Worship: Preaching in a Liturgical Context.* Nashville: Abingdon, 1981.

Smail, Tom. "Can One Man Die for the People?" In *Atonement Today*, edited by John Goldingay, 73-92. London: SPCK, 1995.

Smith, Christian. *American Evangelicalism: Embattled and Thriving.* Chicago: University of Chicago Press, 1998.

Smith, Christian, and Melinda Lundquist Denton. *Soul Searching: The Religious and Spiritual Lives of American Teenagers.* Oxford: Oxford University Press, 2005.

Smith, Christine M. *Weaving the Sermon: Preaching in a Feminist Perspective.* Louisville: Westminster John Knox, 1989.

Snow, John H. *The Impossible Vocation: Ministry in the Mean Time.* Cambridge, MA: Cowley, 1998.

Soskice, Janet. *Metaphor and Religious Language.* Oxford: Clarendon, 1965.

Stanfield, Vernon L., ed. *Favorite Sermons of John A. Broadus.* New York: Harper, 1959.

Steiner, George. *Real Presences.* Chicago: University of Chicago Press, 1989.

Stevenson, Leslie. "Twelve Conceptions of Imagination." *British Journal of Aesthetics* 43/3 (July 2003) 238–59.

Stott, John R. W. *The Contemporary Christian Thinker.* Leicester: InterVarsity, 1992.

Suppe, Frederick, ed. *The Structure of Scientific Theories.* 2nd ed. Urbana: University of Illinois Press, 1977.

Taylor, Charles. *Sources of the Self: The Making of the Modern Identity.* Cambridge: Cambridge University Press, 1989.

Tertullian. "Prescriptions Against the Heretics." In *Early Latin Theology*, edited by S. L. Greenslade, 31–64. Philadelphia: Westminster, 1956.

Torrance, James B. *Worship, Community, and the Triune God of Grace.* Downers Grove, IL: InterVarsity, 1996.

Torrance, Thomas F. *Incarnation: The Person and Life of Christ.* Colorado Springs: Helmers and Howard, 1992.

———. "The Mind of Christ in Worship: The Problem of Apollinarianism in the Liturgy." In *Theology in Reconciliation*, 139–214. Eugene, OR: Wipf & Stock, 1996.

———. *Preaching Christ Today: The Gospel and Scientific Thinking.* Grand Rapids: Eerdmans, 1994.

Toulmin, Stephen. *Cosmopolis: The Hidden Agenda of Modernity.* Chicago: University of Chicago Press, 1990.

———. *Return to Reason.* Cambridge, MA: Harvard University Press, 2001.

Troeger, Thomas. *Creating Fresh Images for Preaching*. Valley Forge, PA: Judson, 1982.
———. *Imagining A Sermon*. Nashville: Abingdon, 1990.

Vaggagini, Cyprian. *The Theological Dimensions of the Liturgy*. Translated by Leonard J. Doyle and W A. Jurgens. Collegeville, MN: Liturgical, 1976.
Meer, Frederik, van der. *Augustine the Bishop: The Life and Work of a Father of the Church*. Translated by Brian Battershaw and G. R. Lamb. New York: Sheed and Ward, 1961.
Vanhoozer, Kevin J. *The Drama of Doctrine: A Canonical Linguistic Approach to Christian Theology*. Louisville: Westminster John Knox, 2005.
———. "The Voice and the Actor." In *Evangelical Futures: A Conversation on Theological Method*, edited by John G. Stackhouse, 61–106. Grand Rapids: Baker, 2000.
Vermes, Geza. *The Religion of Jesus the Jew*. Minneapolis: Fortress, 1993.
Voltaire. *The Works of Voltaire: A Contemporary Version*. Translated by W. F. Fleming. London: St. Hubert's Guild, n.d.
Waldrop, C. T. *Karl Barth's Christology: Its Basic Alexandrian Character*. Berlin: Mouton, 1984.
Walker, Andrew. *Telling the Story: Gospel, Mission, and Culture*. London: SPCK, 1996.
Walls, Andrew F. *The Missionary Movement In Christian History: Studies in the Transmission of Faith*. Edinburgh: T. & T. Clark, 2007.
Walton, Janet. *Art in Worship: A Vital Connection*. Wilmington, DE: Michael Glazier, 1988.
Wardlaw, Don M. *Learning Preaching: Understanding and Participating in the Process*. Lincoln, IL: Lincoln Christian College and Seminary Press, 1992.
Warnock, Mary. *Imagination*. Berkeley: University of California Press, 1976.
Warren, Rick. *The Purpose-Driven Church: Growth Without Compromising Your Message and Mission*. Grand Rapids: Zondervan, 1995.
———. *The Purpose-Driven Life: What on Earth Am I Here For?* Grand Rapids: Zondervan, 2002.
Watson, Francis. "Bible." In *Cambridge Companion to Karl Barth*, edited by John Webster, 57–71. Cambridge: Cambridge University Press, 2000.
Webb, Stephen. *The Divine Voice: Christian Proclamation and The Theology of Sound*. Grand Rapids: Brazos, 2004.
Webber, Robert E. *Ancient-Future Faith: Rethinking Evangelicalism for a Postmodern World*. Grand Rapids: Baker, 1999.
Webster, John. *Barth's Ethics of Reconciliation*. Cambridge: Cambridge University Press, 1995.
———. *Barth's Moral Theology: Human Action in Barth's Thought*. Edinburgh: T. & T. Clark, 1998.
Wells, Samuel. *Improvisation: The Drama of Christian Ethics*. Grand Rapids: Brazos, 2004.
Westerhoff, John H. "Teaching and Preaching." In *Concise Encyclopedia of Preaching*, edited by William Willimon and Richard Lischer, 467–69. 2nd ed. Louisville: Westminster John Knox, 1995.
Whitsitt, W. H. "John Albert Broadus." *Review and Expositor* (July 1907) 347.
Wilder, Amos N. *Early Christian Rhetoric: The Language of the Gospel*. London: SCM, 1964.

Williams, Rowan. *Grace and Necessity: Reflections on Art and Love*. Harrisburg, PA: Morehouse, 2005.

———. *On Christian Theology*. Malden, MA: Blackwell, 2000.

Williamson, Clark M., and Ronald J. Allen. *The Teaching Minister*. Louisville,: Westminster John Knox, 1991.

———. *The Vital Church: Teaching, Worship, Community, Service*. St. Louis: Chalice, 1998.

Willimon, William. *Conversation with Barth on Preaching*. Nashville: Abingdon, 2006.

Wilson, Marvin. *Our Father Abraham: Jewish Roots of the Christian Faith*. Grand Rapids: Eerdmans, 1989.

Wilson, Paul Scott. *God Sense: Reading the Bible for Preaching*. Nashville: Abingdon, 2001.

———. *The Practice of Preaching*. Nashville: Abingdon, 1995.

Wittgenstein, Ludwig. *Philosophical Investigations*. 2nd ed. Translated by G. E. M. Anscombe. New York: Macmillan, 1958.

Witvliet, John. "Metaphor in Liturgical Studies: Lessons from Philosophical and Theological Theories of Language." *Liturgy Digest* 4/1 (1997) 28–30.

Wolterstorff, Nicholas. *Art in Action: Toward a Christian Aesthetic*. Grand Rapids: Eerdmans, 1980.

———. "Barth on Evil." *Faith and Philosophy: Journal of the Society of Christian Philosophers* 13/4 (1996) 584–608.

———. *Divine Discourse: Philosophical Reflections on the Claim that God Speaks*. Cambridge: Cambridge University Press, 1995.

———. "What Is this Thing—Liturgical Art." In *Art in Worship: Clay and Fiber*. Grand Rapids: Calvin College Center Art Gallery, 1988.

———. "The Work of Making a Work of Music." In *What Is Music? An Introduction to the Philosophy of Music*, edited by Philip Alperson, 101–31. New York: Haven, 1987.

Work, Telford. *Living and Active: Scripture in the Economy of Salvation*. Grand Rapids: Eerdmans, 2002.

Worley, Robert C. *Preaching and Teaching in the Early Church*. Philadelphia: Westminster, 1967.

Young, Brad. *Jesus The Jewish Theologian*. Peabody, MA: Hendrickson, 1995.

Young, Frances. *The Art of Performance: Towards a Theology of Holy Scripture*. London: Darton, Longman and Todd, 1990.

Name/Subject Index

Scripture Index